I0812137

POSTCARD HISTORY SERIES

Laurens County

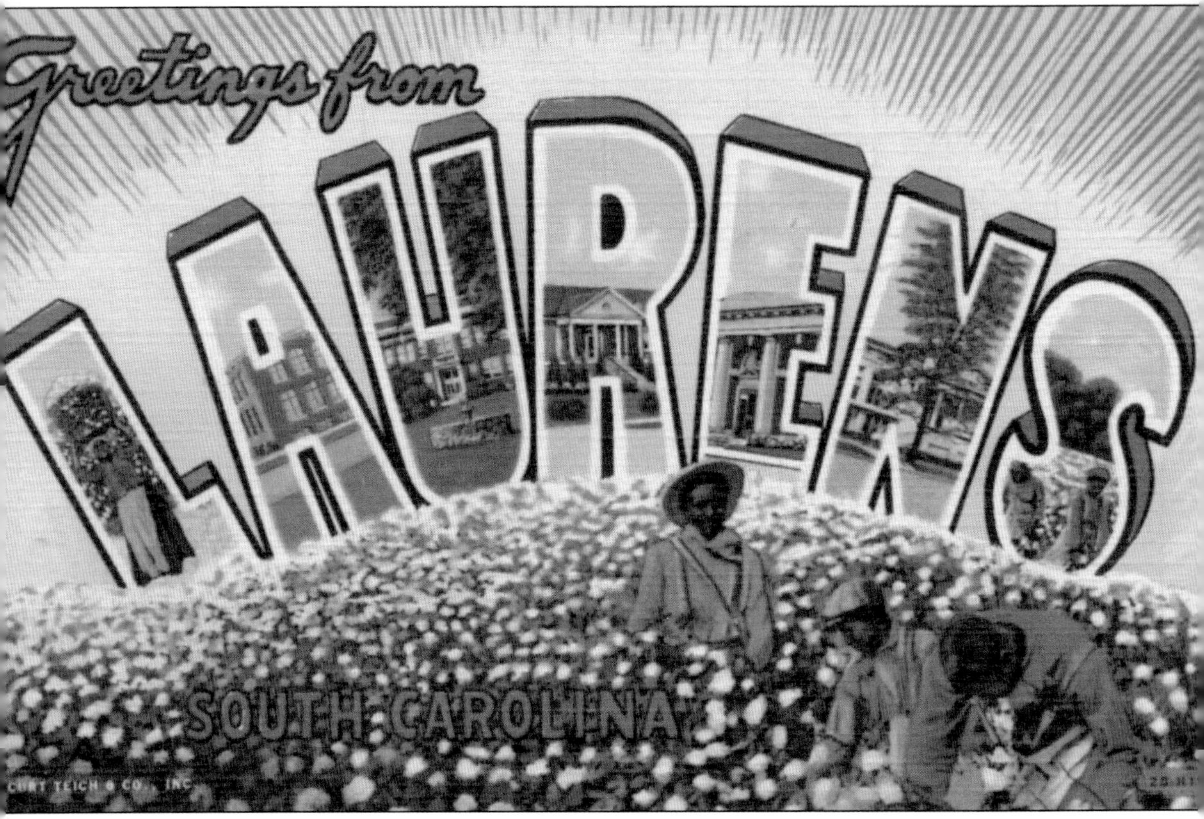

On March 12, 1785, Laurens became one of six South Carolina counties created from the Ninety Six District. Located in the piedmont region of upper South Carolina, the county was divided into nine townships: Laurens, Dials, Waterloo, Sullivan, Scuffletown, Hunter, Cross Hill, Jacks, and Youngs. The county derived its name from a distinguished statesman, Henry Laurens of Charleston. (Courtesy Elaine Martin.)

On the Front Cover: The first courthouse constructed for Laurens County was a log structure. The county seat, or "Laurens Court House Square" as it was called in the early days, soon developed into a flourishing town. A new courthouse was constructed in 1815 and was replaced in 1840 by the present structure, with additions made in 1858 and 1911. (Courtesy Elaine Martin.)

On the Back Cover: When automobiles replaced the horse and buggy, a new era came into being. The historic Laurens courthouse and square remained as the center of activity for Laurens County. (Courtesy Elaine Martin.)

POSTCARD HISTORY SERIES

Laurens County

Laurens County Museum Association

ARCADIA PUBLISHING

ISBN 978-0-7385-4441-0

Published by Arcadia Publishing
Charleston, South Carolina

Printed in the United States of America

Library of Congress Catalog Card Number: 2007920802

For all general information contact Arcadia Publishing at:
Telephone 843-853-2070
Fax 843-853-0044
E-mail sales@arcadiapublishing.com
For customer service and orders:
Toll-Free 1-888-313-2665

Visit us on the Internet at www.arcadiapublishing.com

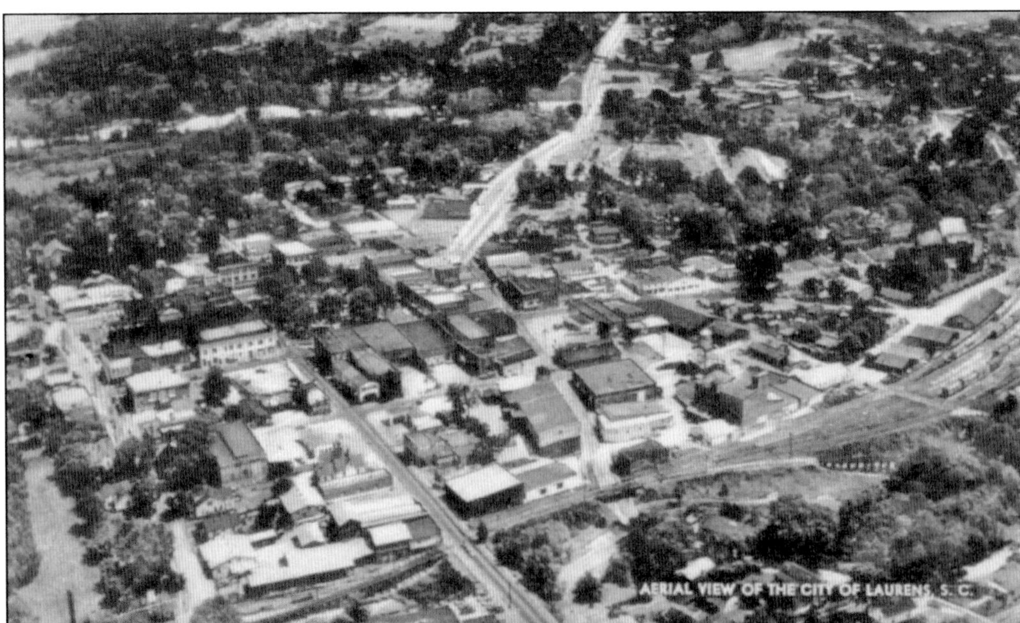

The aerial view shows the town of Laurens including mills, schools, railroads, churches, residences, and the Laurens Court House Square. Located near the center of the county, the town of Laurens serves as the county seat. (Courtesy Elaine Martin.)

Contents

Acknowledgments

Compiling *Laurens County* has been a team effort by Libby C. Rhodes, Julius D. Bolt, Elaine Martin, and Kathryn W. Johnson, all members of the Laurens County Museum Association. We, the team, are honored to have been a part of the museum's first publication.

Also we are appreciative of numerous postcard collectors, libraries, and museums for providing information and lending postcards for *Laurens County* and for their enthusiasm and willingness to trust the Laurens County Museum Association with treasured vintage postcards.

Telling the story of Laurens County in these few pages proved to be an impossible task. Perhaps at a later date we can create another book in our efforts to preserve the rich heritage of the county we know, love, and call home.

Grateful acknowledgment is given to the Laurens County Library for providing access to books, documents, and other materials used to verify names, dates, and locations of postcards and for allowing us to use the South Carolina Room as headquarters from start to finish of the book.

Appreciation is given to the *Laurens County Advertiser* for supporting and encouraging the Laurens County Museum Association's endeavors in publishing *Laurens County* by printing numerous articles and photographs.

To Maggie Tiller Bullwinkel, our acquisitions editor at Arcadia, we wish to offer a sincere thank-you for advice and patience during the publishing of *Laurens County.*

Laurens County has been written with the heartfelt desire that the book will inspire memories of the past for those who turn the pages.

Learning more about our county and meeting new people has been a rewarding experience for us. What is more, this venture has been great fun.

INTRODUCTION

Our desire is to have you open *Laurens County*, turn the pages, read the captions, get lost in the postcard images, and then stop, close your eyes for a moment, and allow yourself to go back in time, back to the heyday of Laurens County.

Perhaps nothing is quite so evocative as the clop-clop of horses' hooves clattering upon the timbers of a wooden bridge, a sunny day's ride in a surrey with everyone dressed in their summer best, men in straw hats, women with parasols and mutton-chop sleeves, or farmers in their wagons at the cotton gin. Possibly you can imagine a family that has arrived in town from the country in a horse-drawn wagon. After leading the horses to the watering trough on the square, Papa heads to the bank while the children dash to the candy counter in the general store to decide upon licorice twists or lemon drops, and Mama steps into the millinery shop to try on a new hat.

This pictorial book is simply a nostalgic journey through a crucial period in Laurens County's history during the beginning of the 20th century.

This book contains more than 200 vintage postcard images and real photographs of local businesses, railroad stations, streetscapes, schools, private homes, churches, landscapes, and textile mills. It documents life during the early 20th century in Laurens County.

As Laurens County was the center of social, religious, and business life of an extensive area of upstate South Carolina, the postcard images tie the past with the present. They might well be studied, as many of them are an indication of the culture and character of a way of life in the early history of our county.

When the 1898 Private Mailing Card Act was passed by the federal government, a viable industry was created for private publishing companies. Postcard production reached its height between 1907 and 1915 in the United States.

For Laurens County, as in every other town in the nation, postcards proved to be an inexpensive and convenient method for keeping in touch with family and friends.

Faded inscriptions on many of the cards offered in this volume interestingly read "Wish you were here—Will see you on Easter—Sister sends her love—Crops are good—Laurens is a pretty little town—Went to church Sunday—Brother is ill" and countless other meaningful words written by citizens of yesteryear. The history of Laurens County is recorded in flourishing script and the short scribbled messages on these cards, and this, in fact, is worth more than 1,000 words in a history book.

During this era, it also was a fashionable hobby to collect and exchange postcards, especially for women. Elaborate gilded postcard albums today are a collector's delight.

At the height of the postcard's popularity, Laurens County, like many other South Carolina counties, was recovering from the devastation of the War Between the States. The county, at long last, was facing economic and physical growth.

Railroads and automobiles provided transportation throughout the county, new schools and colleges were being established, churches were expanding, and crops were thriving. As stated earlier, all of these new trends are documented in the postcard images within these pages.

Because of traveling photographers, these postcards tell the story of people who performed hard work and how they did it. It is about people who wrenched a living from behind a plow, from a loom in the textile mill, and at numerous other businesses and establishments. It is a chronicle of people who remembered what it was like before the telephone, the automobile, and the airplane. It is a story about a way of life that has practically disappeared, but it is Americana at its best and we should all remember that.

Almost every facet of life in Laurens County was captured in a postcard print during the first half of the 20th century. It is our good fortune that these works of art have survived.

In collecting these postcards, both grand and humble, we have endeavored to provide readers with the industry, character, charm, and romance of a small upstate Carolina county.

The postcard images are a testament to a blend of people who have cherished Laurens County through the bright and dark days of its history and remind us that we must look back before we move forward.

One

LAURENS
County Seat and Court House Square

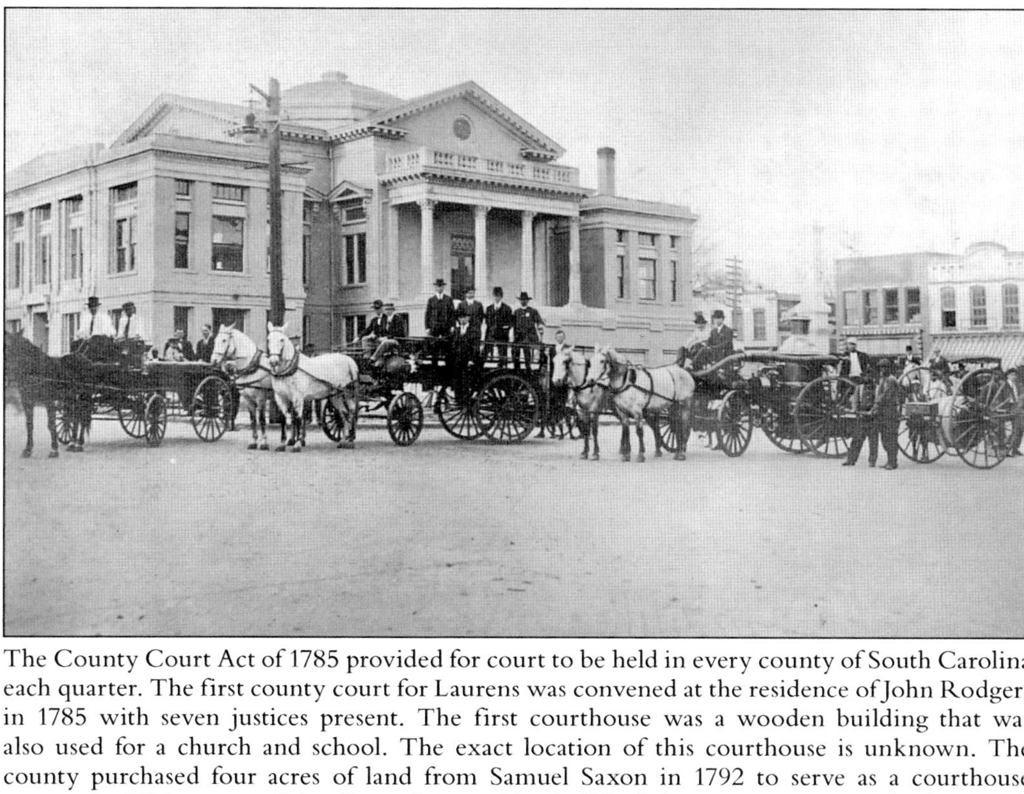

The County Court Act of 1785 provided for court to be held in every county of South Carolina each quarter. The first county court for Laurens was convened at the residence of John Rodgers in 1785 with seven justices present. The first courthouse was a wooden building that was also used for a church and school. The exact location of this courthouse is unknown. The county purchased four acres of land from Samuel Saxon in 1792 to serve as a courthouse square. In 1799, an act of the General Assembly abolished the county courts and, along with them, the judges. The General Assembly appropriated $5,000 for the construction of a new courthouse and jail in 1815. Dr. John Wells Simpson constructed the central portion of the Laurens County Courthouse *c.* 1838, and in February 1840, it was ready for court. (Courtesy South Caroliniana Library, University of South Carolina, Columbia.)

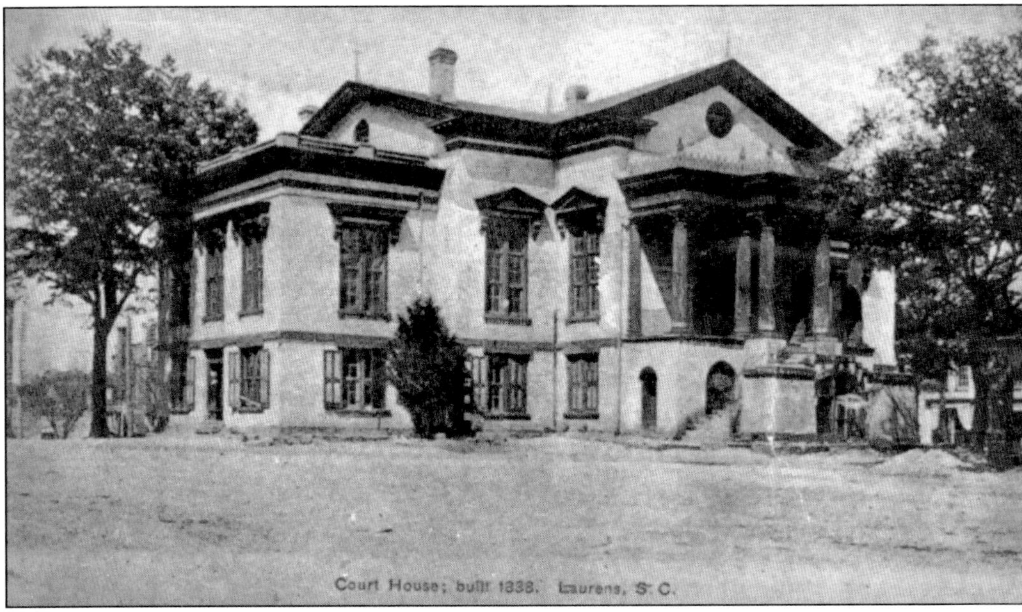

Architect Thomas C. Veal designed the Laurens County Courthouse, and Dr. John Wells Simpson, a leading building contractor in Laurensville, was the builder. The Laurens County Courthouse illustrates an example of Greek Revival architecture in rural South Carolina. The central portion was constructed *c.* 1837–1838; wings to the northwest and southwest were added in 1858; and in 1911, additions were made to the wings, windows remodeled, Palladian stairs added, and the elliptical dome constructed. The building is constructed of brick and granite. W. T. Crews, in his personal diary, wrote that one of the columns supporting the portico roof of the courthouse served as the public whipping post. Even though court is no longer held in the historic building, it remains the focal point of Laurens Court House Square. (Above courtesy Libby C. Rhodes; below courtesy Richard B. Taylor Jr.)

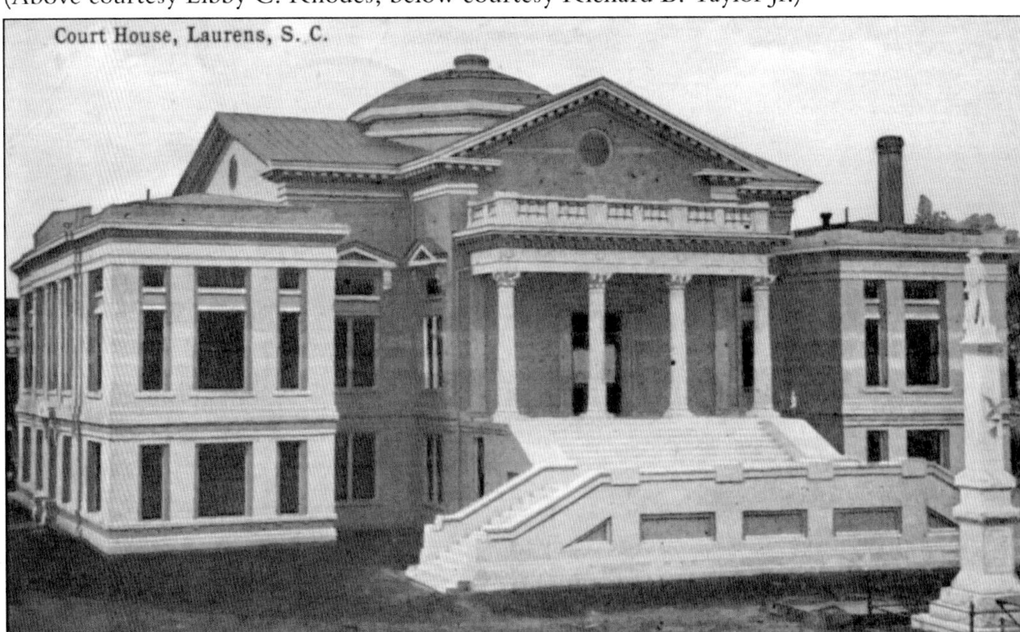

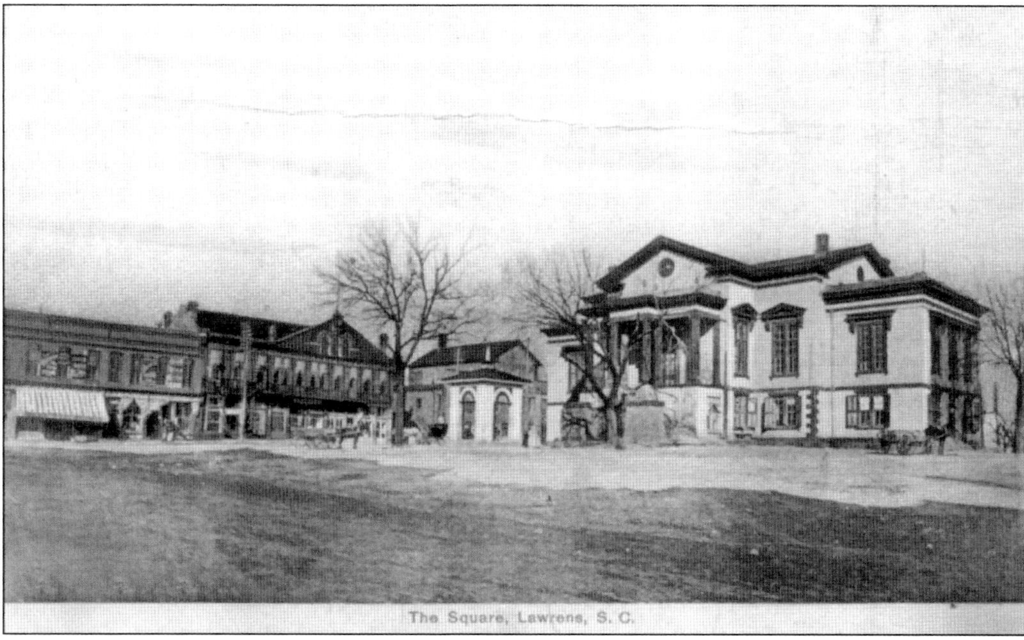

Originally the county seat was called Laurens Court House, later Laurensville, and eventually Laurens. Historical data states that when the first county-wide sales day was being planned, legal sales were advertised in front of the courthouse. The larger plot needed to accommodate those interested in trading was on the south side; thus the south side became known as the front side. Covered public wells were located on the north and south sides of the courthouse. There were also watering troughs for mules and horses. The wells and troughs were removed in 1907, when the Laurens Court House Square was paved for the first time. When automobiles replaced the horse and buggy, a new era came into being, and marble water fountains replaced the wells on the courthouse grounds. (Above courtesy Libby C. Rhodes; below courtesy Elaine Martin.)

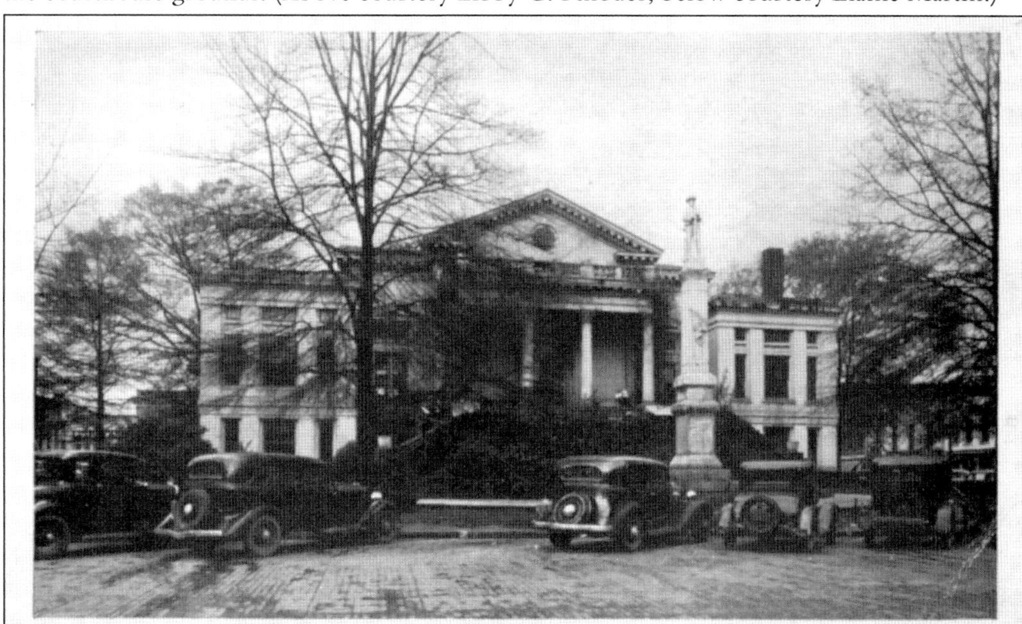

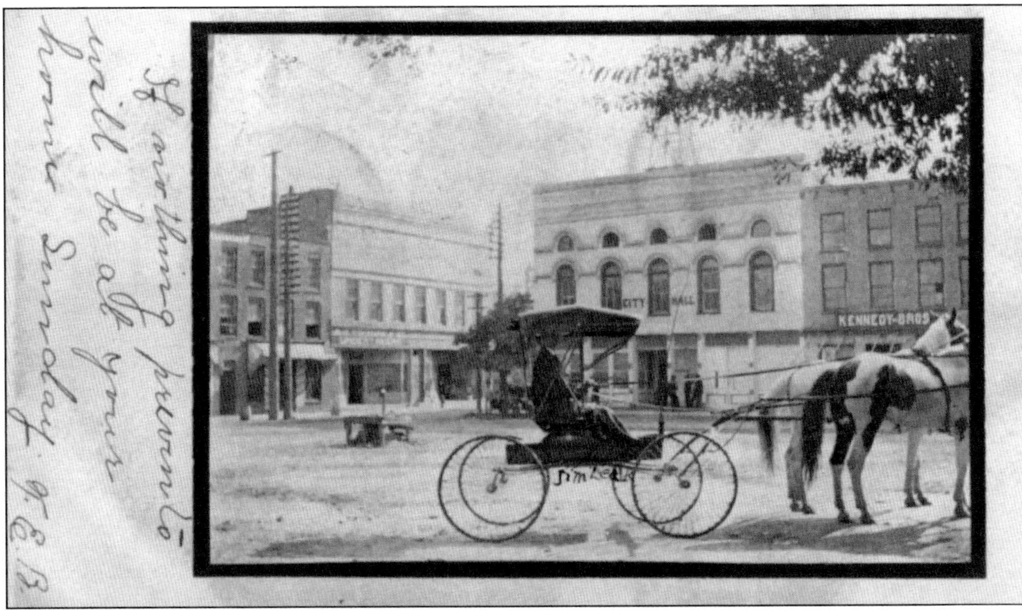

A horse-drawn carriage driven by Jim Leak is captured by a photographer on the east side of the Laurens Court House Square. Kennedy Brothers Store and Laurens City Hall are also in the photograph. The Laurens Opera House occupied the upper story of city hall. A well, used for human consumption and also for watering livestock, is pictured opposite the carriage. (Courtesy Richard B. Taylor Jr.)

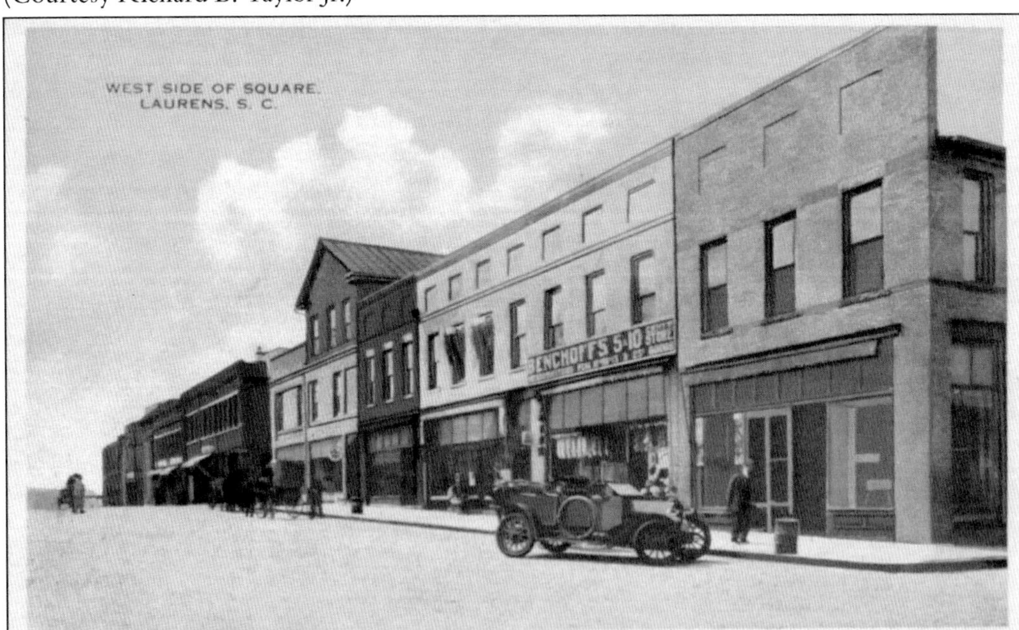

An early automobile and a horse and carriage are parked on the west side of the Laurens Court House Square. Benchoff's Five and Dime Store, the Ben Della Hotel, drugstores, mercantile companies, and numerous other establishments were located on the square and served the needs of Laurens residents. Jail House Alley led from the west side of the square to the Laurens County Jail. (Courtesy Frances C. Weathers.)

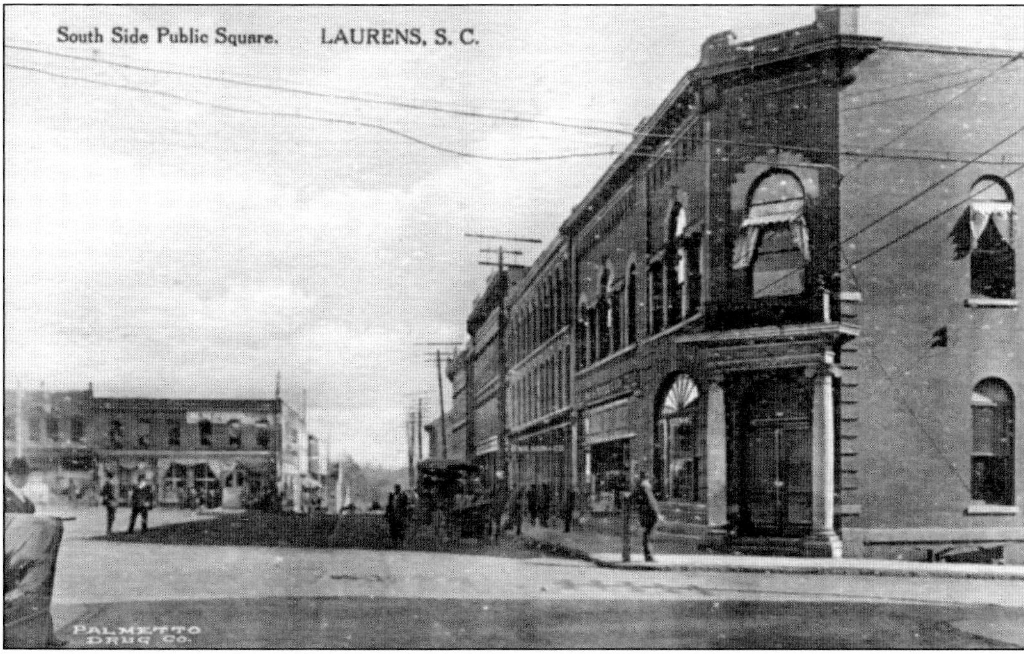

Printed for Palmetto Drug Company, this early-1900s postcard depicts a streetscape of the corner of South Harper and West Main Streets on the south side of the Laurens Court House Square. Included in the row of buildings are Davis and Roper Company, Inc.; G. Wilson and Company; and the People's Loan and Exchange Bank. (Courtesy Kathryn W. Johnson.)

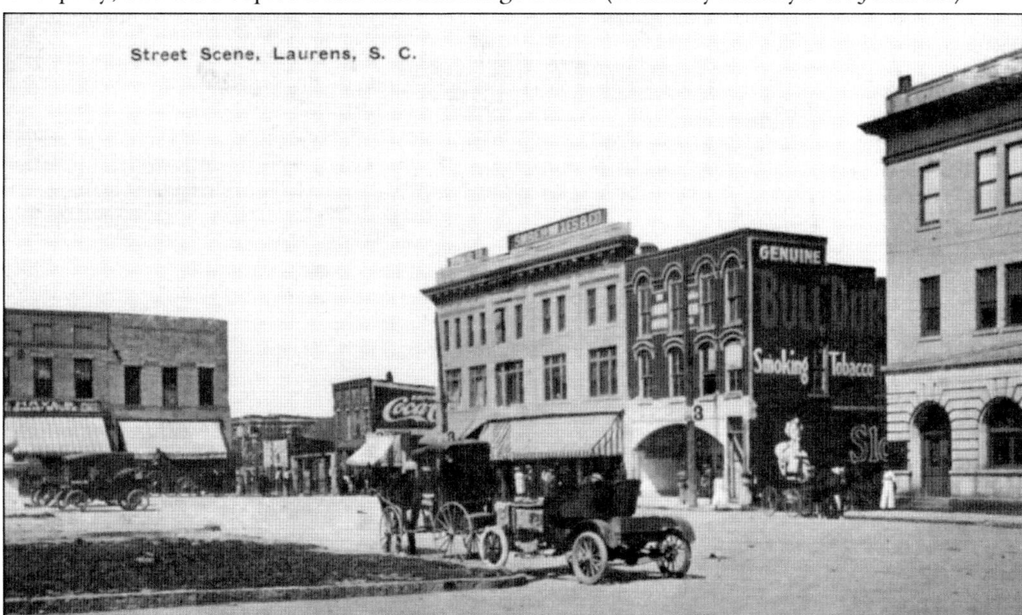

Complete with a horse and buggy and an early automobile, this street scene shows the north side of the Laurens Court House Square. The Enterprise Bank, *Laurens Advertiser*, and S. M. and E. H. Wilkes, all on the north side of town, were noted establishments of the era. Painted on the brick buildings are advertisements for Coca-Cola and Bull Durham Smoking Tobacco. Also shown is the street corner of Silver and Laurens Streets. (Courtesy Richard B. Taylor Jr.)

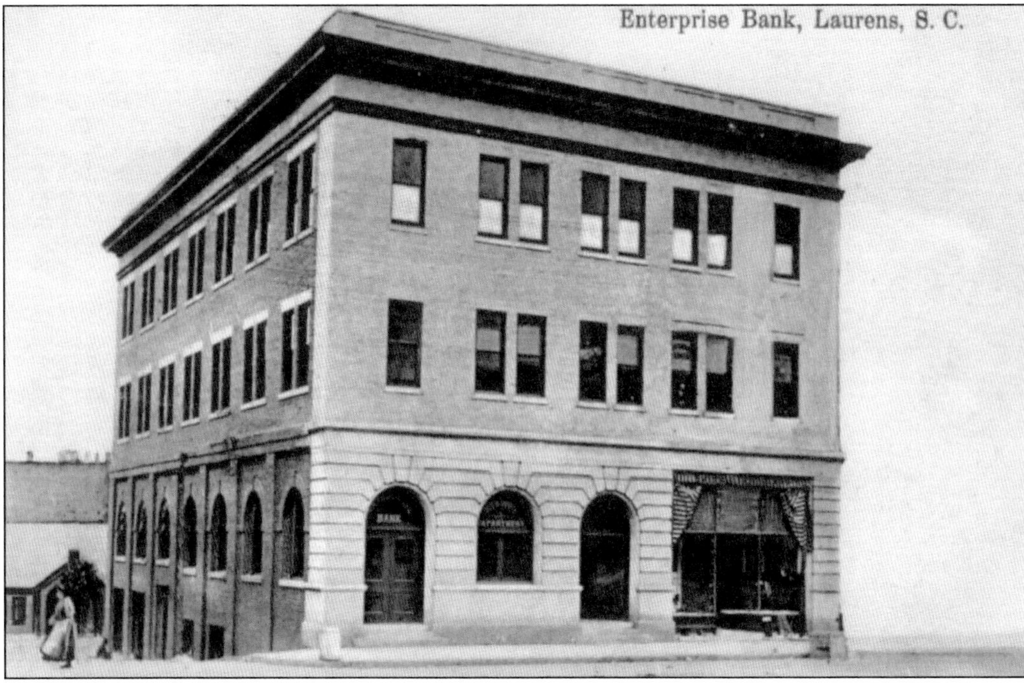

In 1901, Charles Houston Roper was instrumental in organizing the Enterprise Bank, which was located on the north side of the Laurens Court House Square on the corner of Laurens and Silver Streets. Roper served as cashier of the financial institution, and Nathaniel B. Dial served as president. When Dial was elected to the U.S. Senate, Roper assumed the presidency and remained in that capacity until the bank consolidated with the Peoples Loan and Enterprise Bank. A postcard advertisement invited customers to visit the new, up-to-date inside-and-out building and to inspect the fireproof vaults and the modern manganese-steel-screw door of the burglarproof safe. The Enterprise Bank was advertised as being handsome, commodious, and secure. (Above courtesy Richard B. Taylor Jr.; below courtesy Billie Lawson Jr.)

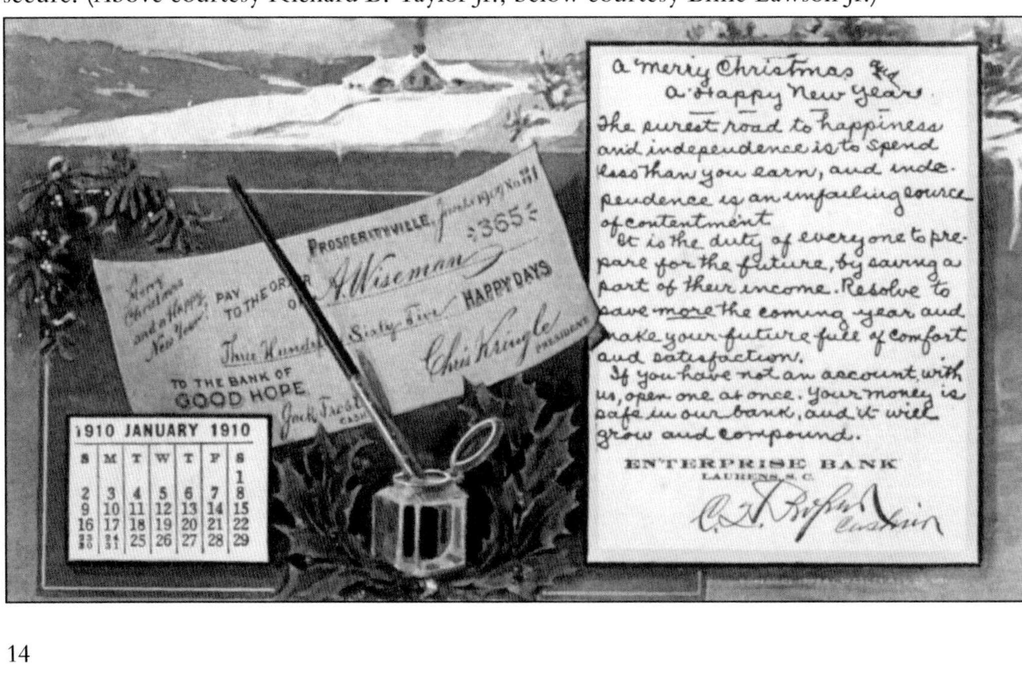

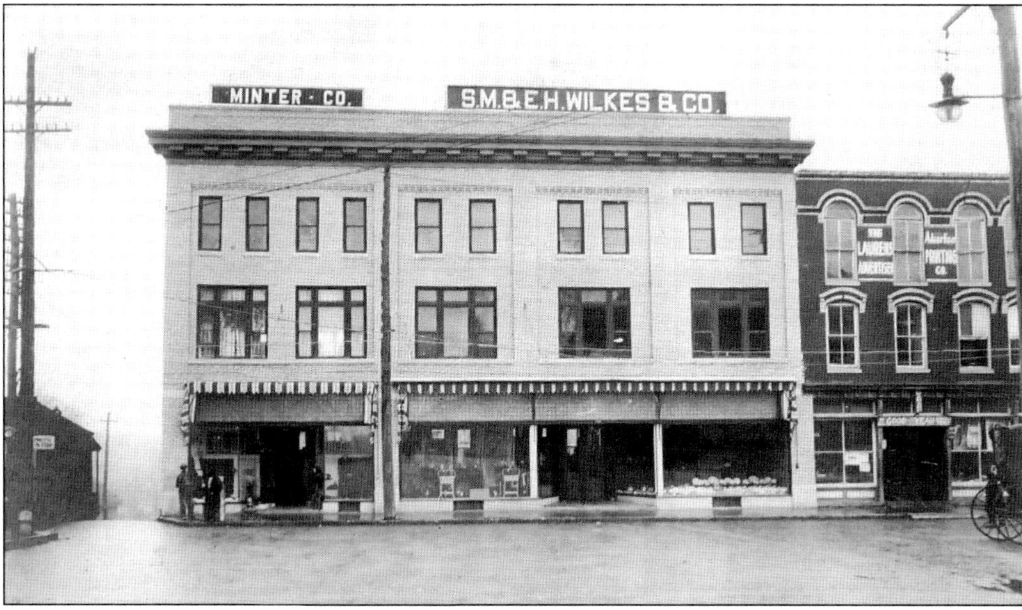

J. E. Minter and Brother, a clothing store; S. M. and E. H. Wilkes, a furniture store; and the *Laurens Advertiser* were located on the north side of the Laurens Court House Square. The *Laurens Advertiser* office and printing press were housed on the second floor of a building located on the corner of Laurens and Silver Streets. The newspaper's first editor was Conway Garlington, and after several years, the paper was sold to Col. B. W. Ball, a Confederate veteran and lawyer. (Courtesy South Caroliniana Library, University of South Carolina, Columbia.)

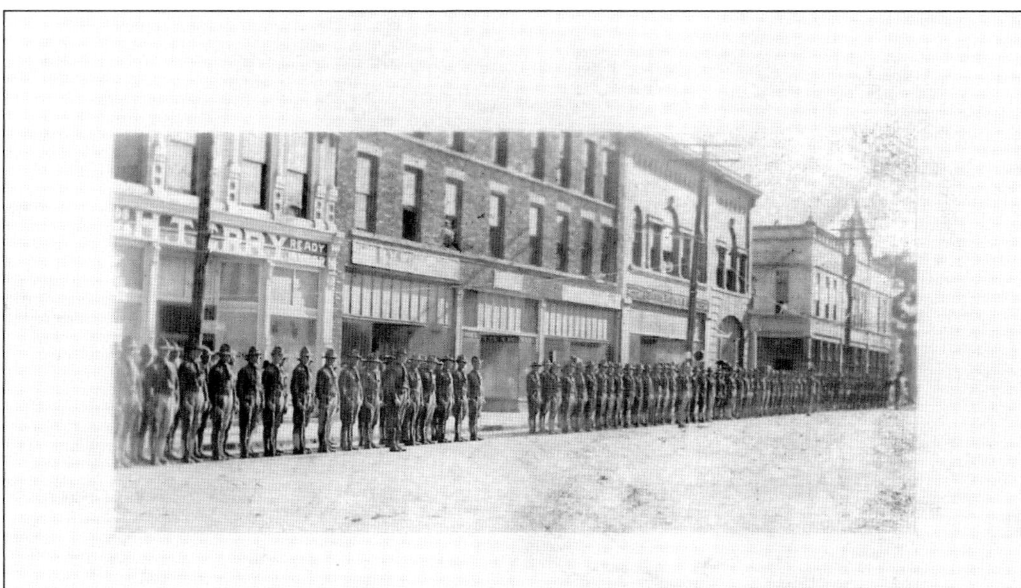

This 1917 photo postcard shows World War I soldiers at a dress parade on the Laurens Court House Square. Numerous soldiers from Laurens fought in World War I as well as in all American wars before and since. (Courtesy South Caroliniana Library, University of South Carolina, Columbia.)

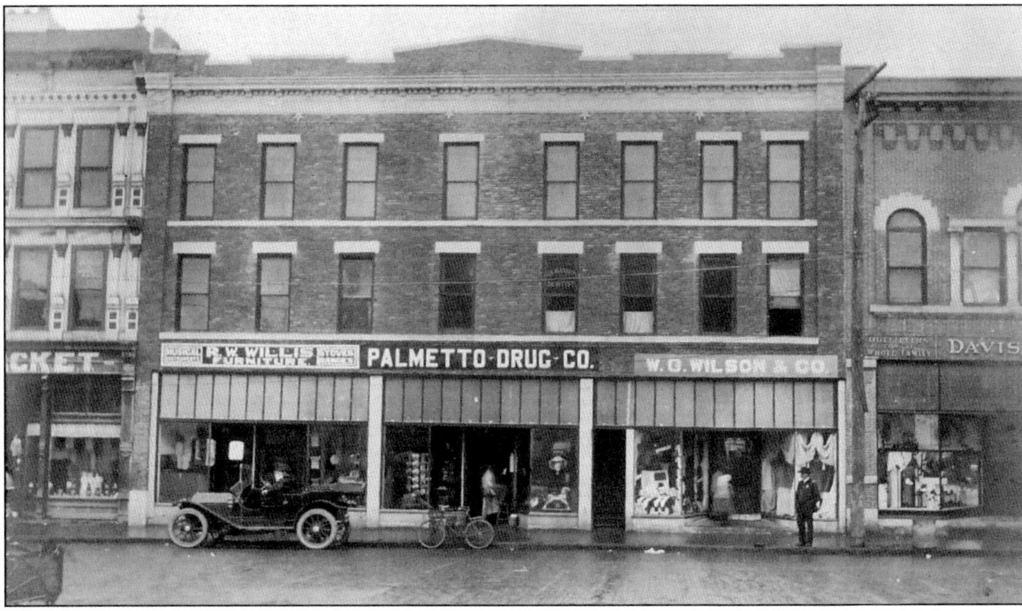

These early-1900s postcards show the Red Iron Racket, Willis Furniture Store, Palmetto Drug Company, W. G. Wilson and Company, and Davis and Roper Company, all of which were located on the south side of the Laurens Court House Square. Many souvenir postcards depicting Laurens scenes were printed and sold by the Palmetto Drug Company. Today these postcards are highly collectible. (Courtesy South Caroliniana Library, University of South Carolina, Columbia.)

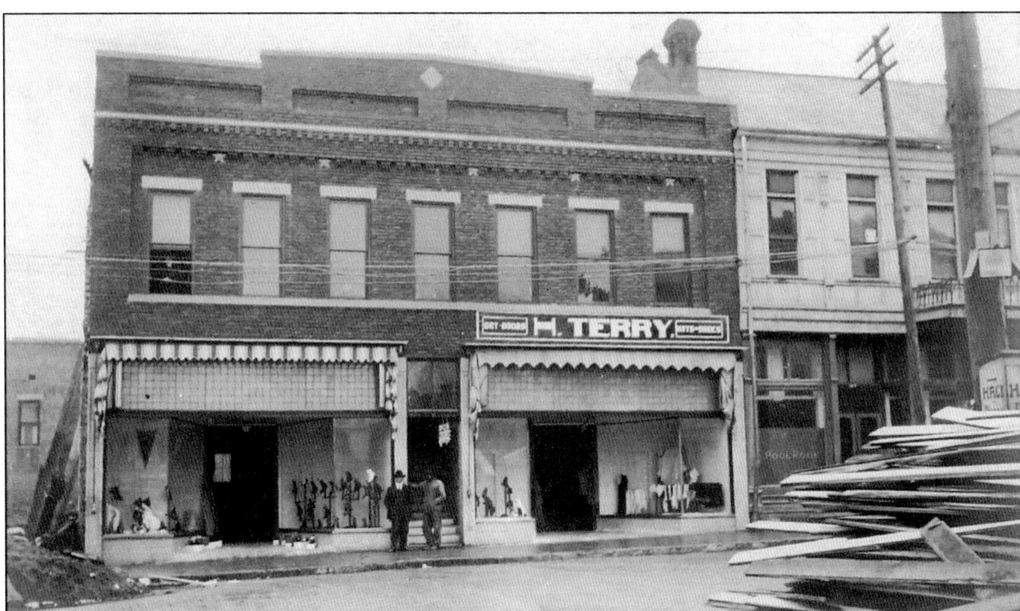

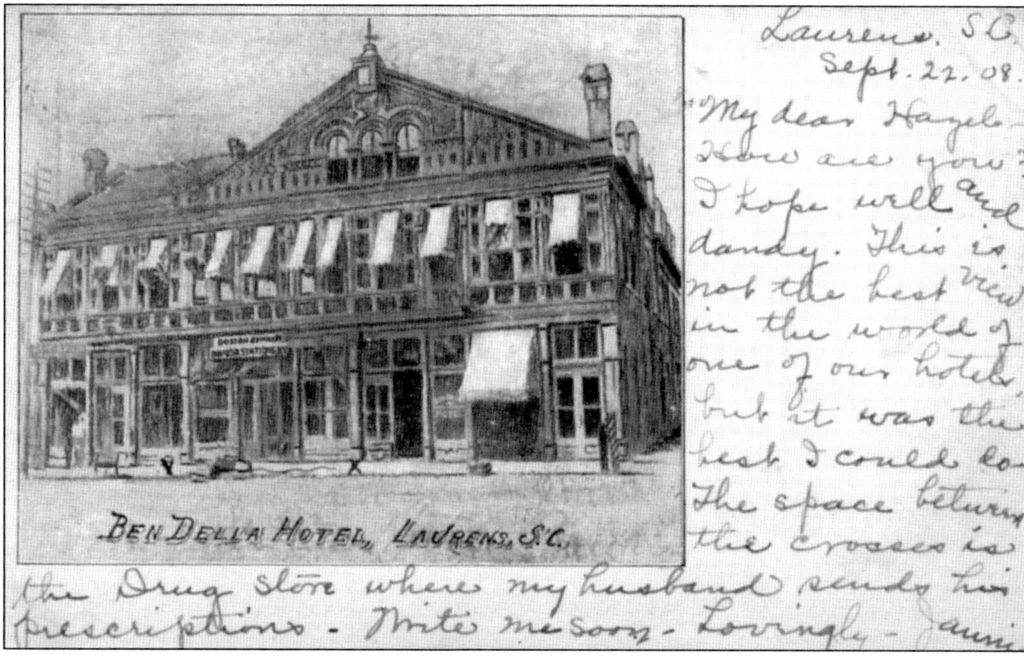

The Ben Della Hotel, located on the west side of the Laurens Court House Square, was erected in 1885. Owned by Dr. Benjamin E. Martin, the hotel derived its name from a union of his and his wife's given names. The building was three stories above ground and 100 feet long by 70 feet wide, and it contained 32 rooms and a basement. A drugstore was located on the first floor. The beautiful building added greatly to the square. This Ben Della Hotel postcard was mailed from Laurens to New York. (Courtesy Kathryn Weathers Johnson.)

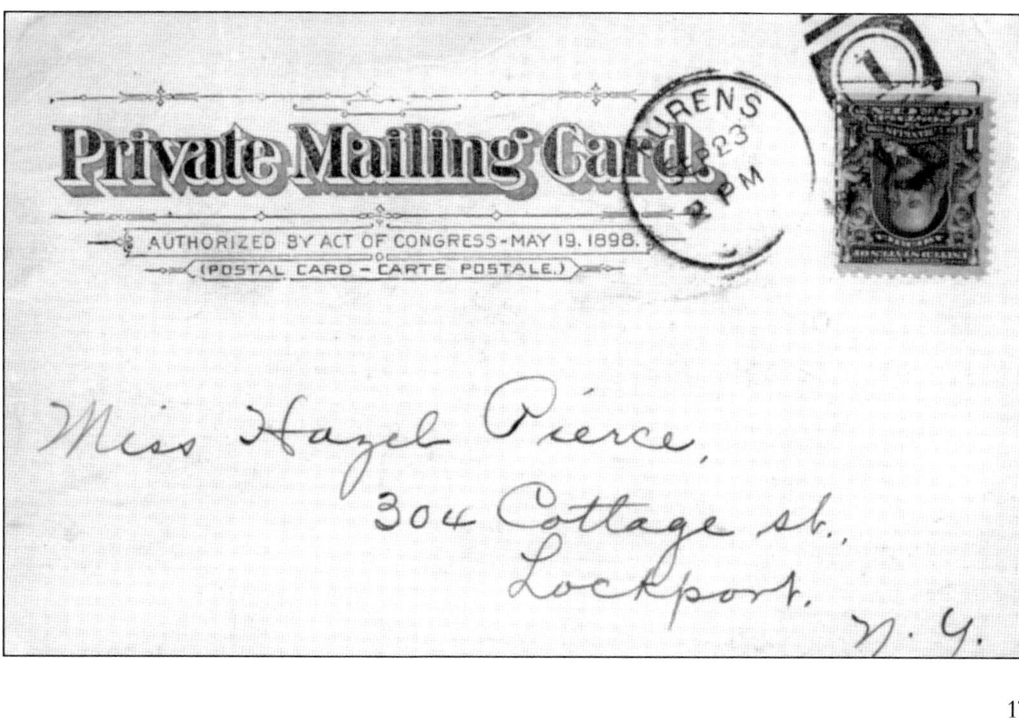

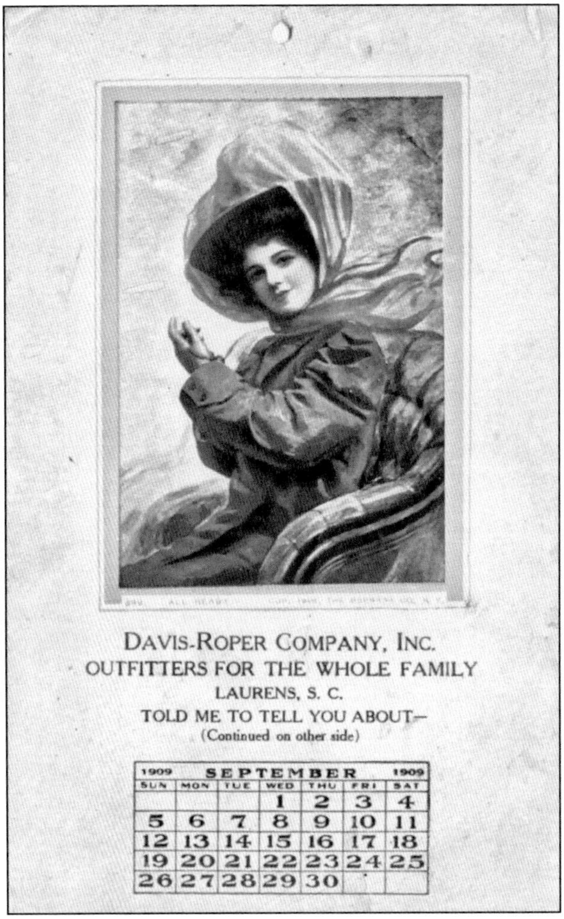

The Davis and Roper Company, Inc., was located on the south side of the Laurens Court House Square. A 1909 calendar postcard from the popular store that was mailed to L. L. Culbertson of Laurens reads, "Fitting the Whole Family—Head To Foot—That's our business—the one thing we do as though it were the only thing worth doing. Clothing, furnishings, shoes, hats, dry goods, millinery, ladies' read-to-wear-suits, coats, skirts. In short, everything worn by either sex from childhood to old age and then trunks and valises. No side lines—no little lots just to talk about, but big, complete stocks, and prices that you'll be perfectly willing to pay. Fall fashions ready, walk in and look around. Davis-Roper Company, Inc. Outfitters for the whole family, Laurens, S.C." (Courtesy Billie E. Lawson Jr.)

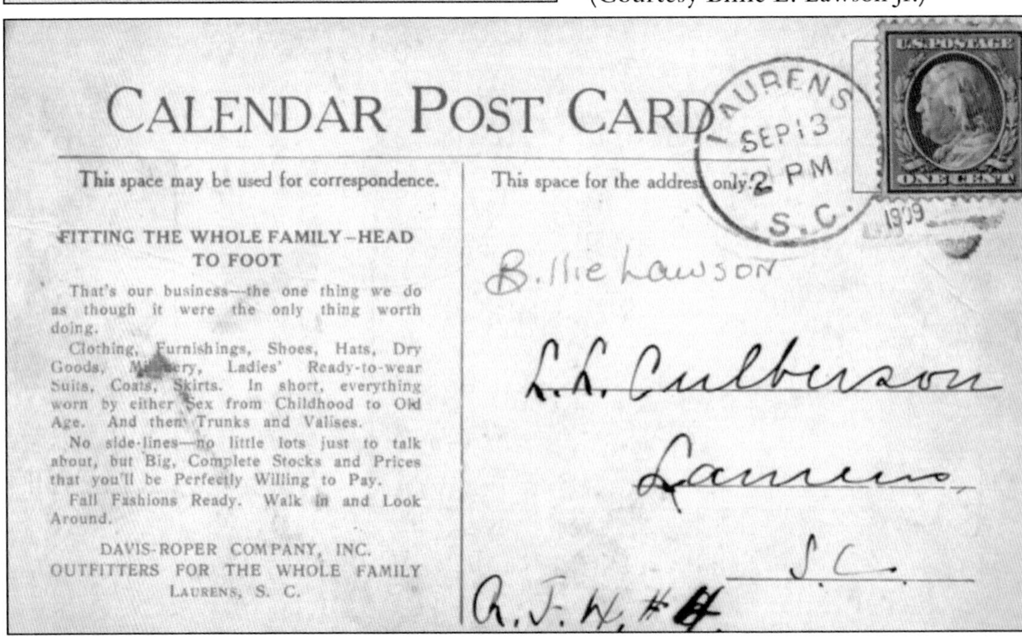

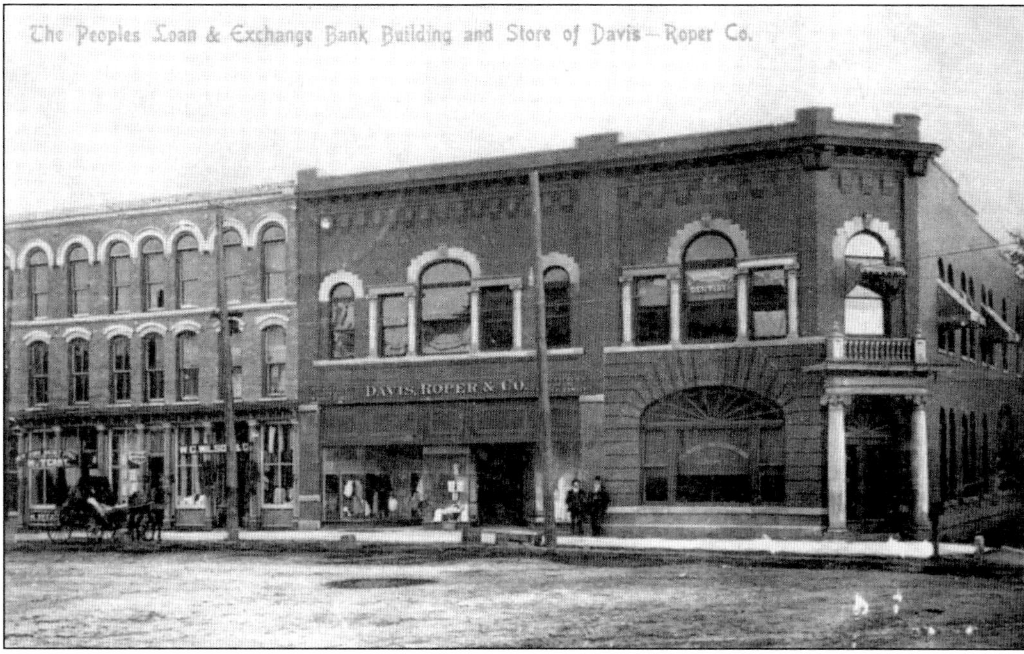

The Peoples Loan and Exchange Bank; Davis and Roper Company, Inc.; W. C. Wilson Company; and the H. Terry Store were some of the establishments located on the south side of the Laurens Court House Square. Dr. G. Albright, a dentist, had an office above the Peoples Loan and Exchange Bank on the second floor. This postcard shows two gentlemen in front of the bank and also a horse and buggy. (Courtesy Kathryn W. Johnson.)

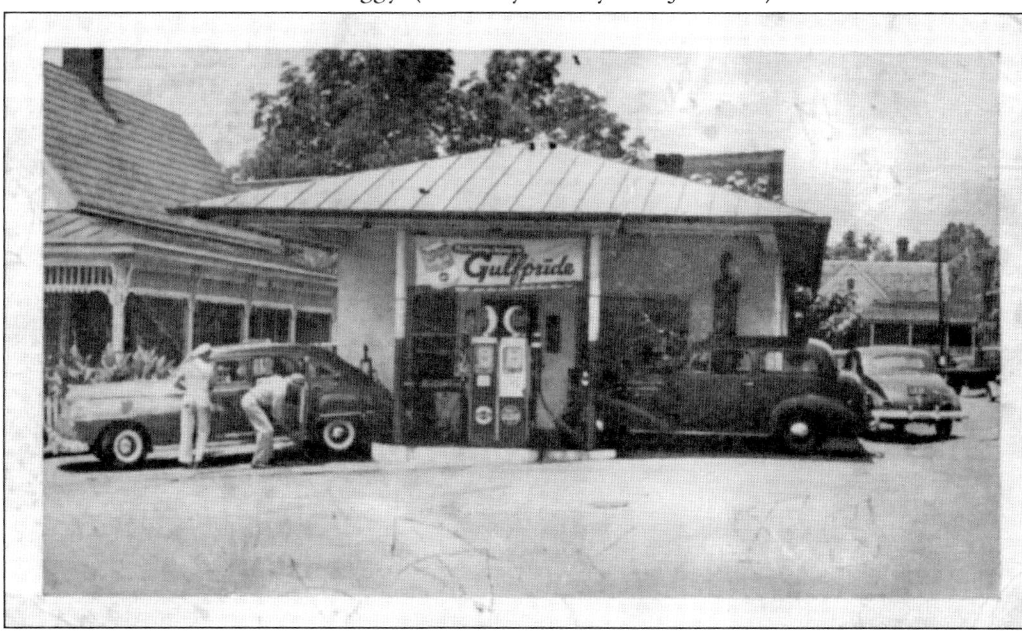

The Harper Street Service Station was located at 8 Harper Street, just off the Laurens Court House Square. This 1947 Gulfpride advertising postcard reads, "For best all-around service, you can't beat this place. It's got everything!" For many years, the service station was owned and operated by the late Wesley Taylor. (Courtesy Laurens County Library.)

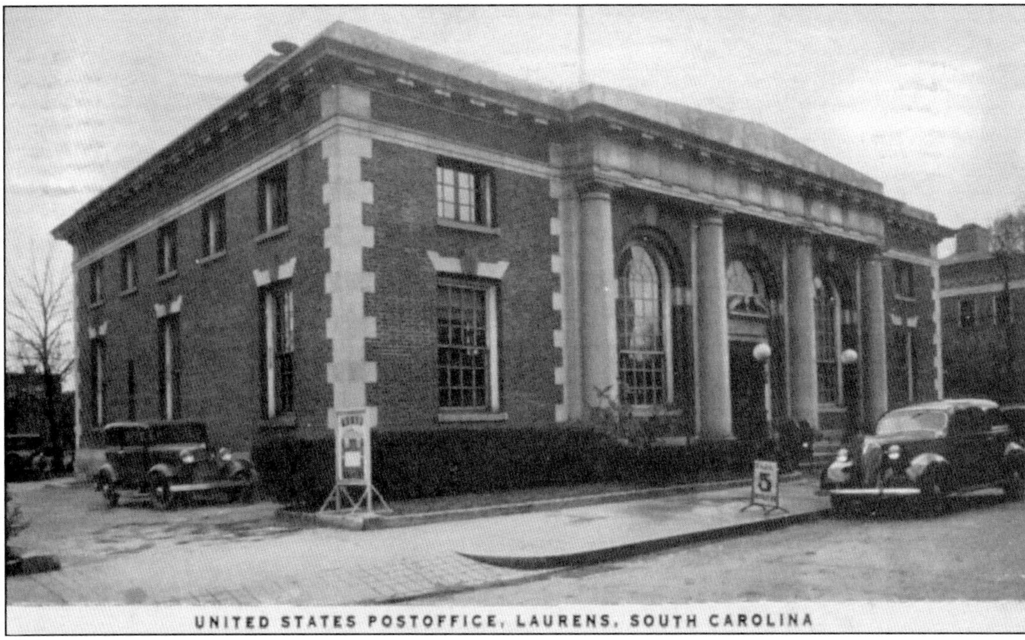

The Laurens Post Office was constructed in 1913 on the corner of West Main and Caroline Streets. This post office replaced a small wooden post office that was located on the Anderson property on West Main Street. The post office served citizens until a new post office was constructed on North Harper Street in 1965. At that time, the Palmetto Bank purchased the building and razed it for a parking lot. (Courtesy Elaine Martin.)

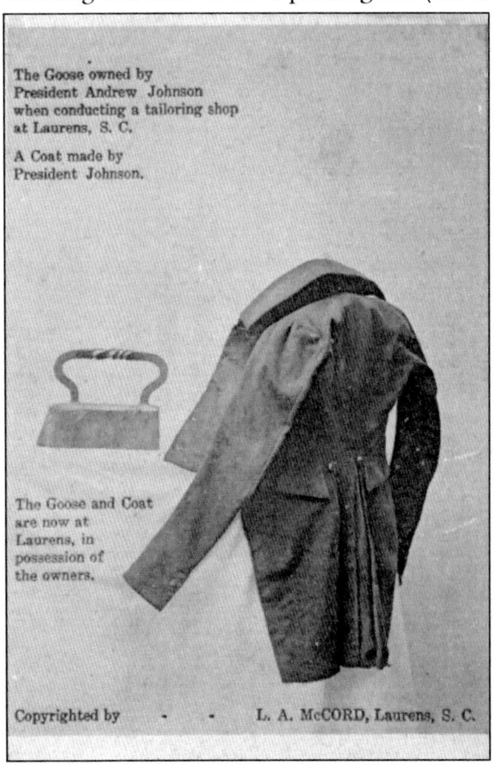

U.S. president Andrew Johnson once was a tailor in Laurens and worked from a shop just off the Laurens Court House Square. This photo postcard was made by Luther A. McCord, a well-known Laurens photographer. The photograph shows a coat that was sewn by Johnson while working in Laurens. (Courtesy Libby C. Rhodes.)

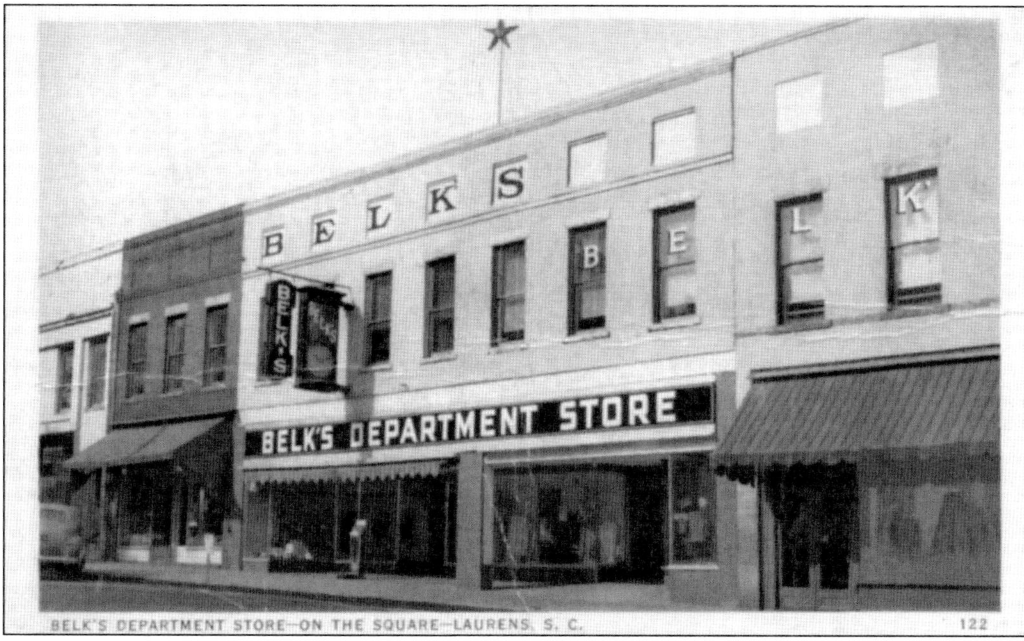

Belk's Department Store, founded by Henry Simpson, opened on the west side of the Laurens Court House Square in October 1931 and quickly sprawled into three buildings. The first store manager was W. P. Putnam. Other managers were J. E. Chandler, Jack Gratz, Tommy Holmes, and David Middleton. In 1970, the popular Laurens store relocated in a new building on Hillcrest Drive and later to the present Highway 76 location. (Courtesy Laurens County Library.)

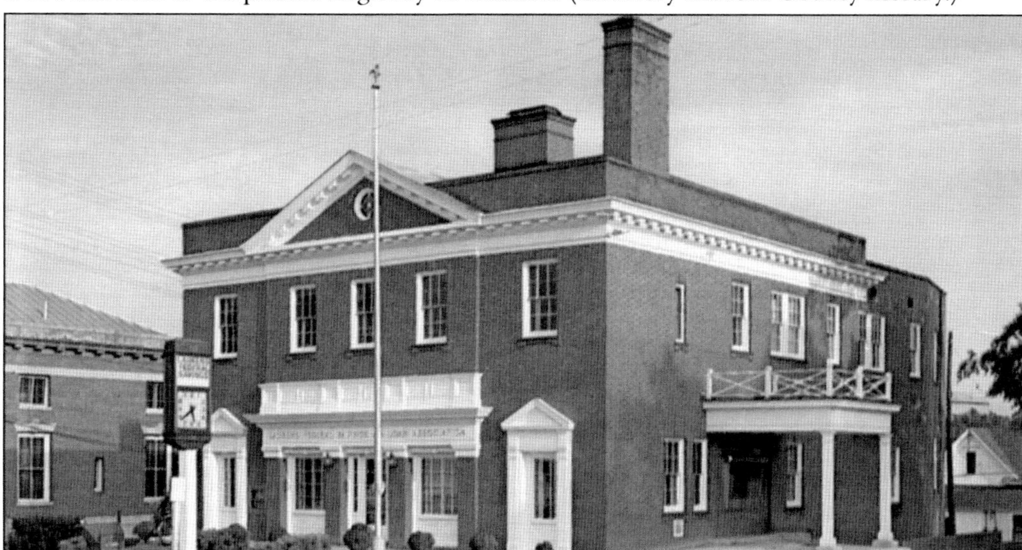

Laurens Federal Savings and Loan Association was organized in 1948. In 1955, the association purchased the Kennedy Mortuary Building at 201 West Main Street and employed the Bank Building and Equipment Corporation of America to redesign and decorate the building. Later the name was changed to Heritage Federal Savings and Loan Association. The large clock out front quickly became a landmark and helped Laurens residents keep track of time. (Courtesy Libby C. Rhodes.)

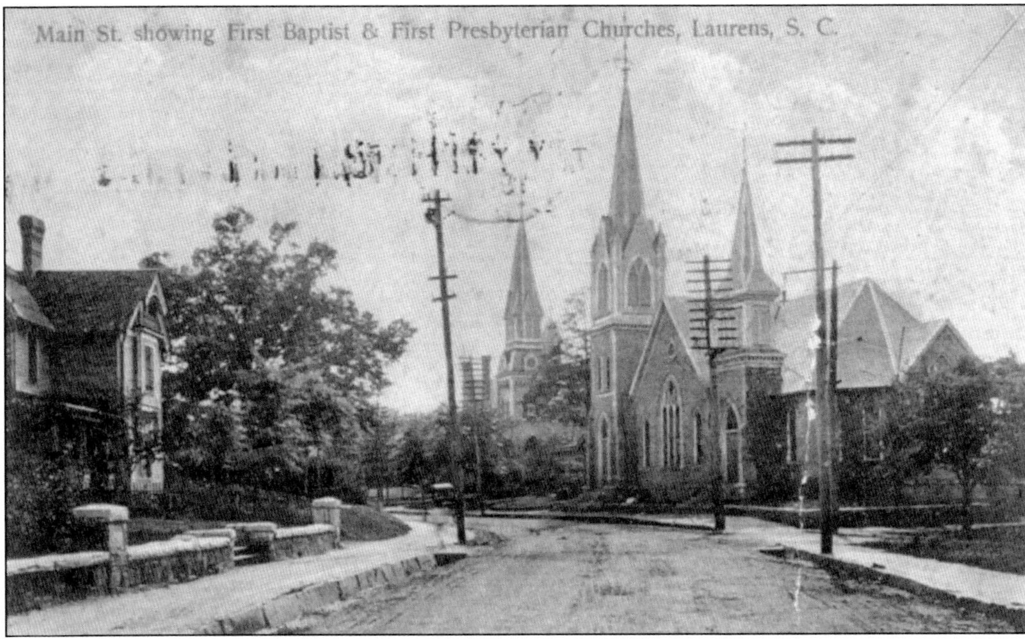

West Main Street was one of four streets that led to Laurens Court House Square. The other streets were East Main, North Harper, and South Harper Streets. The residential area extended a mile from the square in all directions, and granite mile markers were placed on each street. The First Baptist Church, First Presbyterian Church, First Methodist Church, and several residences are captured in the streetscape of West Main Street. Even though buggy tracks are seen in the dirt street, Laurens boasted paved sidewalks complete with granite curbing. Utility poles shown in these scenes indicate that electric lights illuminated the homes and businesses of Laurens residents in 1910. (Above courtesy Frances C. Weathers; below courtesy Elaine Martin.)

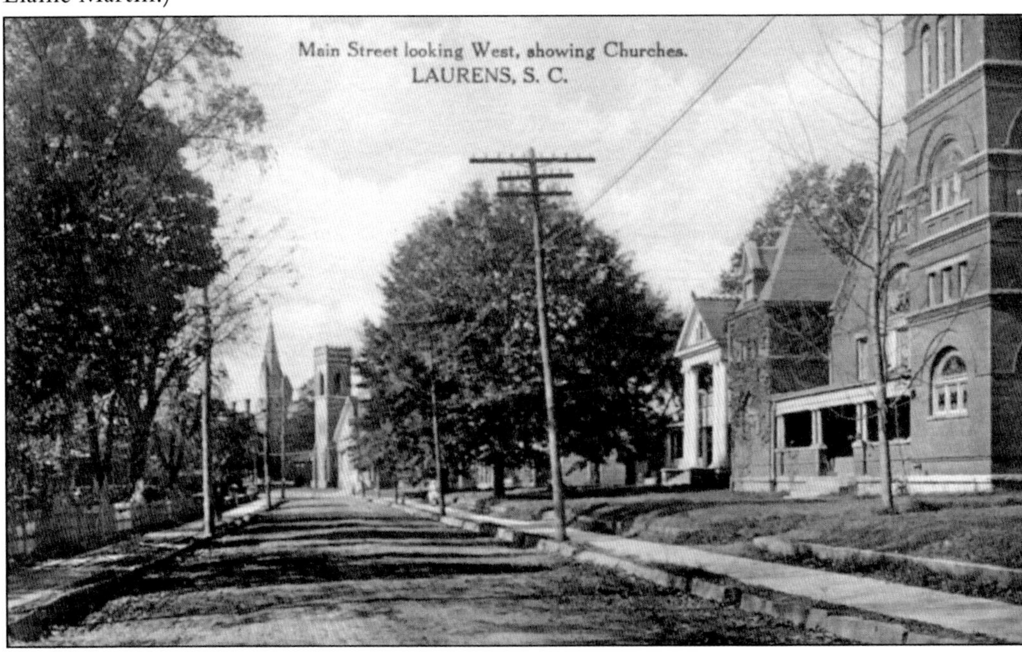

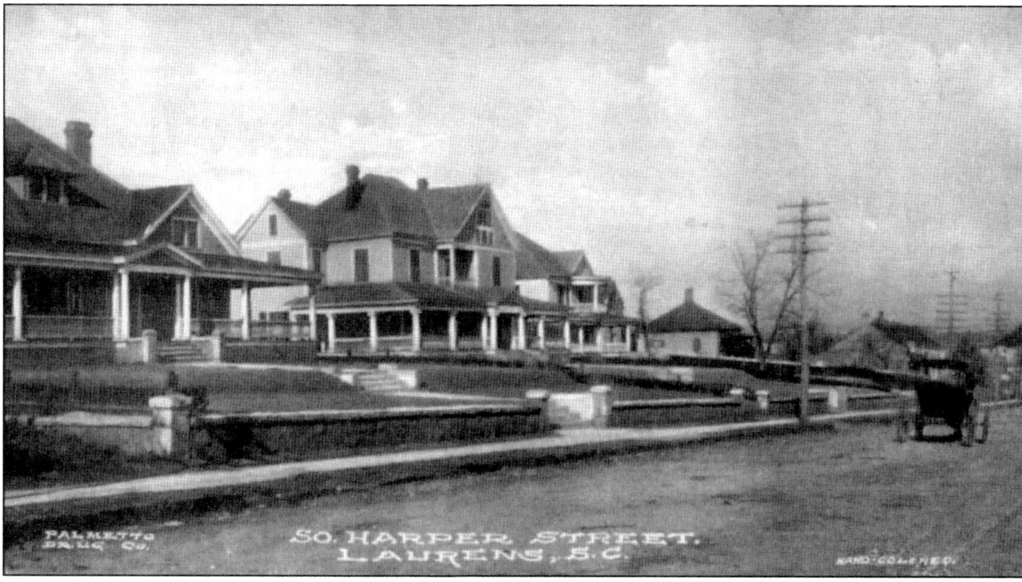

South Harper Street, one of four main thoroughfares that lead to the Laurens Court House Square, was named for Robert Goodloe Harper, who in 1800, prior to moving to Maryland, subdivided and sold his property. The early-1900s postcard shows newly constructed two-story homes on South Harper Street before it was paved. Three of the residences were the Terry, Brown, Barnett House; the Babb, Cook House; and the Hudgens, Sullivan House. (Courtesy Richard B. Taylor Jr.)

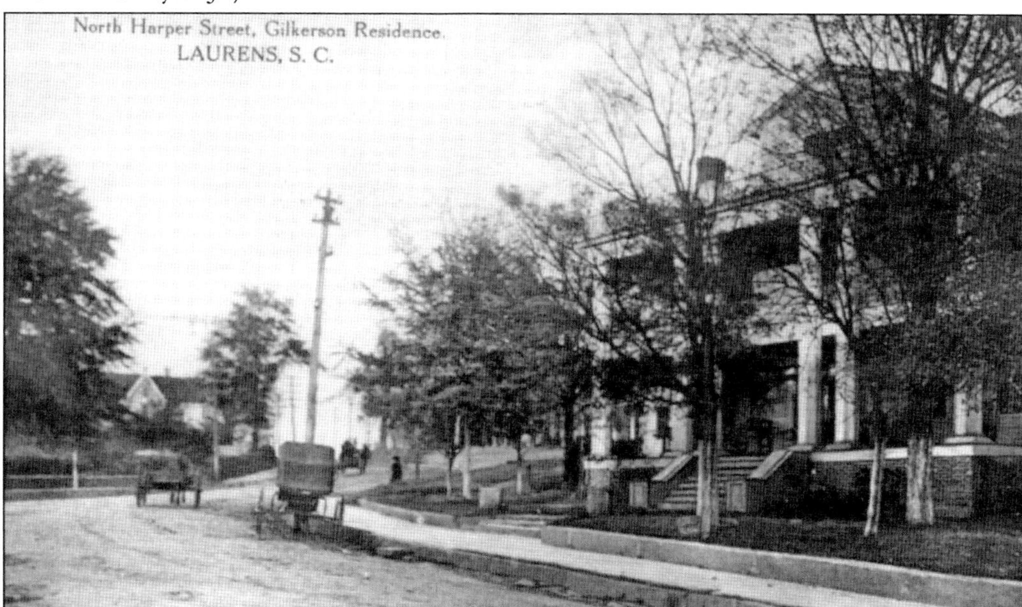

North Harper Street was also named for Robert Goodloe Harper. The postcard by Palmetto Drug Company shows the Black Bear Inn. The inn, so named because North Harper Street was on a tourist route called the Black Bear Trail, was once a popular stopping place for travelers. The Garlington, Richardson, and Bryson families were associated with the large two-story residence before it was torn down. (Courtesy Kathryn W. Johnson.)

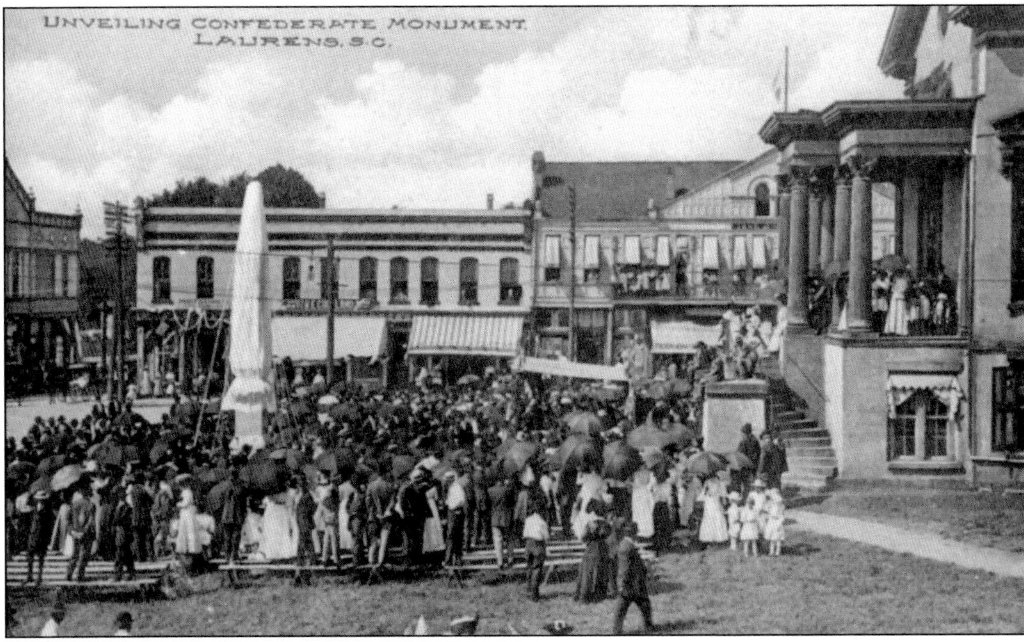

On an April morning in 1861, the first soldiers left Laurens for the War Between the States. These soldiers were the state guards commanded by Capt. Conway Garlington. Also on that memorable Sunday, Capt. Rutherford P. Todd's company of "Briars" came into town to take the train for the war the following Monday morning. On that eventful day, a number of ladies, even though it was Sunday, went to W. C. Dunn's tailor shop and worked all day making caps for Captain Todd's company. From that time on, different companies from every section of Laurens County left for the war from Laurens. Forty-nine years later, a monument to the sacred glory and memory of those patriots was erected and unveiled by the ladies of Laurens, the daughters and granddaughters of those brave soldiers. (Courtesy Richard B. Taylor Jr.)

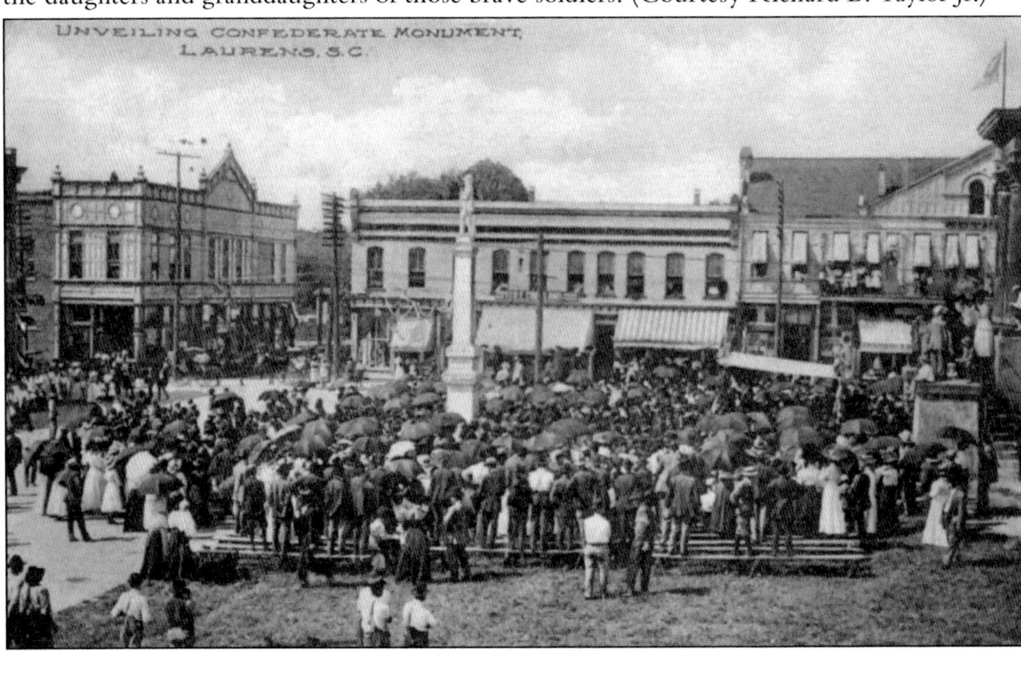

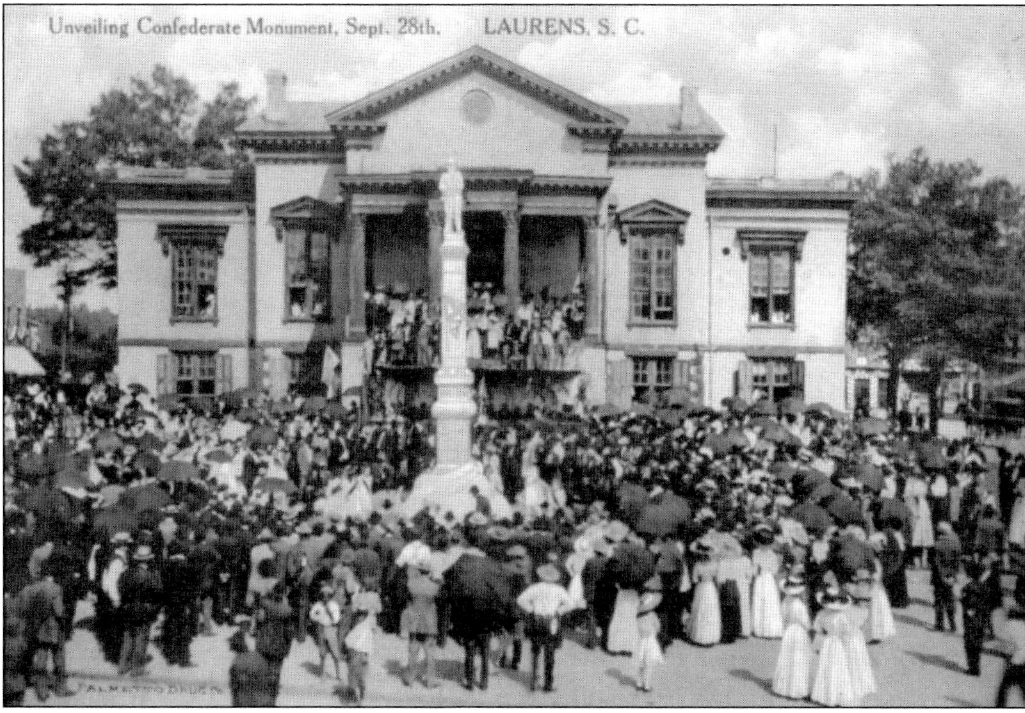

The handsome memorial to the soldiers who participated in the War Between the States was a gift from the people of Laurens County. Mrs. R. B. Bell, president of the John B. Kershaw Chapter of the United Daughters of the Confederacy, along with other members, inaugurated and carried out the movement towards the monument's purchase and erection. After several years of loving toil, the funds to purchase the monument slowly increased until the desired amount was subscribed. It was a grand day on September 28, 1910, the occasion of the unveiling of the Confederate monument to the dead heroes of Laurens County. Laurens, town and county, did themselves proud. The building decorations around the Laurens Court House Square were elaborate, tasteful, and appropriate. (Above courtesy Kathryn W. Johnson; below courtesy Richard B. Taylor Jr.)

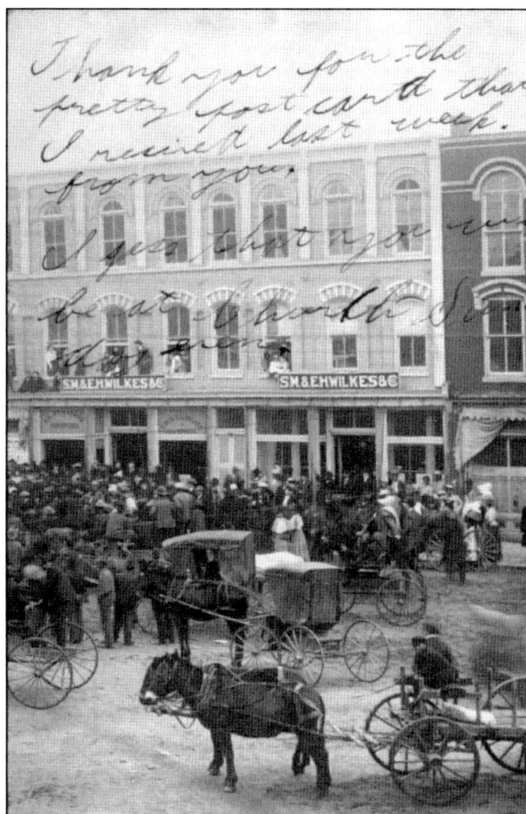

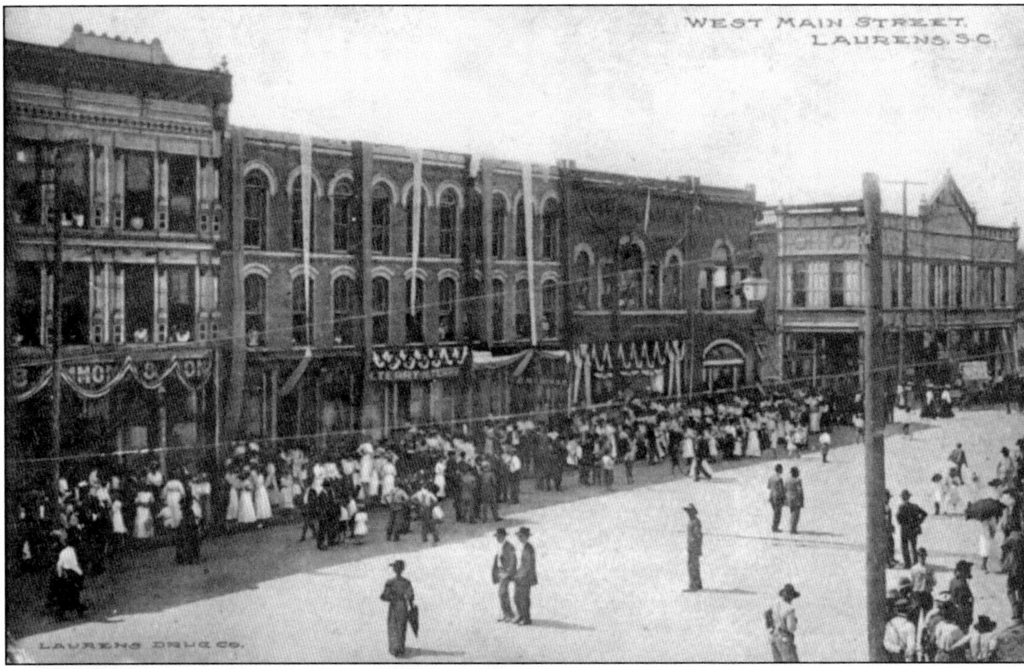

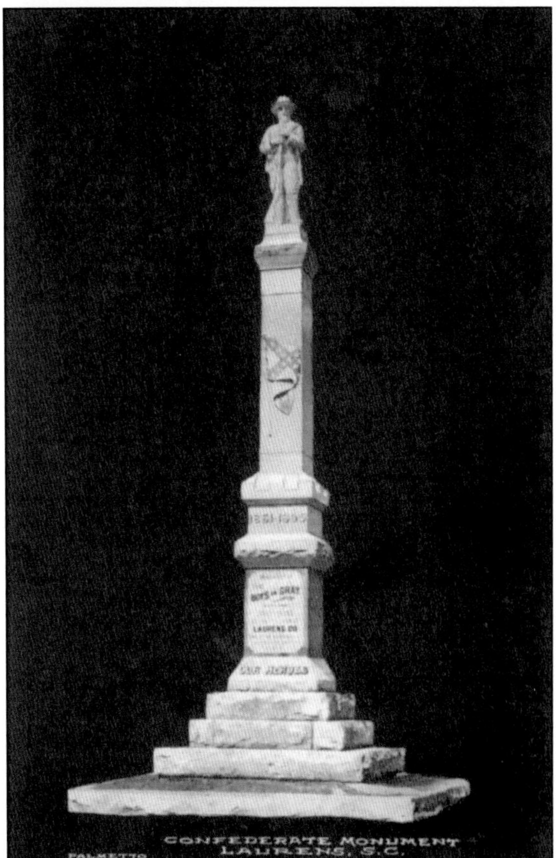

The day, September 28, 1910, was a propitious one for the unveiling of the Confederate monument, and at an early hour, people began to flock into town from all parts of the county; by 9:00, the city was filled with hundreds of people. One of the most beautiful and touching sights was the marching of 600 schoolchildren with 125 old, grizzled war veterans. Fully 3,000 people were in attendance for the exercises. Gov. M. F. Ansel gave the presentation speech and praised both the veterans and the women responsible for the monument. Crowning the 32-foot-high monument is the figure of a Southern soldier, a private, standing erect and almost in the attitude of parade rest. The soldier is facing south. Thirteen little girls, representing the 13 Confederate states, unveiled the monument. (Above courtesy Frances C. Weathers; below courtesy Kathryn W. Johnson.)

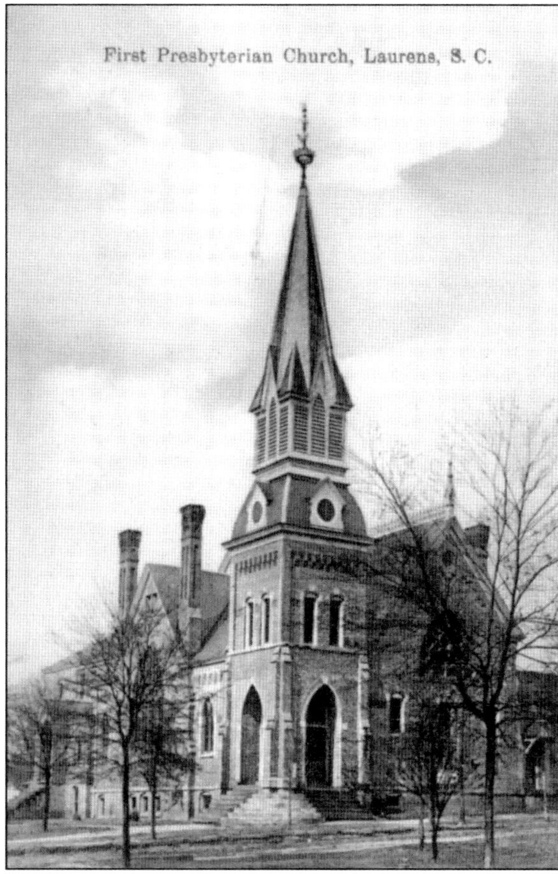

The First Presbyterian Church of Laurens gives credit for its beginning to God's power and the work of Rev. Samuel B. Lewers, who met with a small group at the Laurens County Courthouse in March 1832 and began the organization with 14 charter members. In 1850, the congregation had its first building, an oblong brick structure located in the pines on Church Street. By 1860, the membership had reached 176, forty-six of whom were African Americans. During the ministry of Rev. A. C. Wardlaw, the sixth minister, who served the church from 1890 until 1895, the present church edifice was built on West Main Street. The men of the church did much of the work in the erection of the building. (Above courtesy Laurens County Library; below courtesy Libby C. Rhodes.)

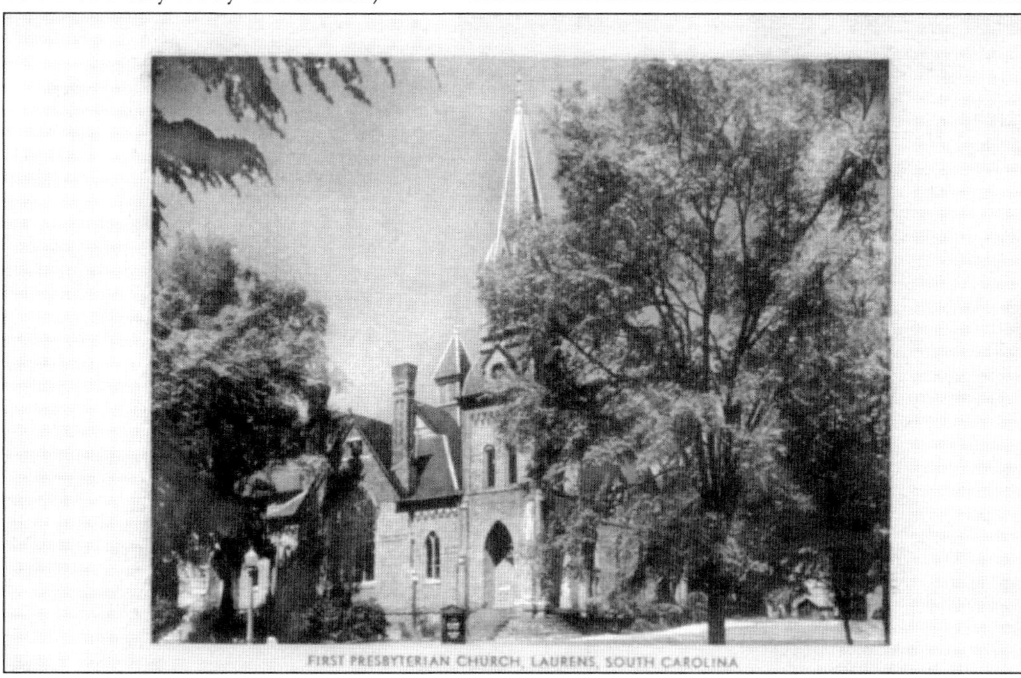

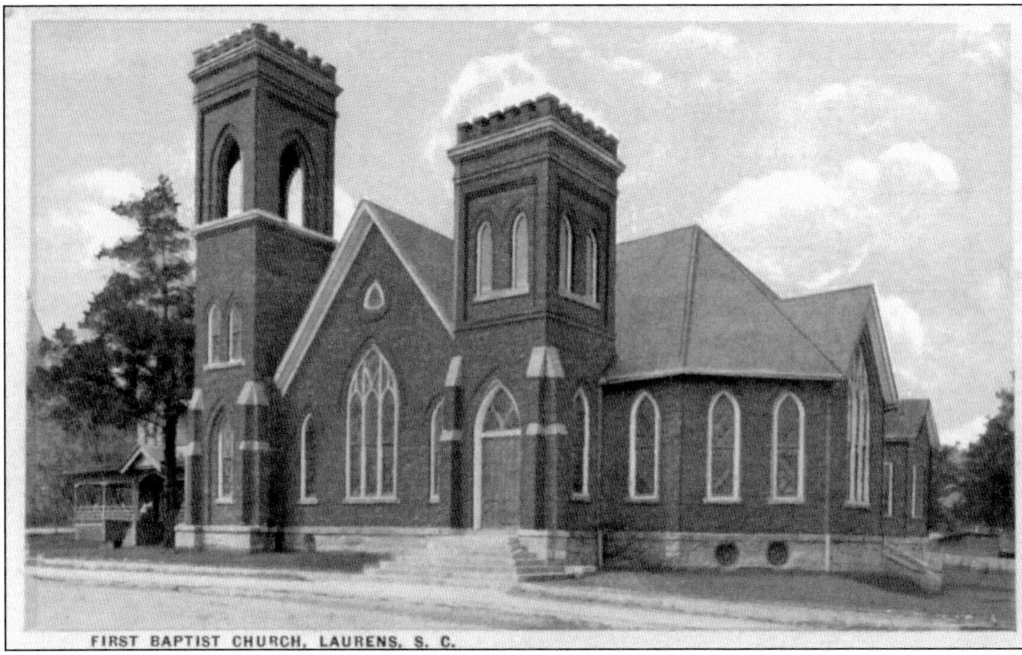

In 1834, the Laurensville Baptist Church was organized with 16 members, 6 by baptism and 10 by letter from other churches. The church was accepted into the Reedy River Association. In 1897, it withdrew to join other Baptist churches in the county to form the Laurens Baptist Association. By 1869, the membership had reached 73. The first house of worship, a small wooden structure, was built in 1850 on the corner of Church and College Streets in Laurens and was dedicated November 18, 1851. During the years and as the congregation increased, several brick churches were constructed. These postcards show the First Baptist Church in 1911 on the corner of West Main and Church Streets and the present-day Laurens First Baptist Church and the Easterby Chapel, which are in the same location. (Courtesy Kathryn Weathers Johnson.)

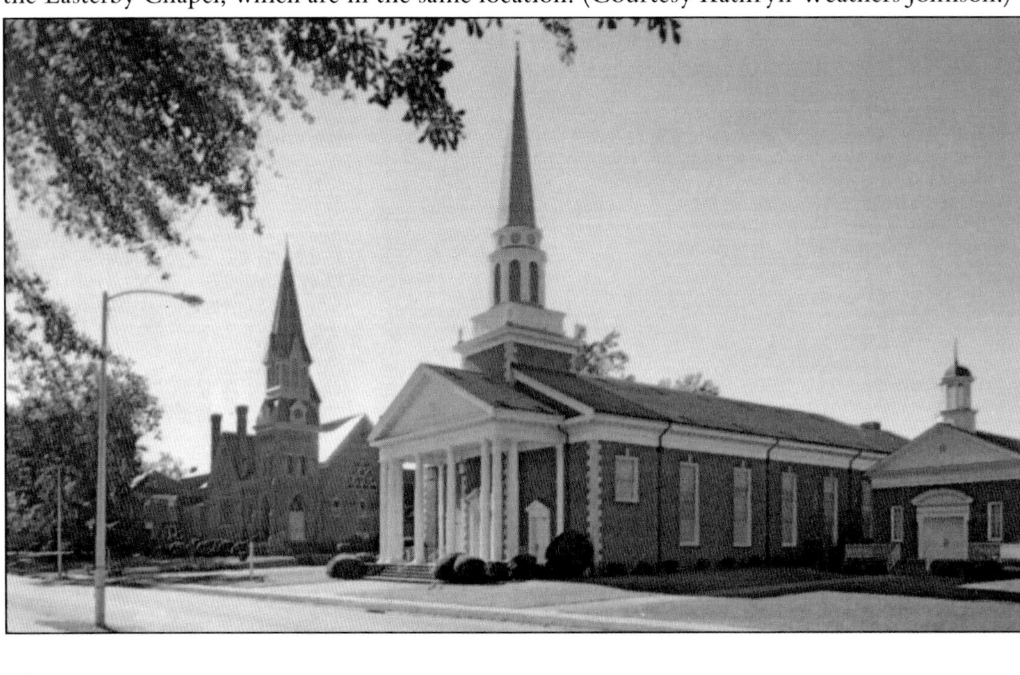

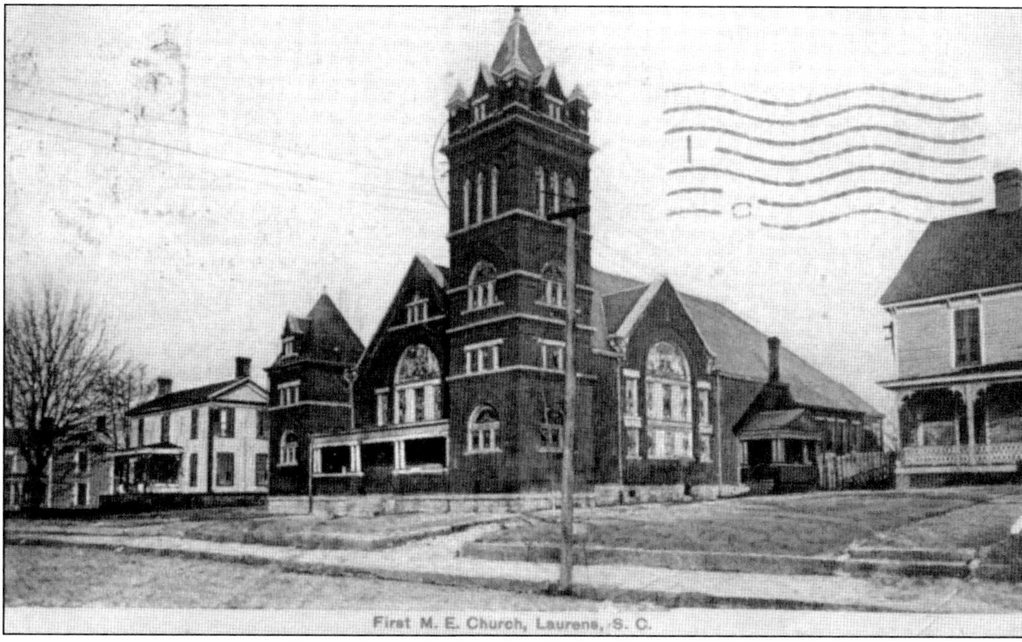

In the year 1819, fifteen earnest Christian men and women organized the First Methodist Church under the guidance of a traveling preacher from Virginia. In 1824, these Methodist friends built a small wooden church on West Main Street. As members and means increased, the small church was torn down and another one built nearby next to the railroad tracks on a lot donated by John Garlington. Garlington's generosity was unlimited. He used his own skilled workmen in helping to erect the building. The First United Methodist Church, located on West Main Street in Laurens, was constructed in 1897–1898 at a cost of $15,000. The first service in the church was held on Christmas Day, 1898, with Rev. R. Herbert Jones delivering the sermon. The first infant to be baptized in the church was Hattie Dunklin Gray. (Above courtesy Frances C. Weathers; below courtesy Ellen D. Simpson.)

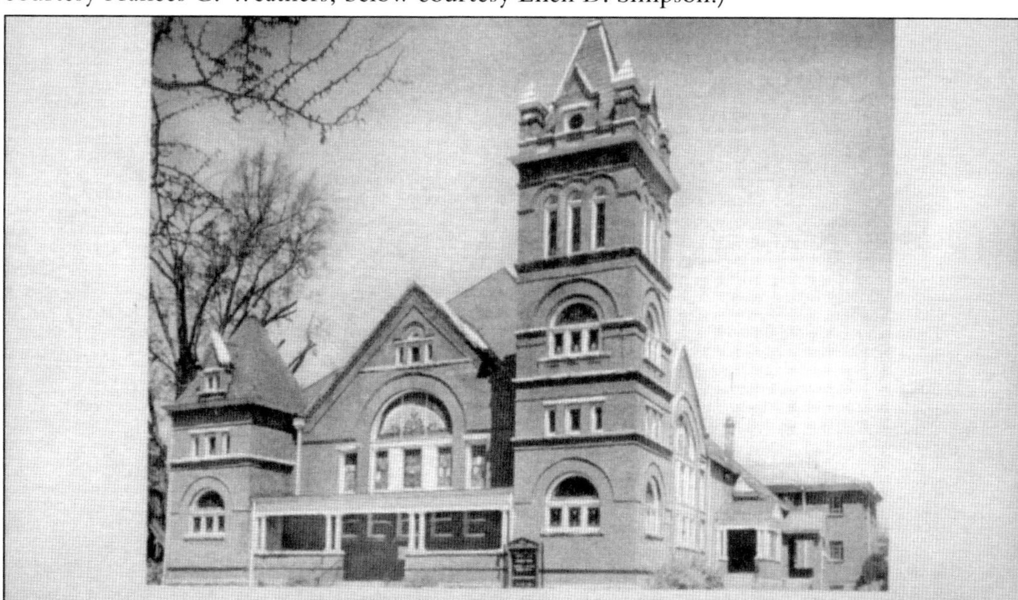

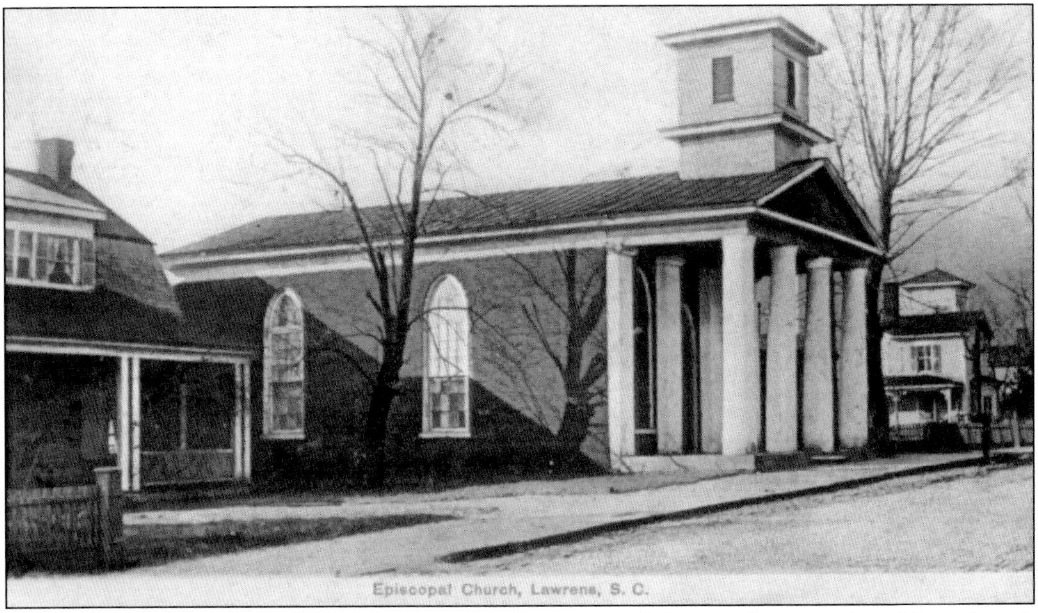

Located on West Main Street in Laurens, the Church of the Epiphany is the oldest church building in the city of Laurens. The church was built in 1846 on land given by Col. James H. Irby, a prominent Laurens citizen. T. R. Badgett constructed the church from bricks made in his brickyard near Wattsville. Refugees from the Lowcountry worshipped in the church during the War Between the States. (Courtesy Richard B. Taylor Jr.)

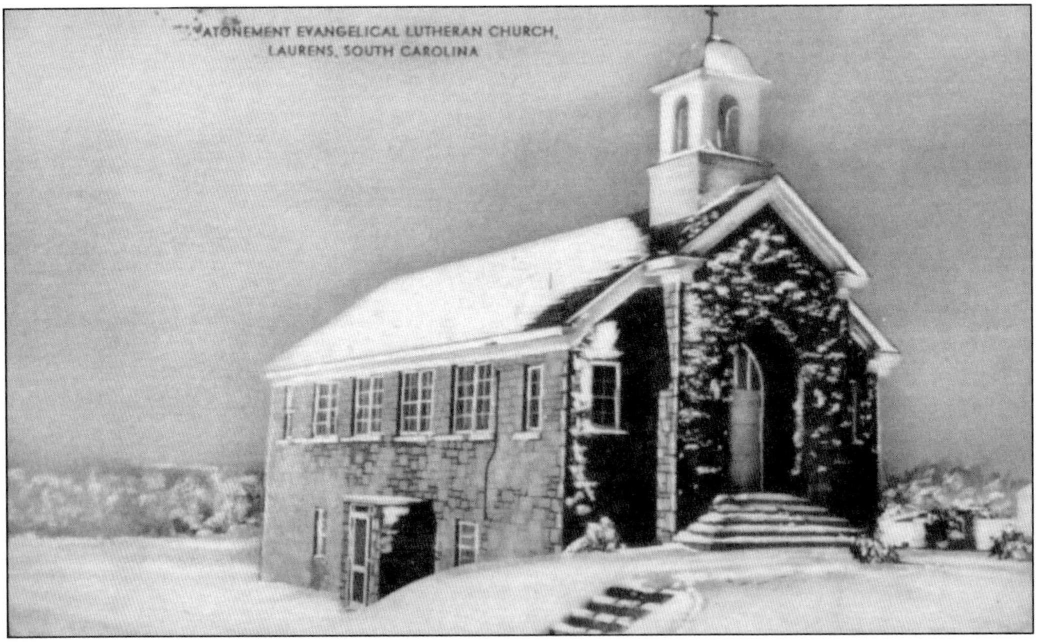

The first Lutheran service was held in Laurens in 1944 at the home of Mrs. J. Turner Martin by Rev. J. Shelton Moose. At this service, the Holy Communion was administered to 20 Lutherans. The Atonement Lutheran Church was organized in 1945 with 43 charter members. By 1946, the membership had reached 50. The stone church is located on Farley Avenue in Laurens. (Courtesy Kathryn W. Johnson.)

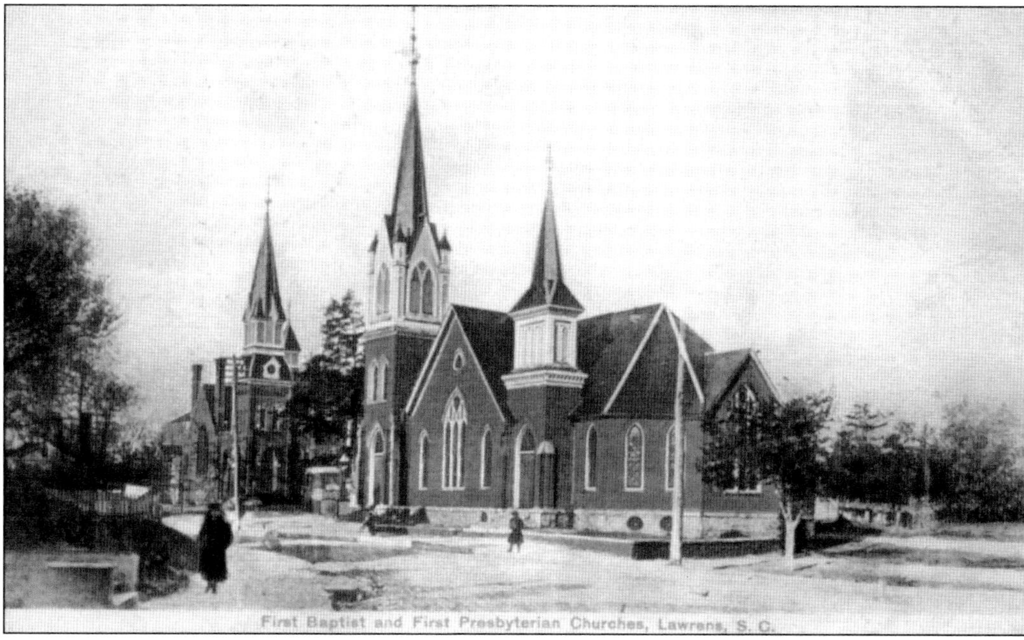

Steeples of the First Baptist Church and the First Presbyterian Church and pedestrians are shown on West Main Street. The church steeples also dot the landscape in a bird's-eye view of Laurens. Two-story West Main Street residences, tenant houses, barns, fences, outbuildings, chicken coops, and garden plots tell the story of men, women, and children and the lives they lived. It was common for city dwellers to have livestock and a variety of fowl contained in lots and pens behind their homes. Shown in the forefront of the early-1900s postcard is a Charleston and Western Carolina (C&WC) railway car. It, too, is a reminder of days gone by and the importance the railroad played in the development of Laurens. (Courtesy Richard B. Taylor Jr.)

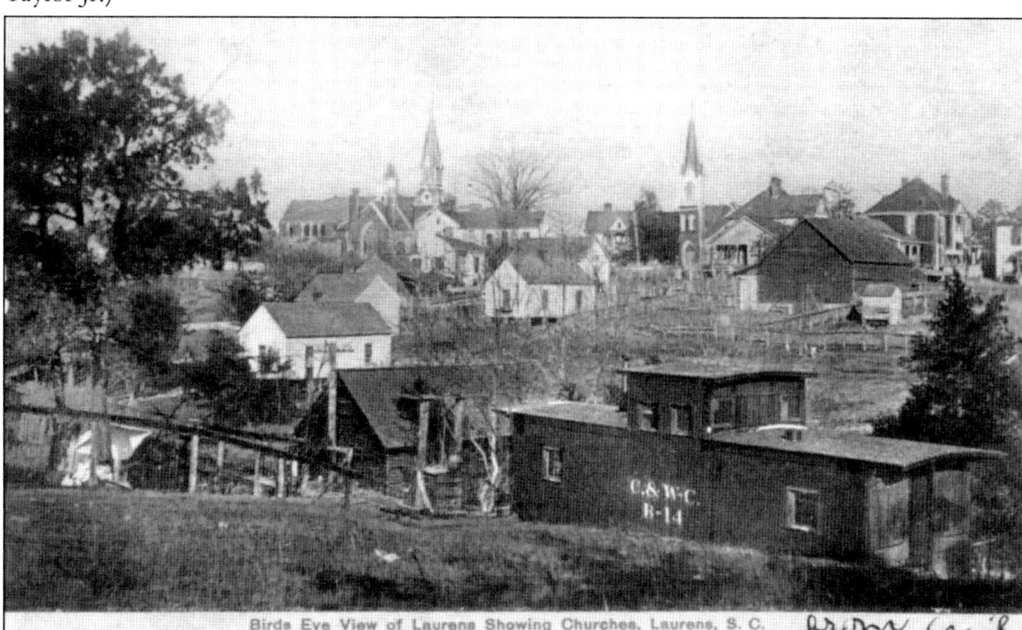

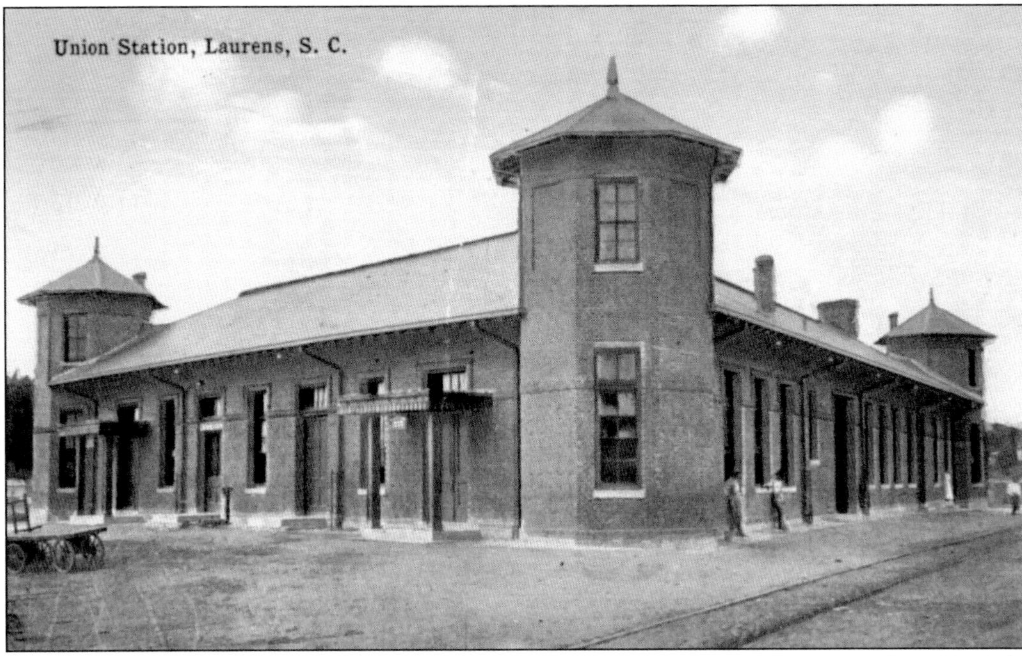

Located on East Main Street, Union Station or the Laurens Depot was constructed *c.* 1908. The unusual, wedge-shaped, brick, triangular station served the C&WC as well as the Columbia, Newberry, and Laurens Railroad (CN&L). The C&WC ran to Spartanburg and was on the left side of the depot, while the CN&L was on the right side. The depot was a vital and necessary part of Laurens. (Courtesy Frances C. Weathers.)

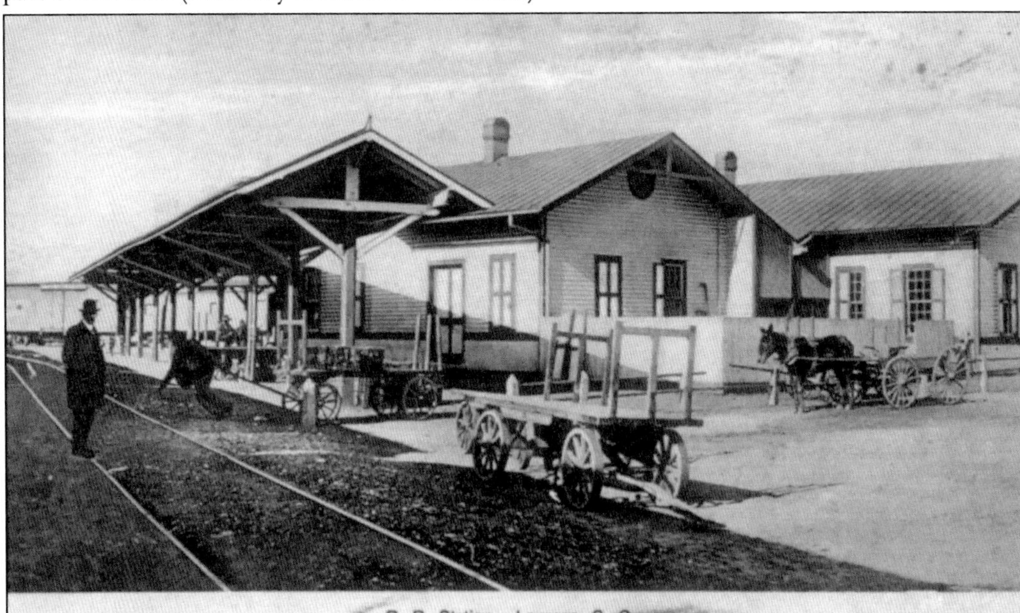

The wooden railway station located on East Main Street in Laurens served mainly as a freight station. Merchants and farmers were dependent upon this station, and mules and wagons were common and familiar sights at the railway station. The railroad played an important factor in the growth of the town of Laurens. (Courtesy Frances C. Weathers.)

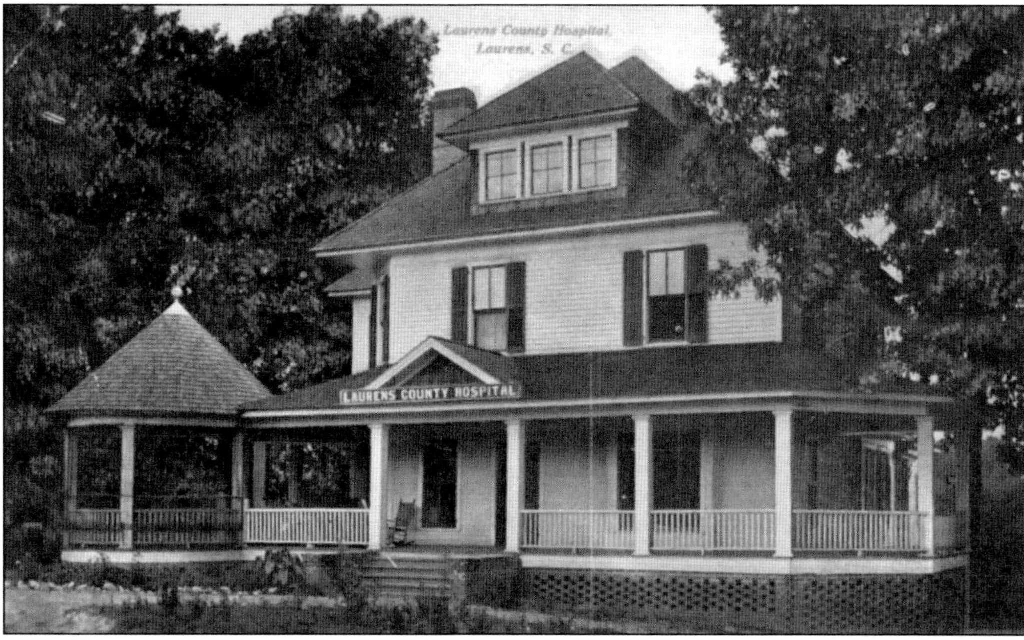

The first hospital registered in Laurens County (above) was organized in 1911 by Julia Irby in a dwelling on Chestnut Street. The hospital moved in 1914 to Irby's home, located between South Harper Street and Irby Avenue Extension in Laurens. The Irby House Hospital did not have an elevator, and patients were carried by hand to the upstairs rooms. Later the hospital became a satellite of the Mary Black Sanitarium of Spartanburg. When a patient required surgery, Dr. Hugh Black traveled from Spartanburg to perform the operation. After Dr. Black decided to give up the hospital, a board of trustees was formed and operated the hospital as a community venture until 1932, when a lack of funds forced the board of trustees to turn the Irby House Hospital over to local physicians. (Above courtesy Frances C. Weathers; below courtesy Elaine Martin.)

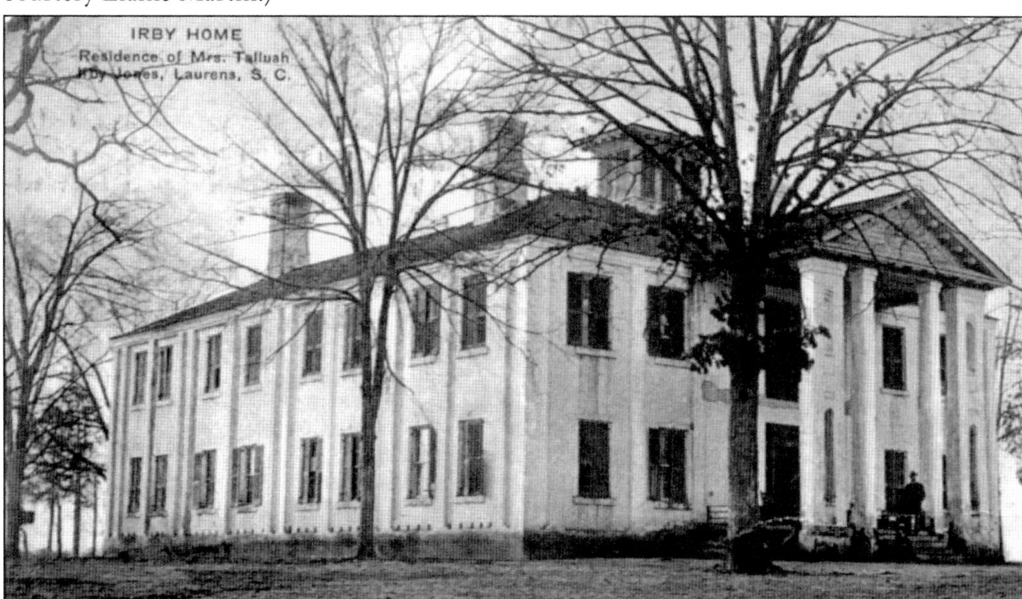

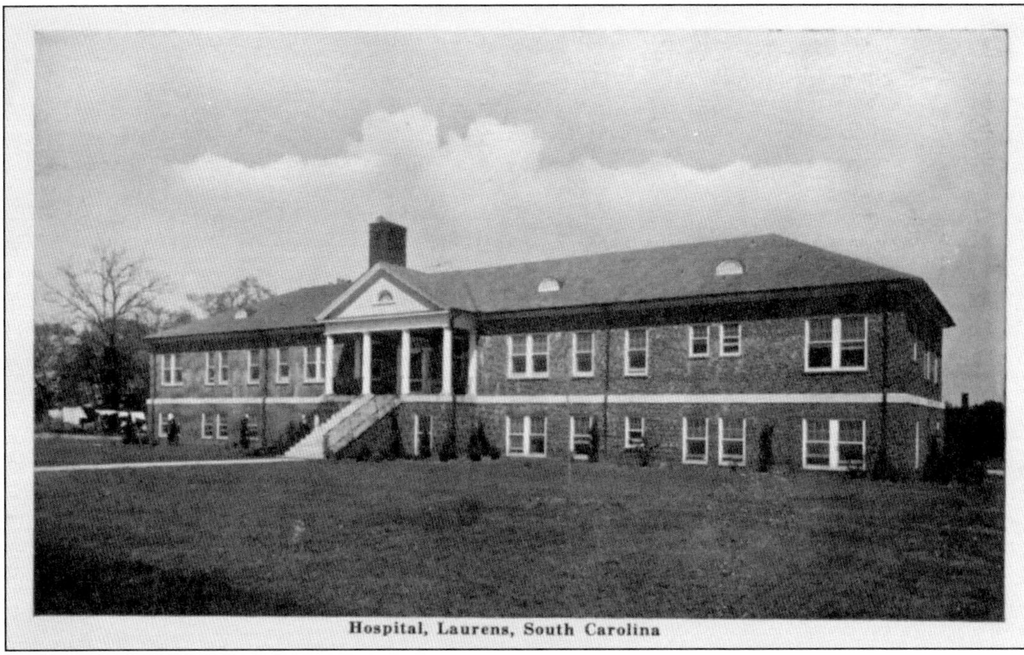

In 1933, Laurens County voted on a bond issue to build a new hospital with public funds. The question was decided in the affirmative. The two-story general hospital was erected on Farley Avenue in 1936 on a lot donated by J. Calvin Owings, using federal and county funds and Works Progress Administration labor. The hospital opened on January 1, 1937, with 29 beds. One patient was transferred from the old Irby House Hospital. (Courtesy Elaine Martin.)

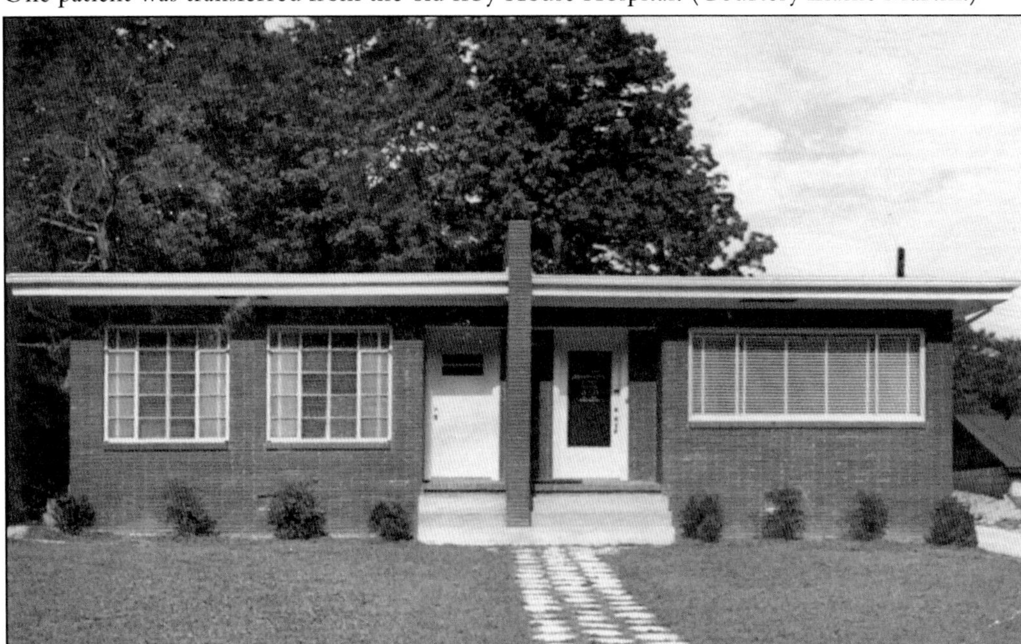

The C. J. Hart Chiropractic Clinic was located at 205 Church Street in Laurens. Dr. Hart kept regular business hours and was open on Sunday by appointment. This advertising Ektachrome postcard was done by Helen S. O'Brien. (Courtesy Elaine Martin.)

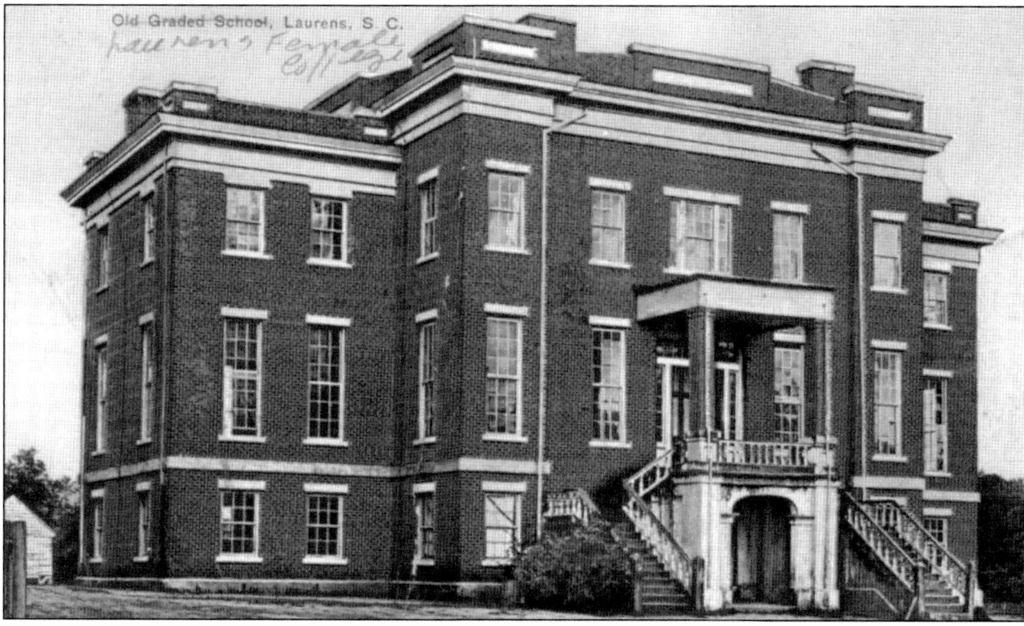

The Laurens Female College, founded in 1858, was situated on a six-acre campus on the outskirts of Laurens near the corner of West Main and Church Streets. The three-story brick structure housed 15 classrooms, a museum, and a library containing approximately 1,000 volumes. The curriculum compared favorably with other female institutions in the South and was one of the most celebrated female institutions in upstate South Carolina. (Courtesy Laurens County Library.)

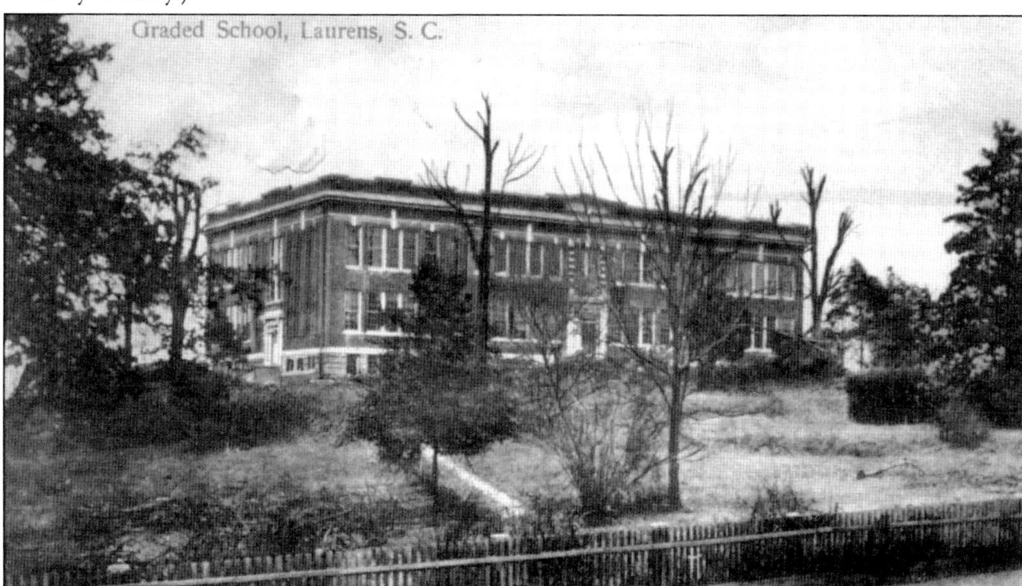

The exact date of the establishment of the first schoolhouse in Laurens is not found in any existing records. However, the first courthouse in Laurens was used for school purposes. In 1908, the Laurens Graded School was constructed on the corner of Church and Laurens Streets, just off the Laurens Court House Square. The Laurens Police and Fire Departments replaced the "Old Central School." (Courtesy Frances C. Weathers.)

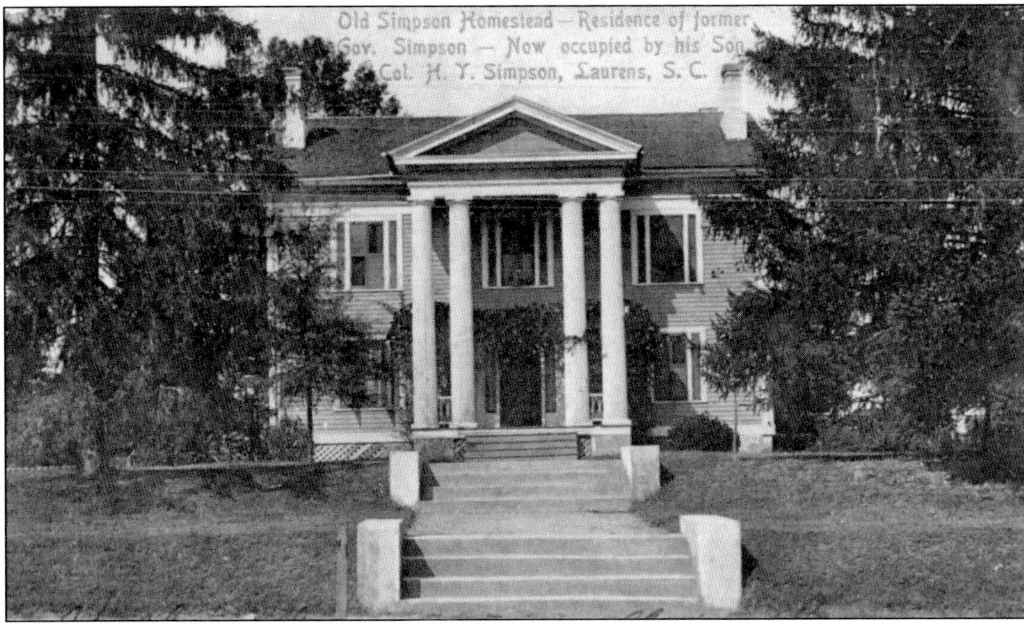

Christopher Garlington constructed the Greek Revival house in 1839 on West Main Street. Maj. Adam Eichelberger became the next owner of the Colonial mansion. William D. Simpson was the third owner of the house in the years following the War Between the States. Simpson later became governor of South Carolina. The late Mason Theodore and Louise Holmes Motes acquired the property in 1939. (Courtesy Frances C. Weathers.)

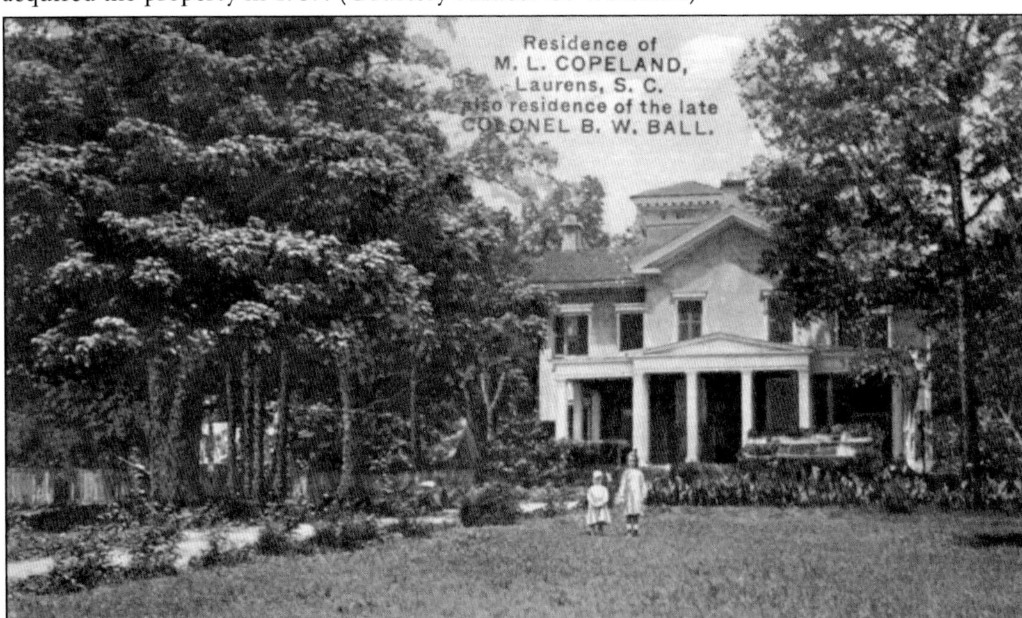

This Italian villa mansion was constructed *c.* 1859 by Col. John D. Williams. B. W. Ball purchased the house in 1875 for his wife, Eliza Watts Ball. Ball's daughter and son-in-law, Sara Ball Copeland and Mason L. Copeland, were the next occupants of the house. Clyde Franks purchased the property in the early 1960s, and today it is the focal point of the Martha Franks Baptist Retirement Center. (Courtesy Frances C. Weathers.)

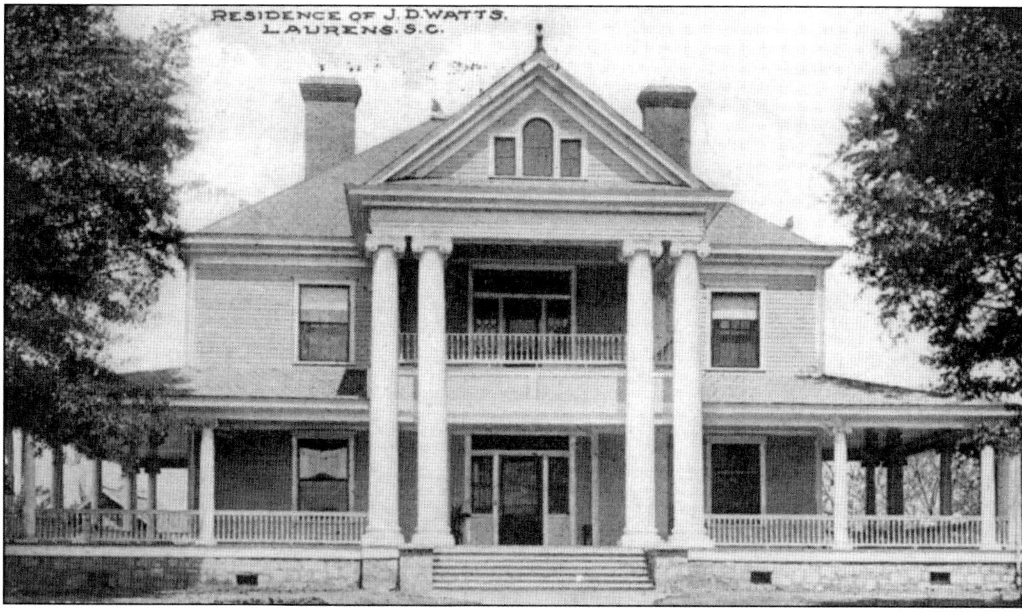

Once located on West Main Street next to the First Methodist Church, this residence belonged to J. Dunklin Watts, a farmer and cotton buyer. He was the son of William Dendy and Sara Cannon Watts and spent his boyhood years on the Watts Plantation on the north side of Laurens. Watts was married to the former Hattie Frierson, a daughter of a First Presbyterian Church minister, E. O. Frierson. (Courtesy Richard B. Taylor Jr.)

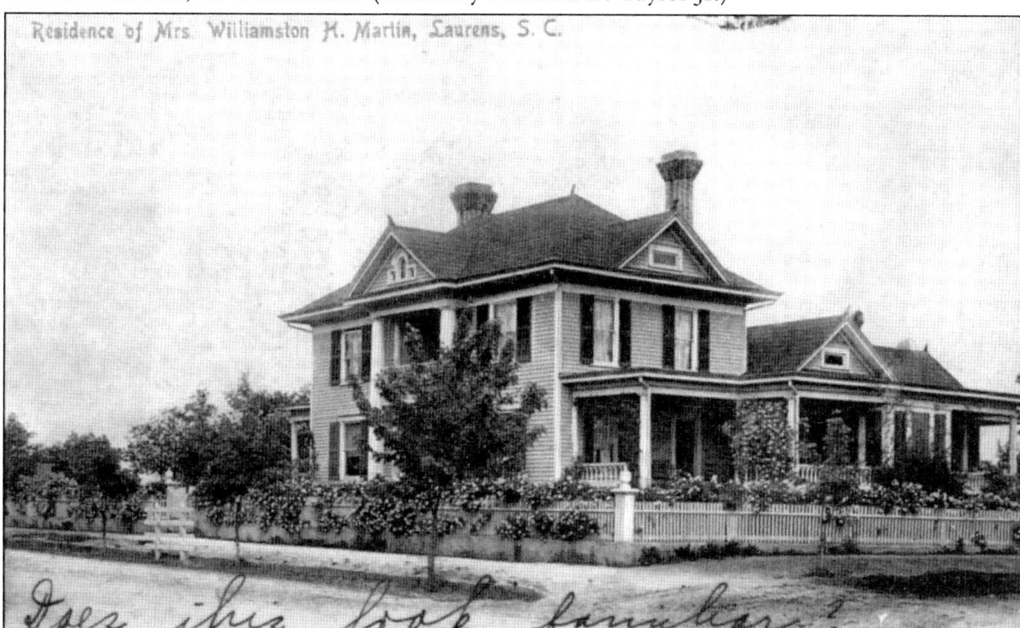

Col. Henry Williamson H. Martin and his wife, the former Anna Sitgreaves, lived in this West Main Street residence. Later Albert and Lucy Dial became owners of the house. Lucy Dial was a niece of Anna Sitgreaves. After Albert Dial's death, Lucy continued to reside in the charming two-story residence, and thus it became known as "Ms. Lucy's House." This postcard shows a front and side view of the residence. (Courtesy Laurens County Library.)

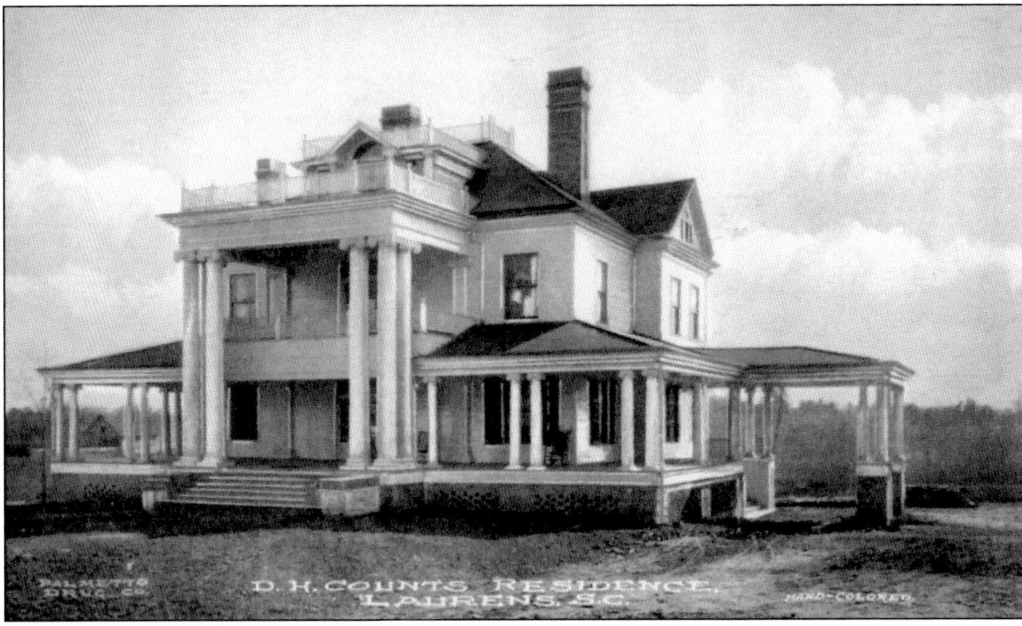

David Henry Counts, originally from Bamberg County, was a prominent livestock dealer in Laurens. He and his wife, the former Bessie Hartzog, resided in the West Main Street house. Later Dr. and Mrs. Graves L. Knight purchased the house. Dr. Knight served as president of Anderson College. Torn down in the 1960s, the house was replaced by Westside Manor Apartments. This postcard was printed and sold by the Palmetto Drug Company in Laurens. (Courtesy Kathryn W. Johnson.)

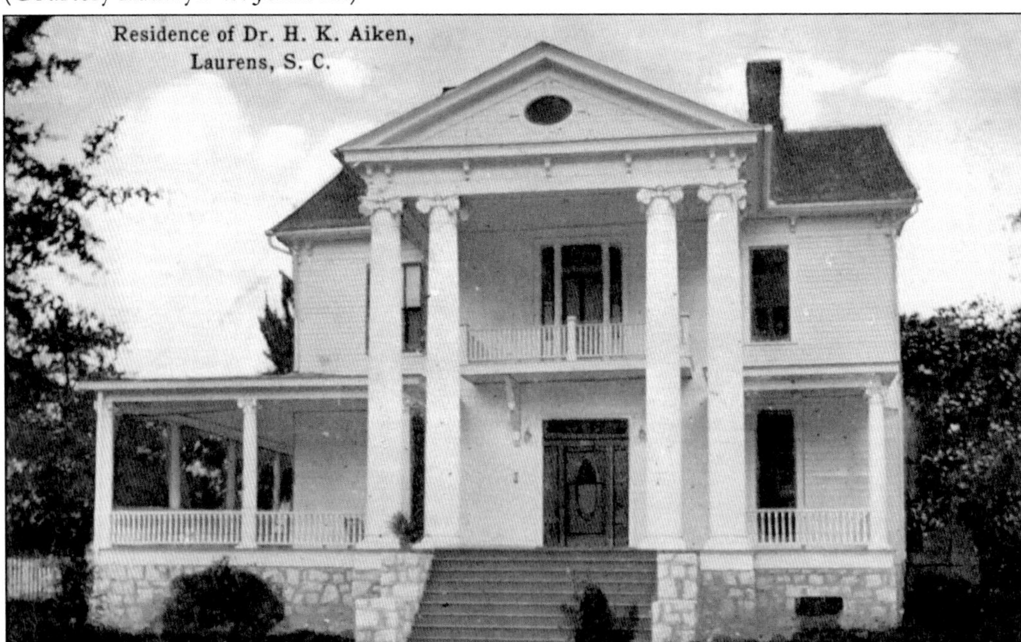

Dr. John D. Pitts began construction on this Greek Revival home on West Main Street in the late 1860s. It was completed *c.* 1870. Dr. H. K. Aiken, a Laurens physician, pharmacist, and later a banker, purchased the residence in the 1930s. (Courtesy Laurens County Library.)

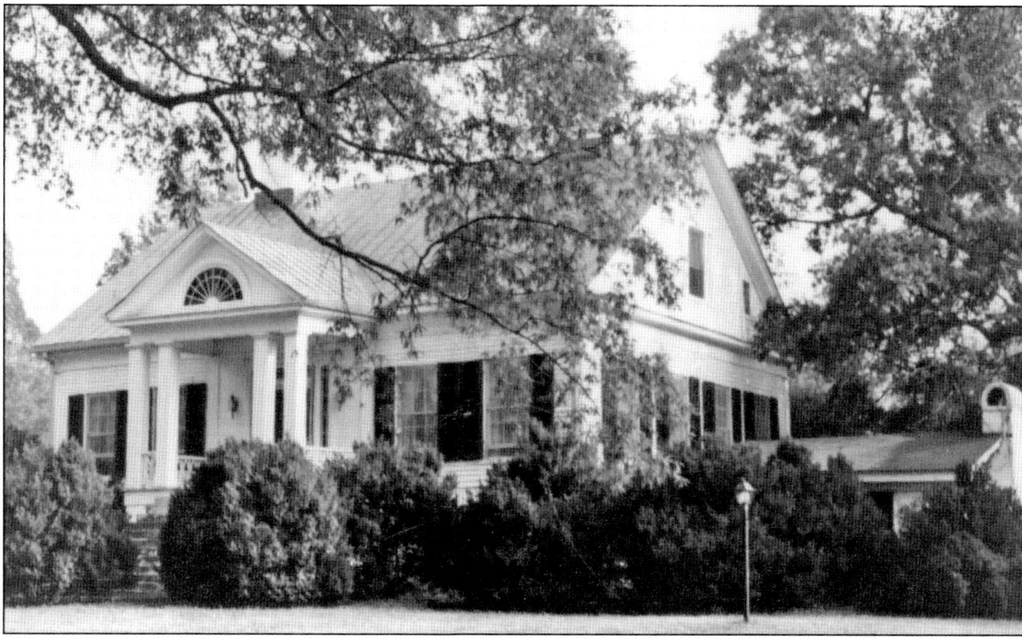

Allen Dial constructed a vernacular Greek Revival cottage *c.* 1855 about six miles west of Laurens. Allen Dial was a farmer, self-taught doctor, and leader in Chestnut Ridge Baptist Church. He was a grandson of Hastings Dial, who settled in what is now Laurens County in 1770. Carrington and Mary Herbert acquired the house and acreage in 1950 and continue to call Cedar Valley Farms home. (Courtesy Ellen D. Simpson.)

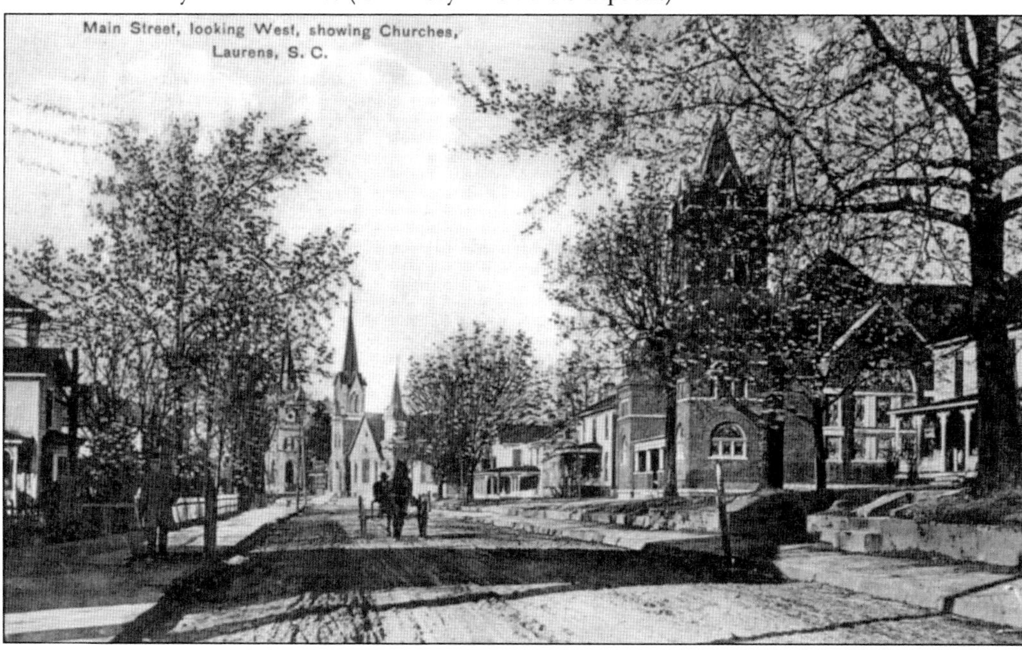

A horse and buggy shown traveling down a dirt West Main Street moves past the Laurens First Methodist Church and residences and is headed in the direction of the Laurens Court House Square. The steeples of the Baptist and Presbyterian churches can be seen in the background as well as gentlemen strolling along West Main Street. (Courtesy Richard B. Taylor Jr.)

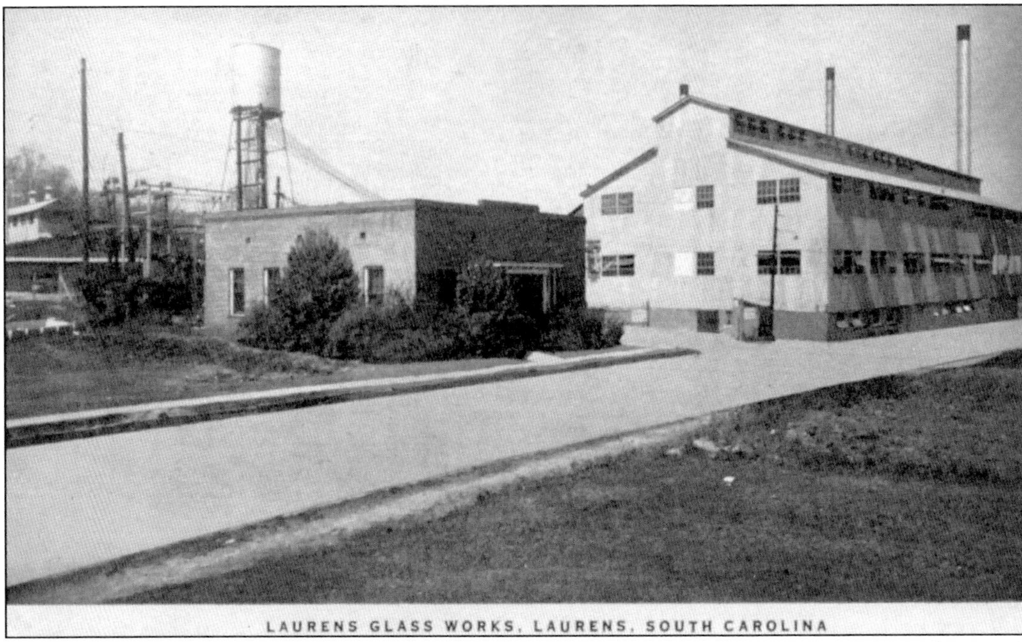

Laurens Glass was originally founded by Luther McCord, a Laurens photographer with mineralogy for a hobby. McCord found silica on "The Little Knob" and "The Big Knob" (hills located near Gray Court) and discovered that silica-sand is valuable to glass workers. Laurens Glass Company was organized by N. B. Dial and a group of businessmen in 1910. The operation was closed in 1911. The company was reorganized in 1913 by Albert Dial, Ernest Easterby, and H. Douglas Gray. Dial served as president until his death in 1928. Albert Dial obtained the first license in the United States to manufacture Coca-Cola bottles. Following Dial's death, Easterby became president of Laurens Glass. Numerous citizens, as shown below, found employment at Laurens Glass during the years of its operation. (Above courtesy Libby C. Rhodes; below courtesy South Caroliniana Library, University of South Carolina, Columbia.)

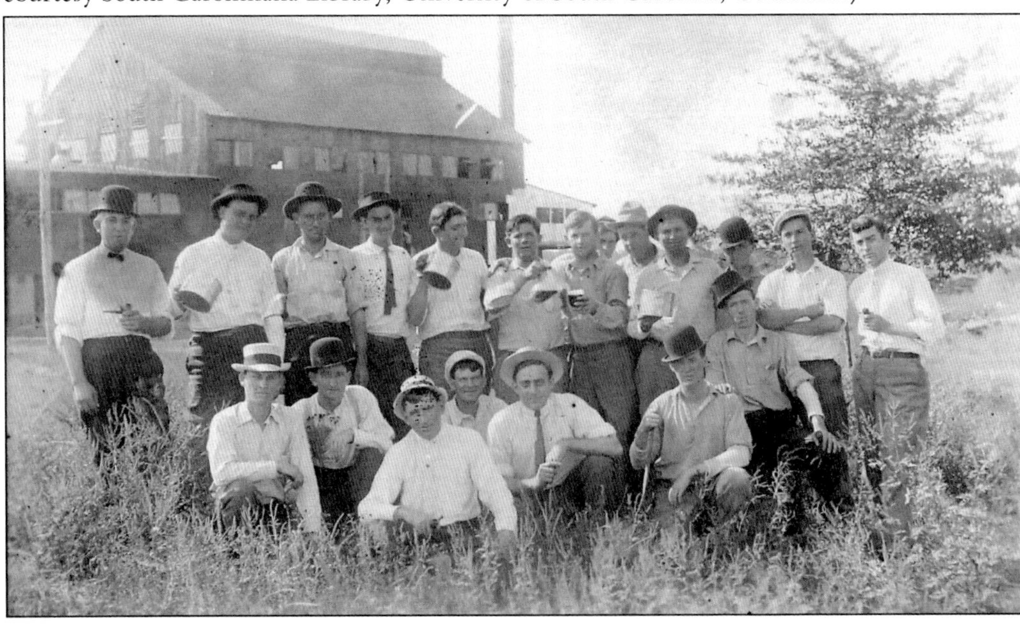

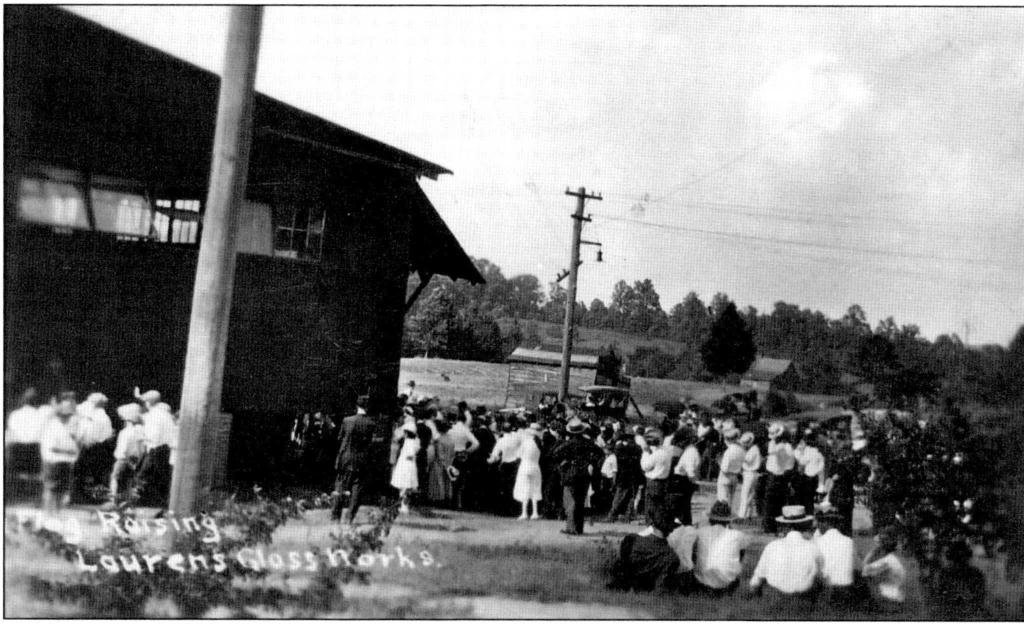

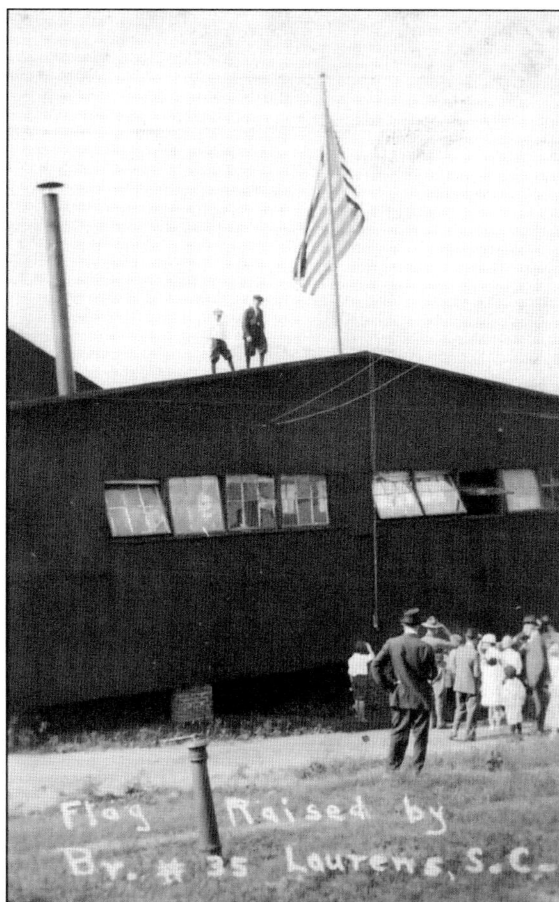

Laurens Glass Works was organized in 1910, with a capital subscription of $50,000, by a group of local businessmen who knew absolutely nothing of the manufacture of glass but were willing to give of their time and risk their money in the growth of an industry that would give much-needed employment to their sons and the younger generations of the community. Most of the first equipment came from the old Carolina Glass Company of Columbia, South Carolina, which had been forced into bankruptcy. After the 1913 reorganization, bottles were made by the hand-blown method, and experienced glass blowers were imported from Ohio and Pennsylvania. The 1900s postcards depict a flag-raising ceremony at Laurens Glass Works. (Courtesy South Caroliniana Library, University of South Carolina, Columbia.)

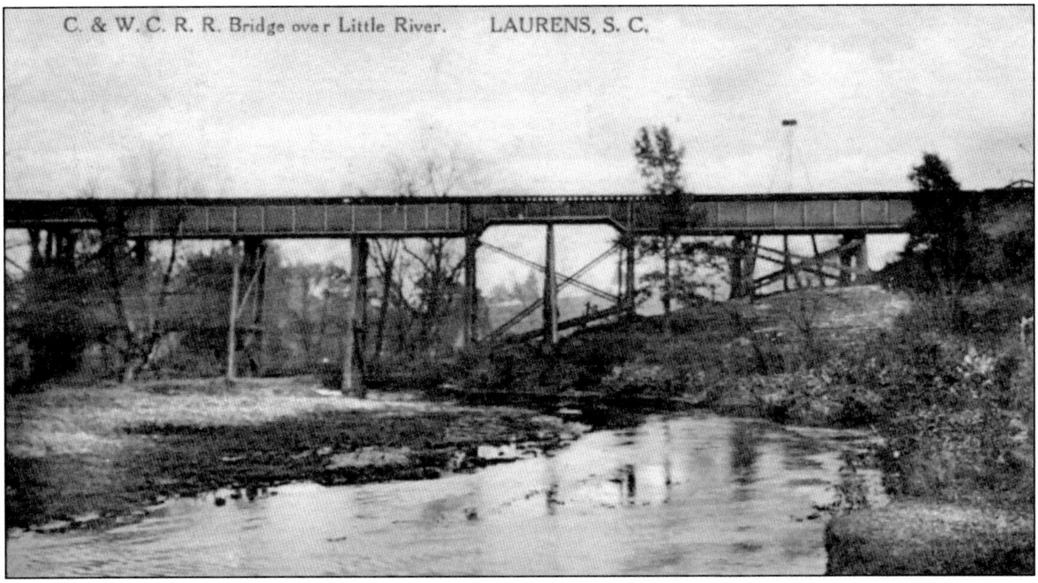

The town of Laurens was built near the banks of Little River because of the accessibility and need of water. Even though it is a small river, Little River has a history of overflowing and damaging homes, businesses, and public properties. Numerous times through the years, Gordon Street homes were flooded by the waters of Little River. This postcard, published and sold by Palmetto Drug Company, shows Little River and the C&WC Railroad Bridge on the east side of Laurens at Gordon Street. (Courtesy Richard B. Taylor Jr.)

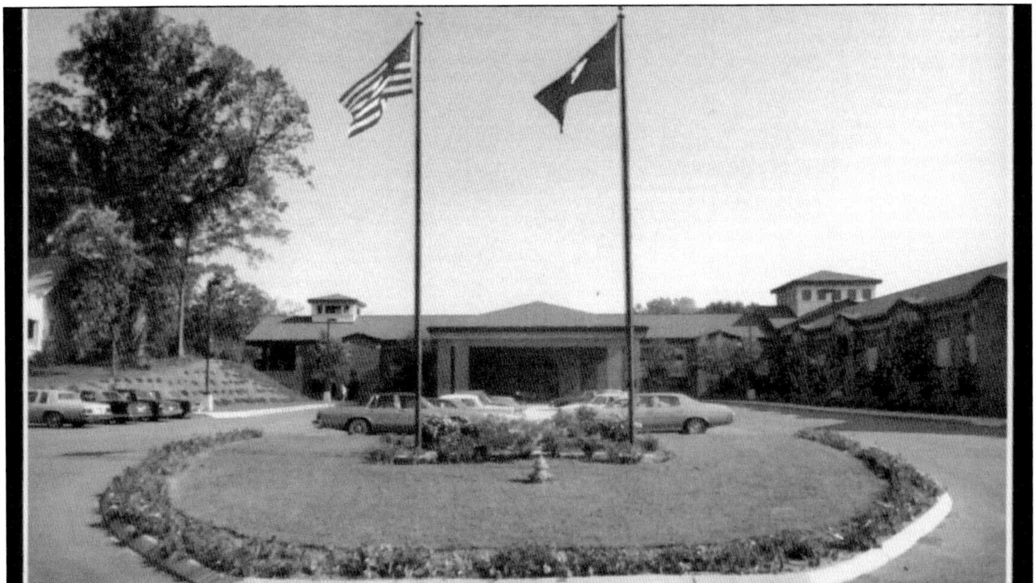

Martha Franks, a retired Baptist missionary to Taiwan, planted the seed for a Baptist retirement center in Laurens *c.* 1965. She and a missionary friend, Olive Lawton, realized the need of a home where older men and women could find companionship and continue with productive lives. After raising $310,000, the dream became a reality in the construction of the Martha Franks Baptist Retirement Center. The Italian villa home, previously owned and occupied by Martha's brother, Clyde Franks, became the hub of activity for the center. (Courtesy Elaine Martin.)

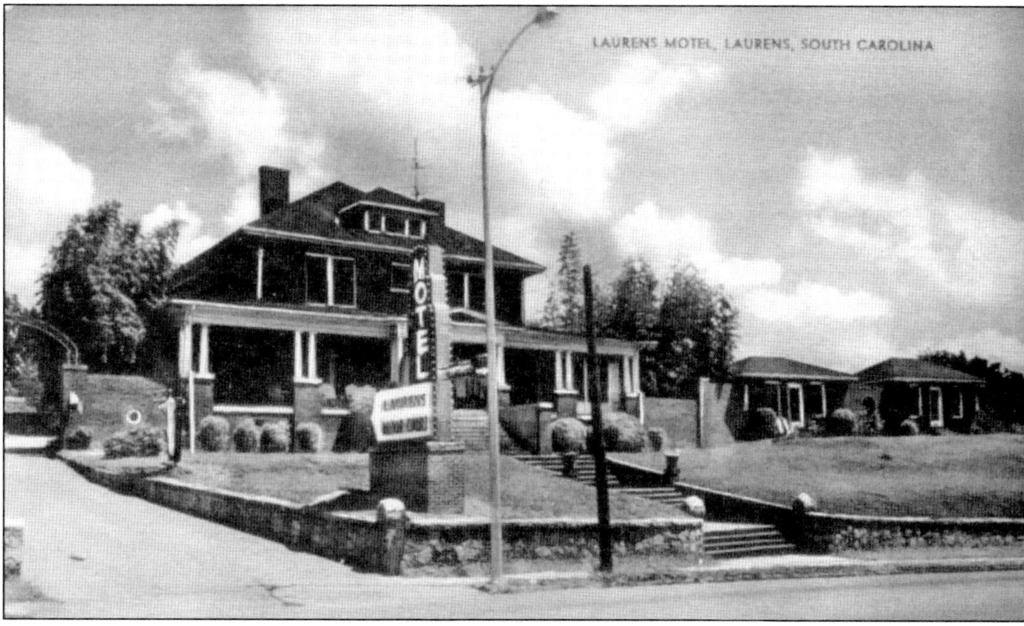

This 1960s postcard describes the Laurens Motel as having 15 modern units, air-conditioning, and tile baths and being located one block from the Laurens Court House Square on East Main Street leading into U.S. Highway 76. The establishment, now the Laurens Motel Apartments, is still open for guests. (Courtesy Kathryn W. Johnson.)

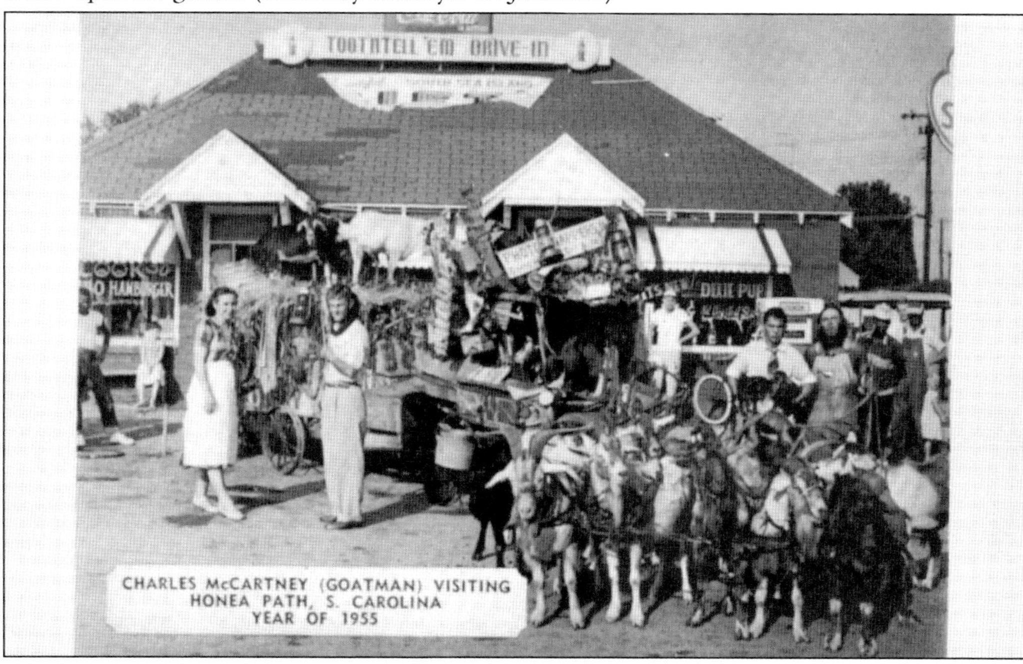

For many years, Charles McCartney ("The Goat Man") made an annual trek through Laurens County. Thrilled by his rickety wagon, pulled by a team of goats and followed by a goat herd, both adults and children extended a cordial welcome to the itinerant traveler. This 1955 postcard shows McCartney in Honea Path, where he was probably on his way to Laurens. (Courtesy Frances C. Weathers.)

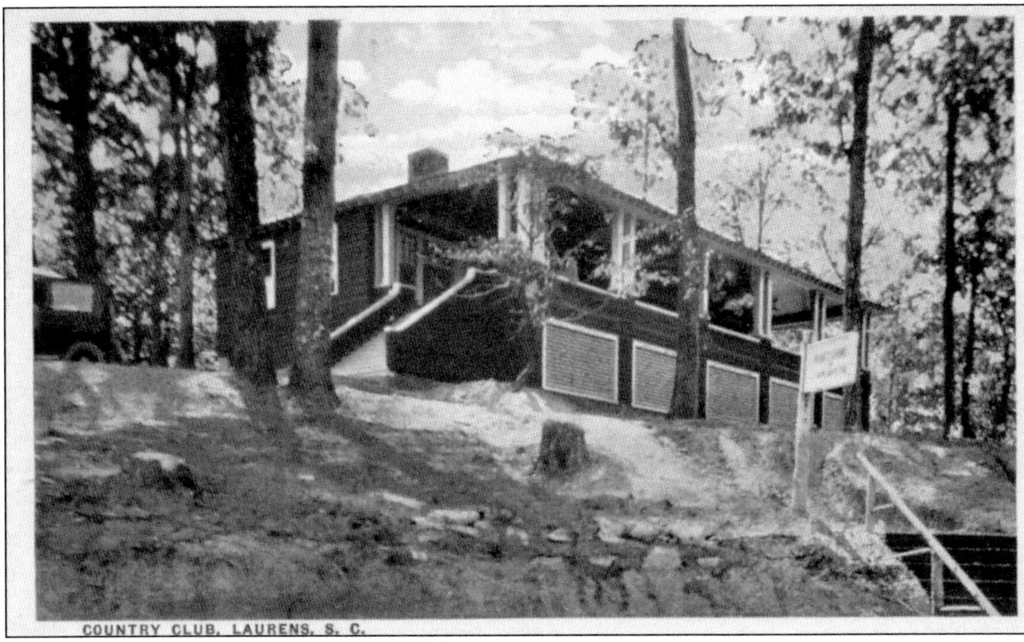

Numerous citizens from throughout Laurens County were members of Lakeside Country Club, located between Laurens and Clinton. In the early days, members enjoyed golfing and attending various social functions, including birthday parties and receptions, in the clubhouse pictured above. In later years, a new clubhouse replaced the old one. (Courtesy Elaine Martin.)

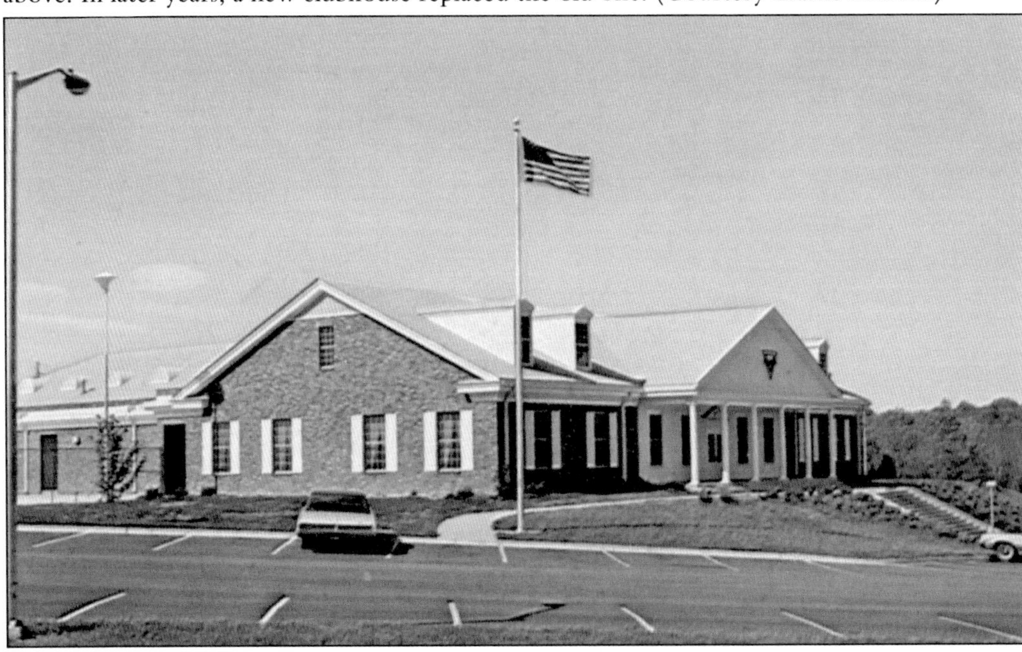

The first YMCA of Laurens was housed in the Lamar Smith Youth Center on Holmes Street in the Laurens Mill Village and became a member of the National Council of YMCA's on August 18, 1969. The current brick facility was constructed and dedicated in 1972 and is located on Anderson Drive in Laurens. The modern health and recreation center serves Laurens School District 55. (Courtesy Kathryn W. Johnson.)

Two

CLINTON
Home of Presbyterian College, Thornwell, and Whitten Center

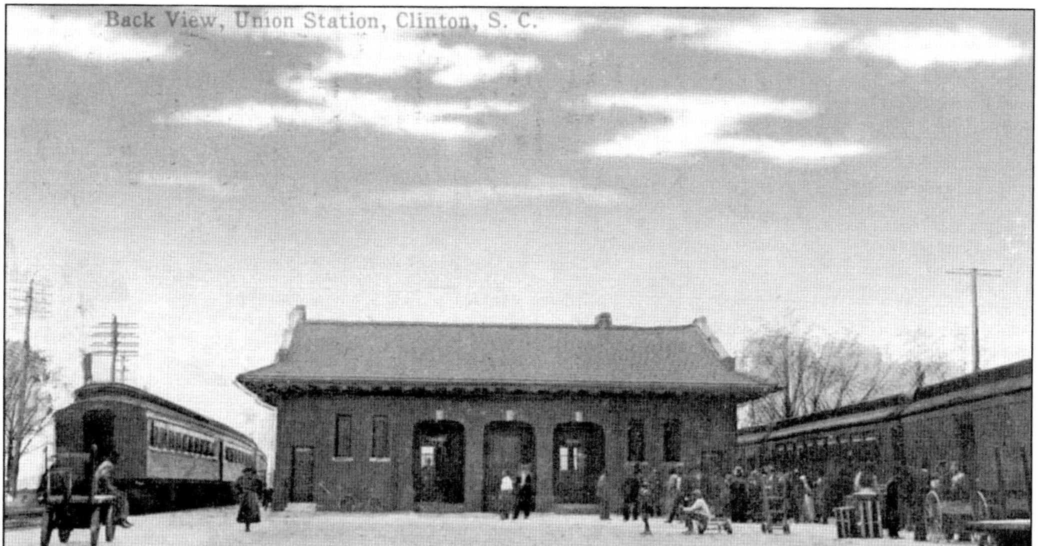

The town of Clinton was once an intersection of the Greenville-Columbia Highway, the Spartanburg-Augusta Highway, and a local road coming from the northwest. These roads formed a junction that became known as Five Points. The junction became a popular spot for drinking, horse racing, and cock fighting. In 1852, the Laurens and Newberry Railroad was scheduled to be built through this junction. Twenty-eight lots were then sold to form a town. Twenty people bought lots for an average of $50 an acre. The first buildings were constructed between Holland's Store and Five Points. As the small community thrived, a name was needed for location purposes. Five Points, Five Forks, and Round Jacket were proposed. It was finally agreed to name the town for Henry Clinton Young, a lawyer from Laurensville who helped to lay out the town's first streets. So, to honor his service, his middle name, Clinton, became the town's name and was so entered on its first charter in 1864. Union Station was constructed in 1908 in Clinton for the CN&L Railroad. The depot was torn down *c.* 1970. (Courtesy South Caroliniana Library, University of South Carolina, Columbia.)

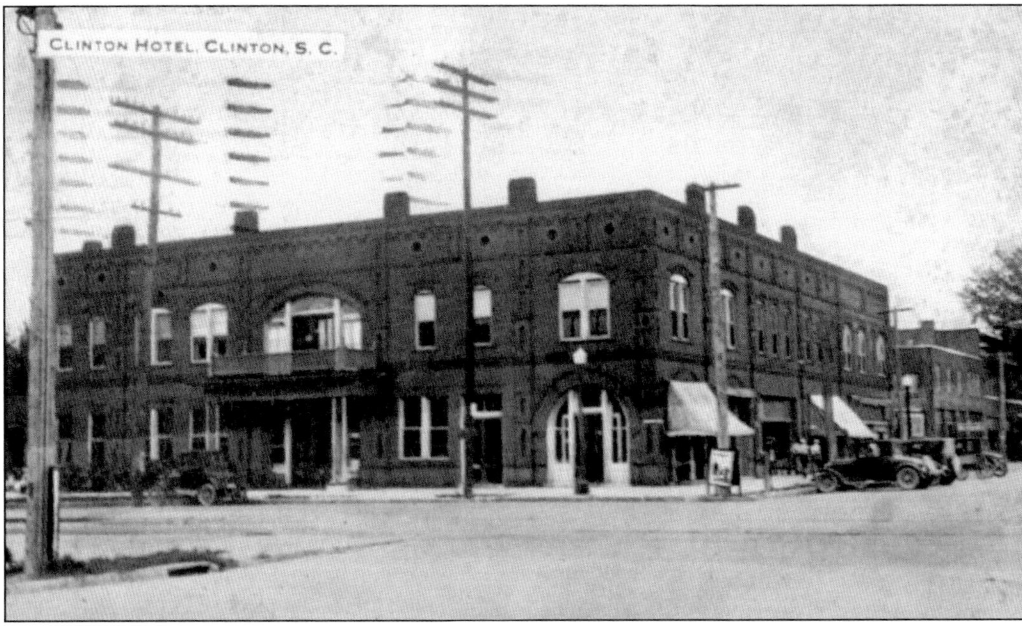

The Clinton Hotel became a landmark in the town of Clinton. Located on the corner of Broad and Main Streets, the establishment had farmers arriving from rural points in the county as well as businessmen, traveling salesmen, and families of Presbyterian College students as frequent guests. The Clinton Hotel was conveniently located near the Clinton Depot or Union Station. With the arrival of the railroad, Clinton became a flourishing town with numerous business establishments. One such store, the Bee Hive, is shown along with other establishments on the Clinton Square. A bicyclist is pictured near the depot. (Above courtesy Laurens County Library; below courtesy Elaine Martin.)

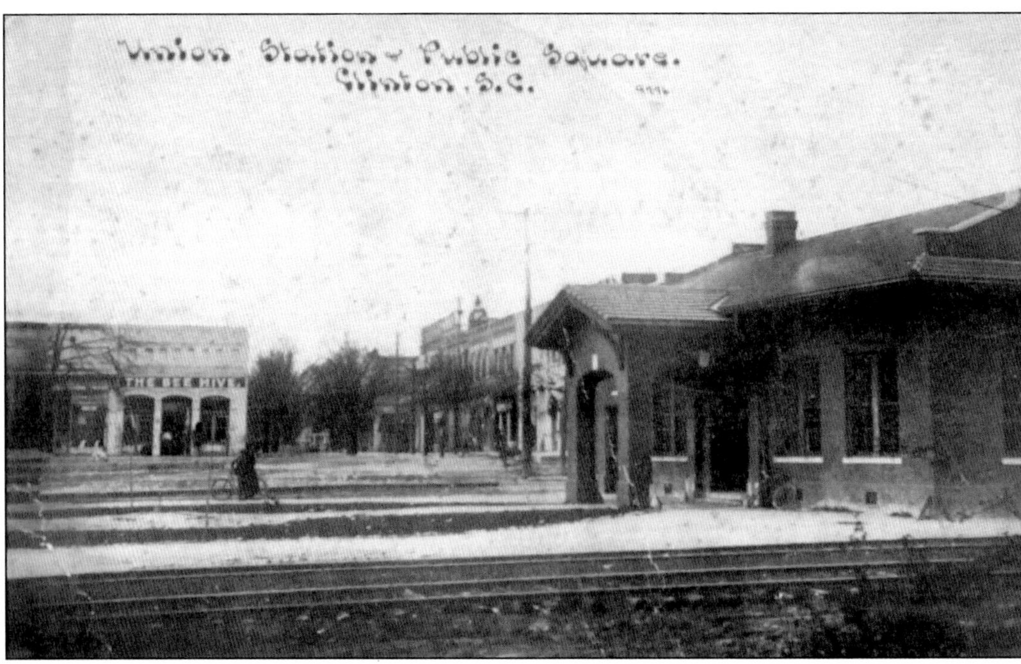

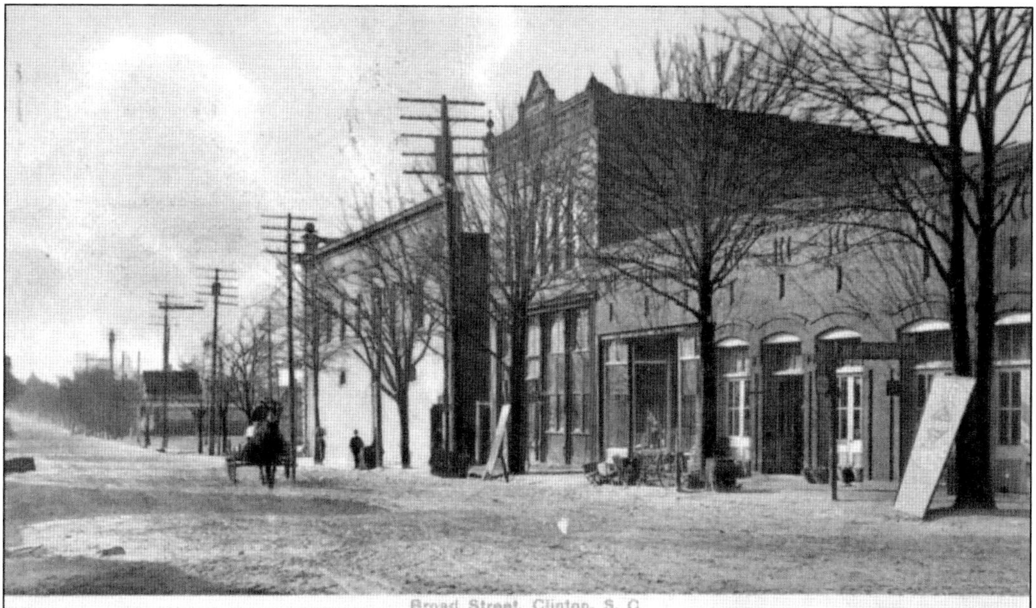
Broad Street, Clinton, S. C.

In 1809, the town of Clinton emerged around Holland's Store, which was the only store and post office in the lower part of Laurens County. Five Points, located approximately one mile west of the store, was a gathering place for men because of the bars, horse track, and chicken fights. Clinton was chartered as a town in 1864. Henry Clinton Young, a Laurens attorney, was chairman of the committee appointed to map the streets and rename the little town; it was named Clinton in his honor. Business establishments quickly began to appear in the small Laurens County town. The thriving little town became the home of Presbyterian College, Thornwell Home for Children, and Whitten Center. These names, even today, remain synonymous with the town. (Courtesy Laurens County Library.)

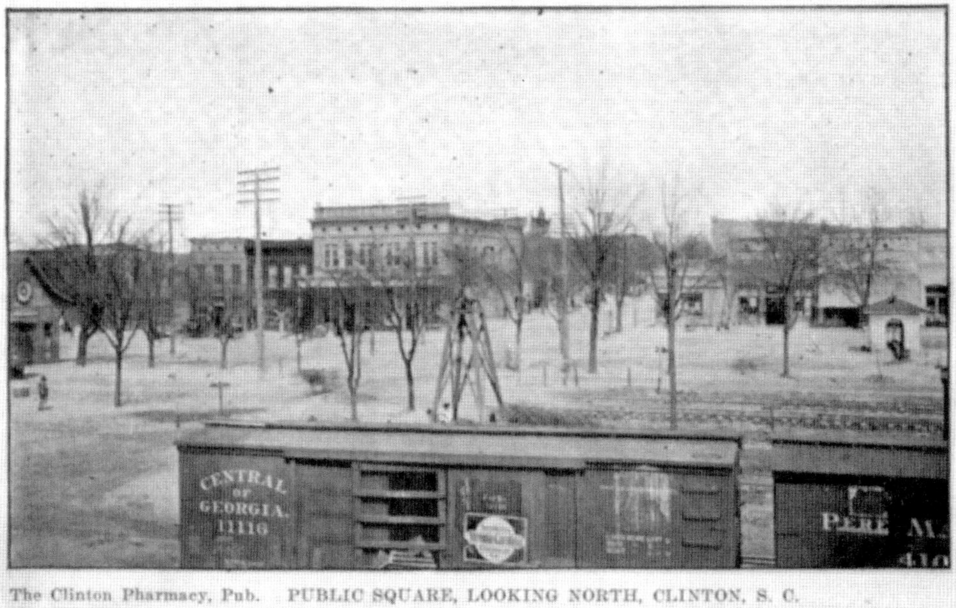

The Clinton Pharmacy, Pub. PUBLIC SQUARE, LOOKING NORTH, CLINTON, S. C.

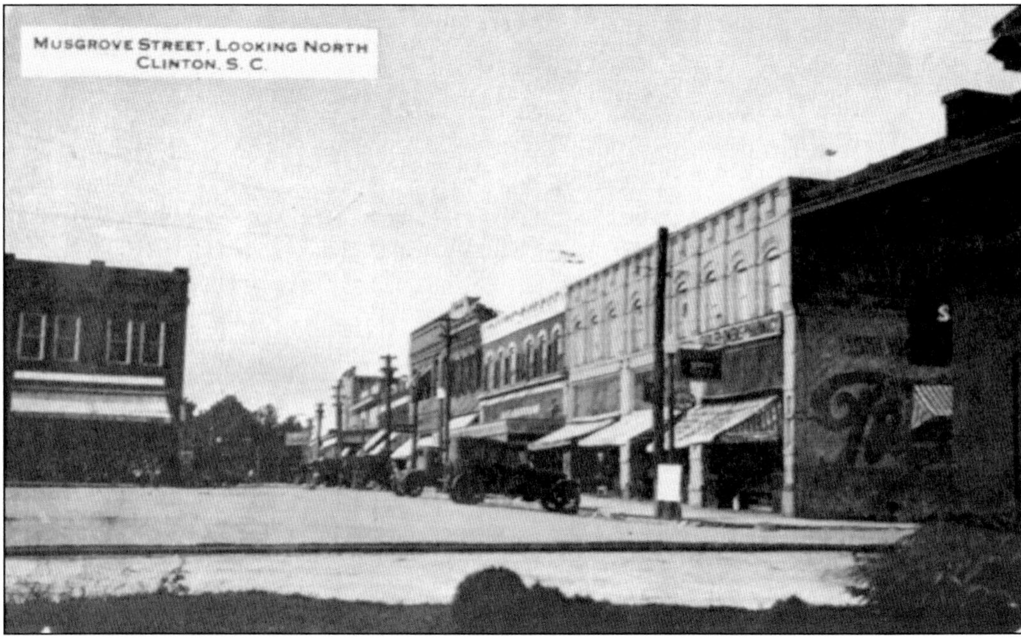

This 1920s postcard of Musgrove Street in Clinton, looking north, shows business establishments of the past including George A. Copeland Hardware Store, Clinton Café, and Sadler-Owens Pharmacy. (Courtesy Laurens County Library.)

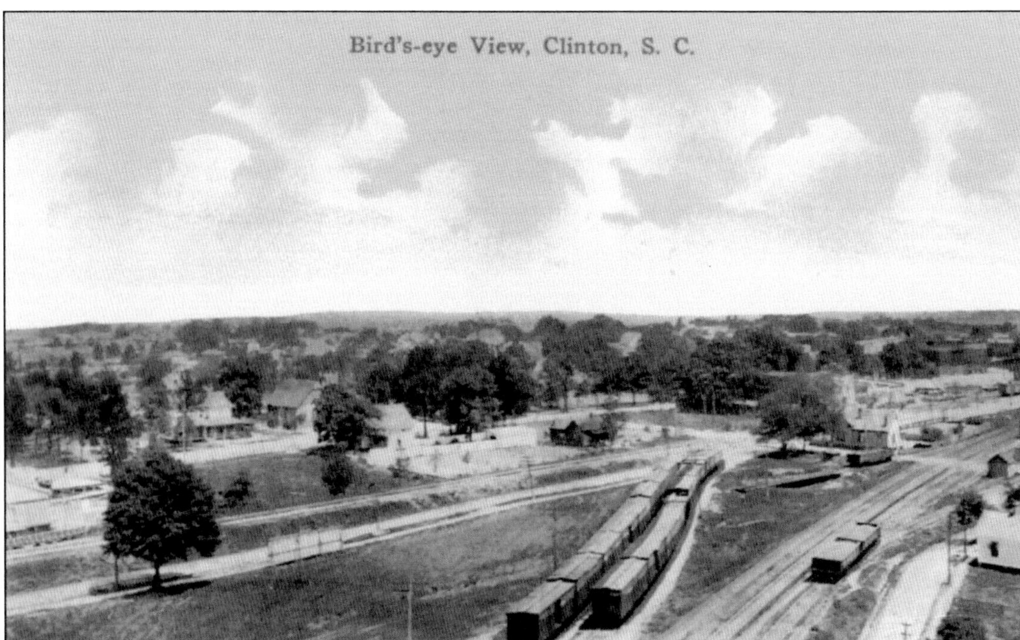

A bird's-eye view of Clinton, looking northeast, was captured by a photographer in the early 1900s. Zion Hill Methodist Church, later named Broad Street Methodist Church, can be seen in the distance. The crossing of the town's two railroads can also be seen. (Courtesy Regan and Riley Freeman.)

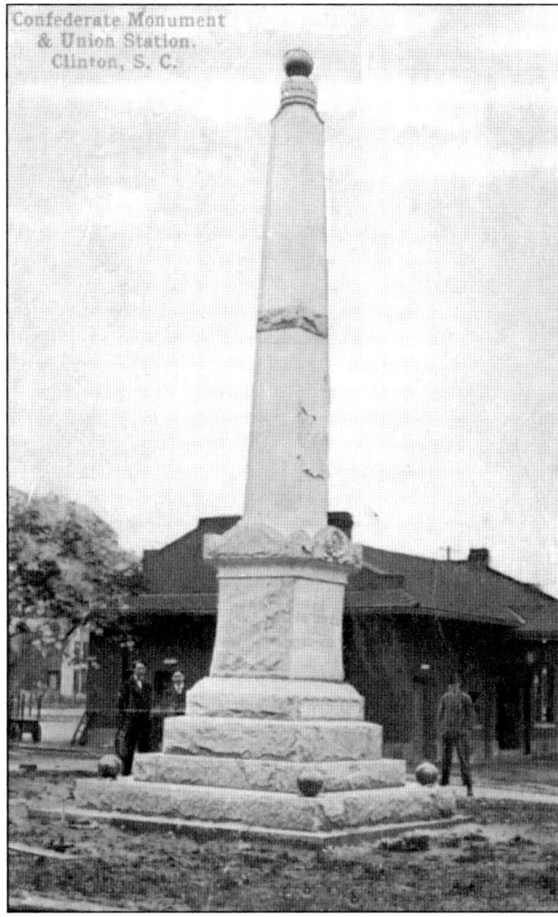

The Stephen D. Lee Chapter, No. 1066 of the United Daughters of the Confederacy (UDC), was organized February 16, 1907. Because of the efforts of Mrs. R. Z. Wright and Mrs. W. M. McCaslin, many daughters became interested in organizing the chapter and raising funds for a monument. The Confederate monument in Clinton was unveiled January 19, 1911. The monument, at a cost of $1,600, represented many hours of labor for the members of the Stephen D. Lee Chapter. Along with the monument on the Clinton Square, the depot and business establishments of the town are shown. (Above courtesy Lawrence E. Young; below courtesy Richard Taylor Jr.)

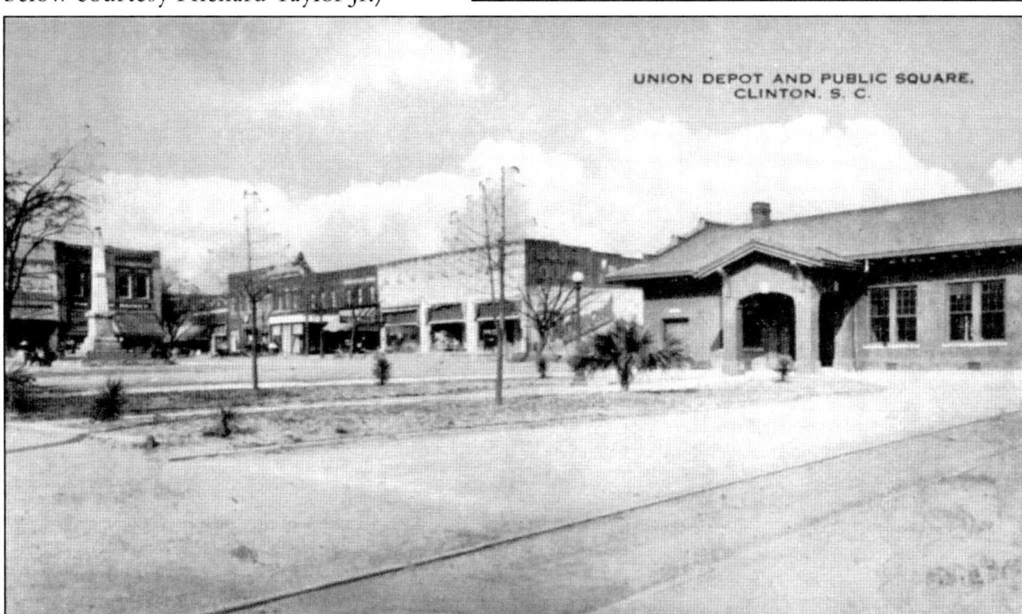

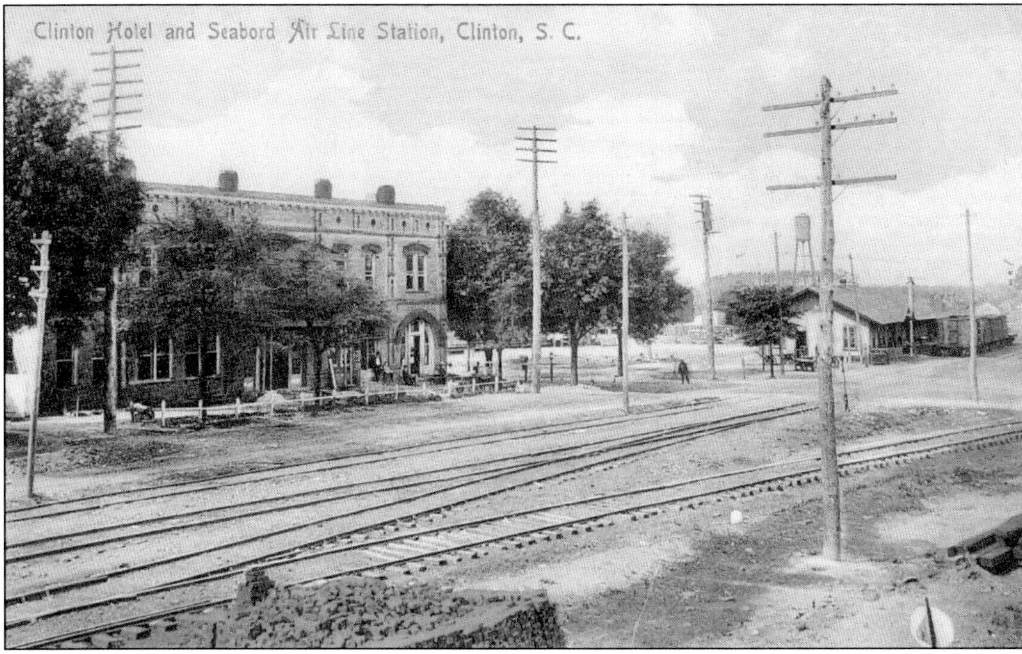

The view of this 1902 postcard is looking southwest toward South Broad Street. The Clinton Hotel, left, was built *c.* 1900, and to the far right is the Seaboard Air Line Station, which was constructed *c.* 1890. In later years, a barber shop, a store owned by Jim Pitts, and the *Clinton Chronicle* were located on the first floor of the hotel. (Courtesy South Caroliniana Library, University of South Carolina, Columbia.)

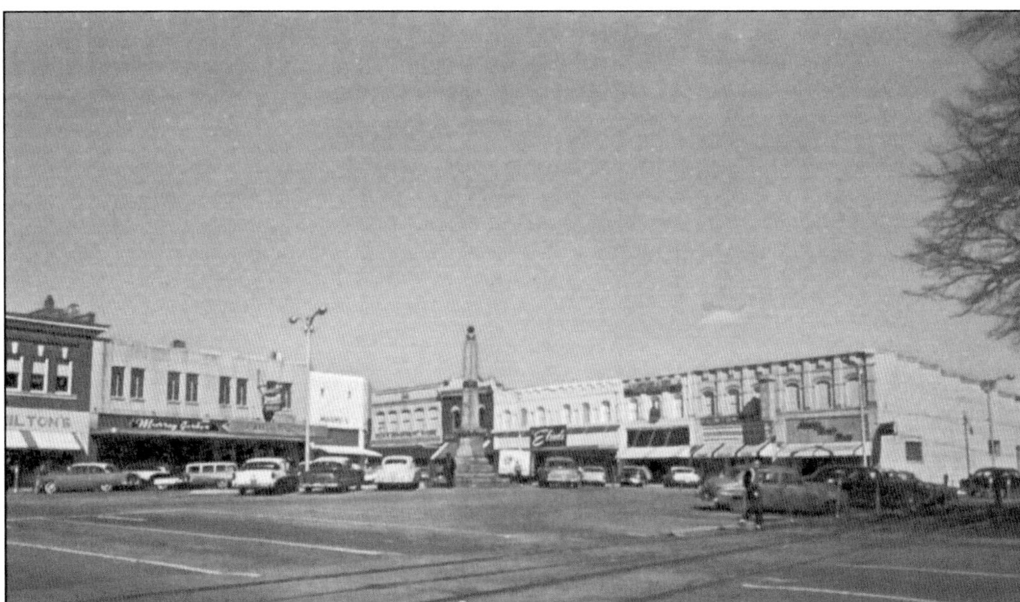

This postcard image was taken in 1959 and shows a busy Clinton Square. Businesses of the day included Hamilton's Jewelry Store, Murray Garber Dress Shop, Moore's Shoe Store, Howard's Pharmacy, Adair's Men Shop, and Effirds Department Store. (Courtesy Clinton Museum.)

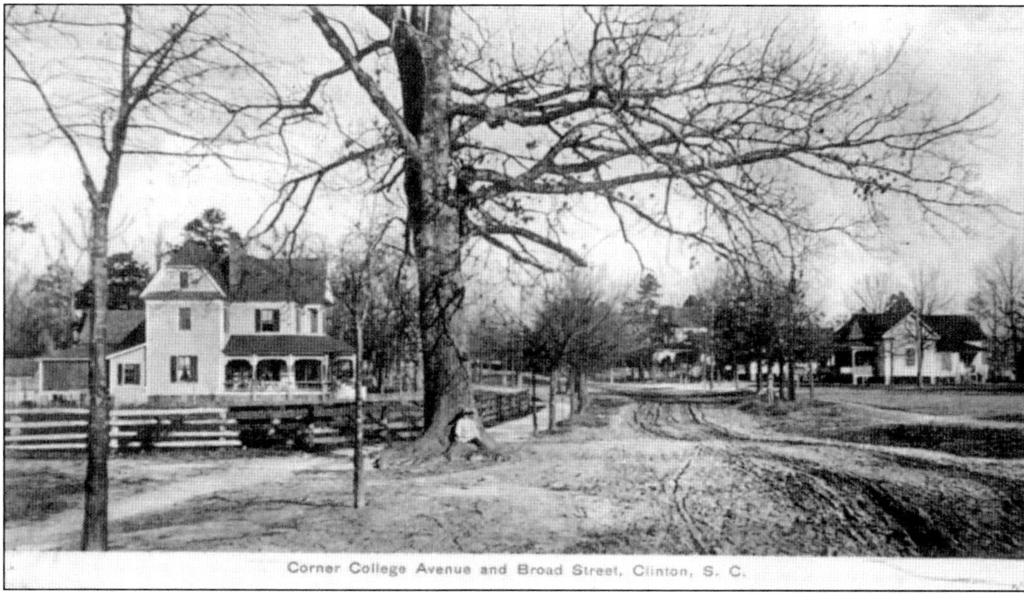

Dirt streets with wagon tracks are shown at the corner of College Avenue and Broad Street in Clinton. The two-story house is believed to be the home of Dr. Jack Young, a Clinton pharmacist. Notice the man sitting beneath the oak tree in this 1909 postcard. (Courtesy Clinton Museum.)

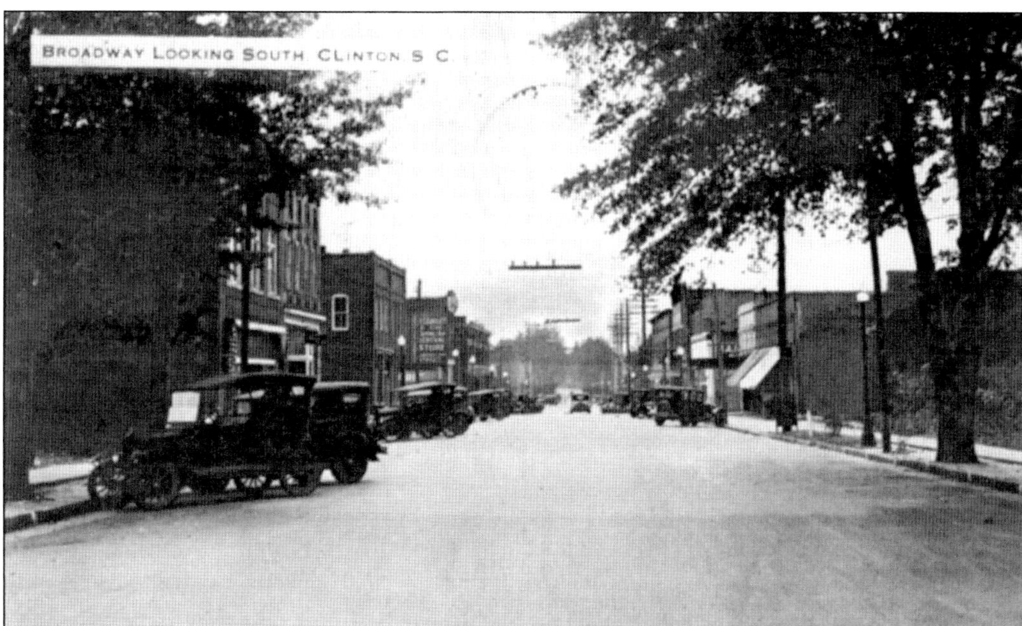

Model A and Model T Ford automobiles are parked on Broadway Street, later named Broad Street, in Clinton. They indicate a flourishing little town. This 1920s postcard shows the 200 block of Broad Street looking south and the Commercial Bank. (Courtesy Clinton Museum.)

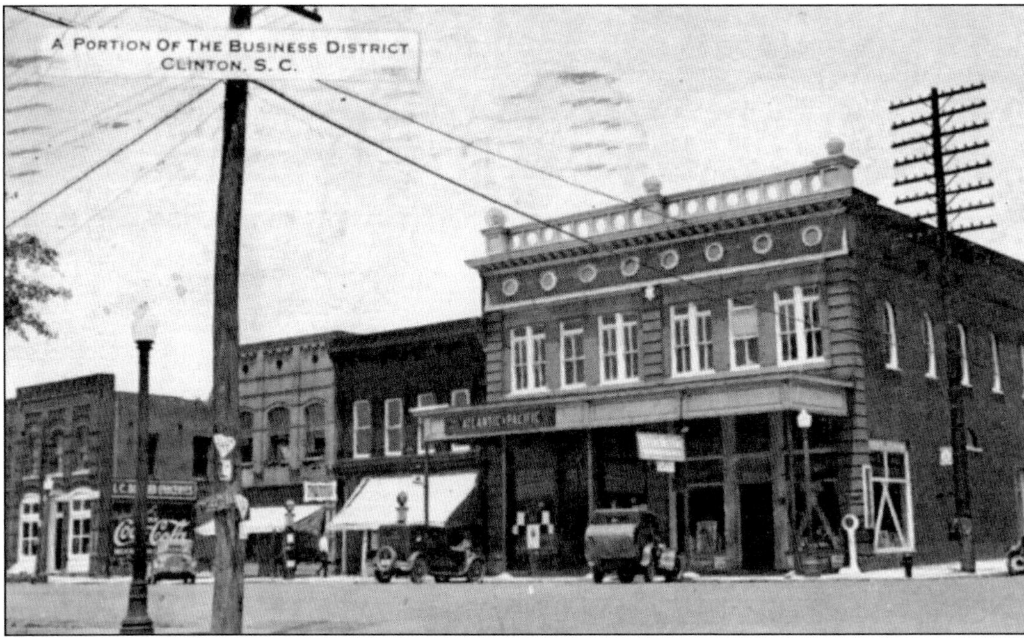

Both postcards feature the J. W. Copeland General Merchandise Store in Clinton. Located on the corner of North Broad and West Main Streets, the J. W. Copeland Building was constructed in 1875. The second floor of the building, known as Copeland Hall, was used for community parties and dances. Copeland, one of Clinton's earliest businessmen, was the son of George Pringle Copeland. He also was a farmer and real estate agent. In later years, located close by were the A&P Grocery Store and the Western Auto Store. (Above courtesy Regan and Riley Freeman; below courtesy Richard B. Taylor Jr.)

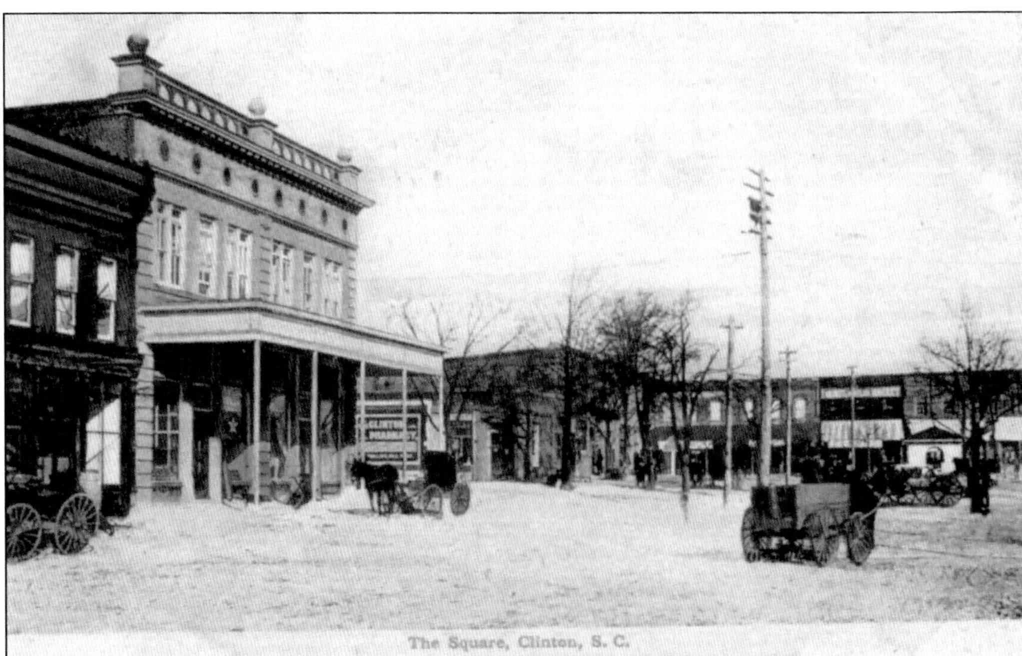

Jacobs Press, Inc., had its beginnings *c.* 1875 shortly after the War Between the States, when Dr. William P. Jacobs, founder of Thornwell Orphanage (now Thornwell Home for Children), set up a print shop on the Thornwell campus to publish material relating to Thornwell's work and activities. Dr. Jacobs's oldest son, James Ferdinand Jacobs, got enough printer's ink in his blood to create a lifelong interest in printing and advertising. In 1914, he purchased a partially completed hotel on East Main Street in Clinton and completed it as a three-story office and plant building for advertising and printing. The building had 18,000 feet of floor space and was the largest advertising plant in the South. (Above courtesy Caroliniana Library, University of South Carolina, Columbia; below courtesy Regan and Riley Freeman.)

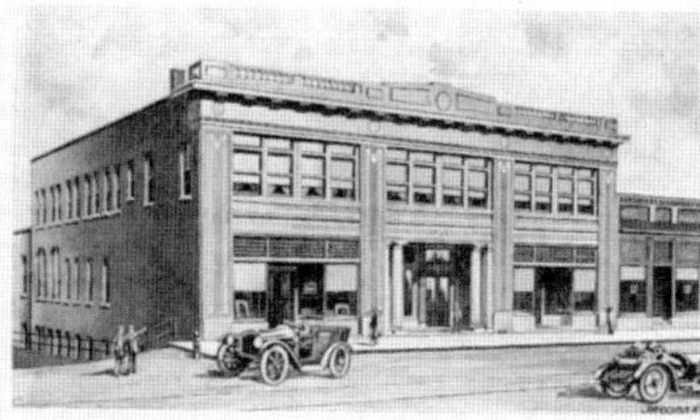

New Fire Proof Office Building of Jacobs & Co., Clinton, S. C.
18,000 feet of floor space. Largest advertising plant in the South.

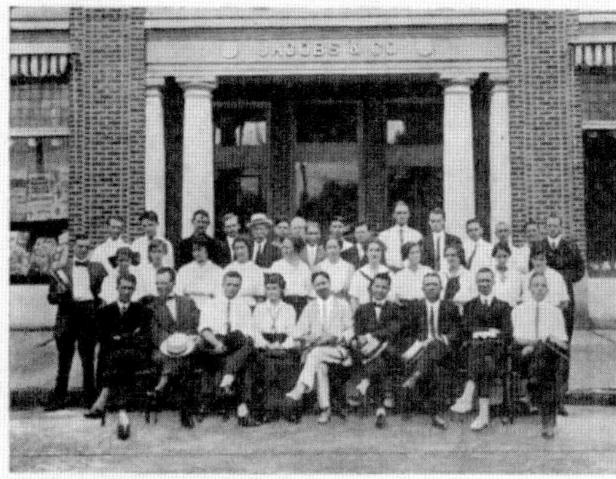

Group View of Jacobs & Company Office Force.

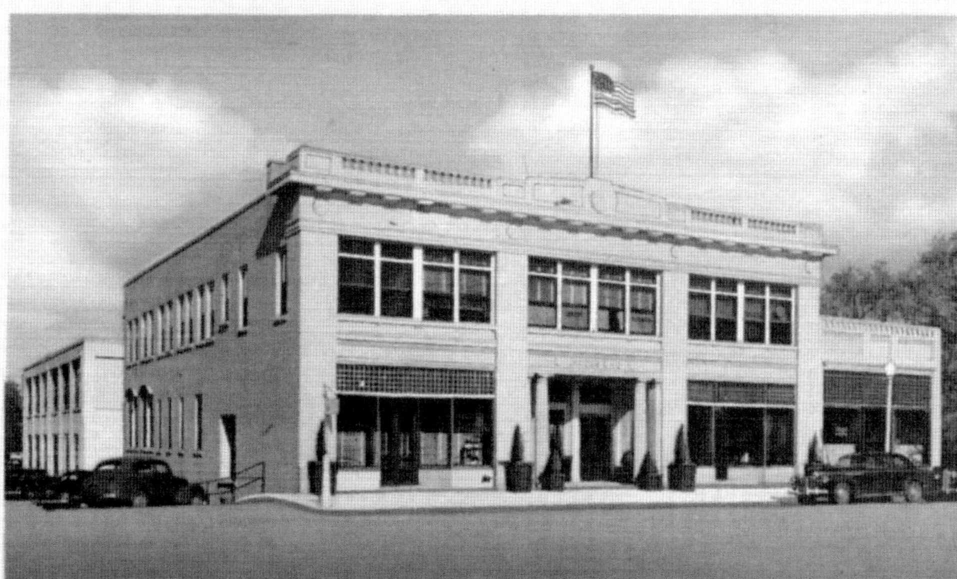

JACOBS PRESS — CLINTON, S. C. 4B-H53

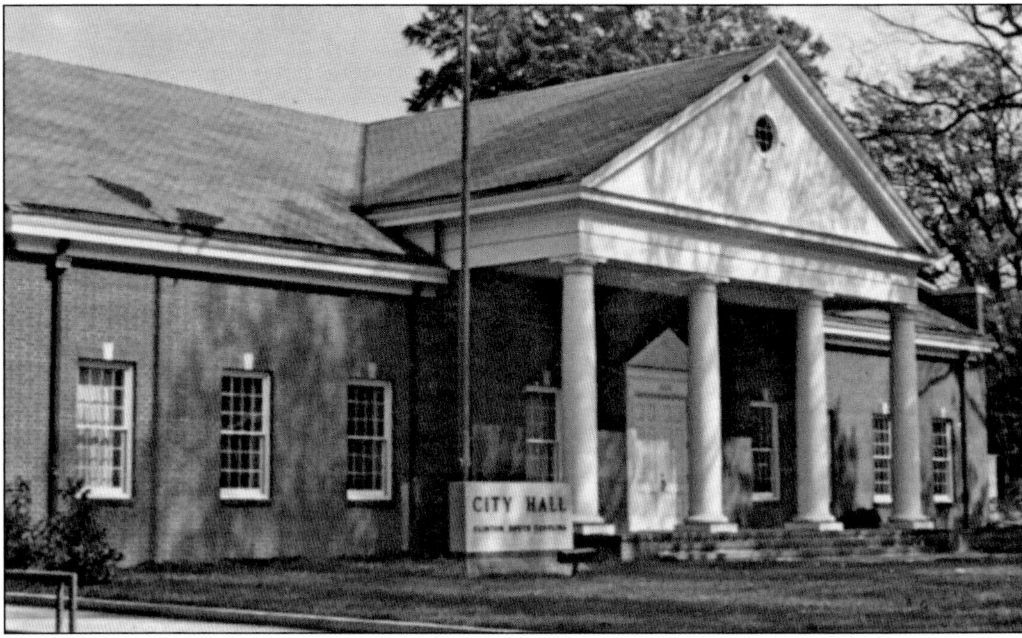

The present Clinton City Hall, located on Broad Street, was built in the early 1970s. It houses the police department, fire department, and administrative offices for the City of Clinton. The new city hall replaced the old city hall, which was located between Maxwell Brothers Furniture Store and Copeland Hardware on the Clinton Square. (Courtesy Elaine Martin.)

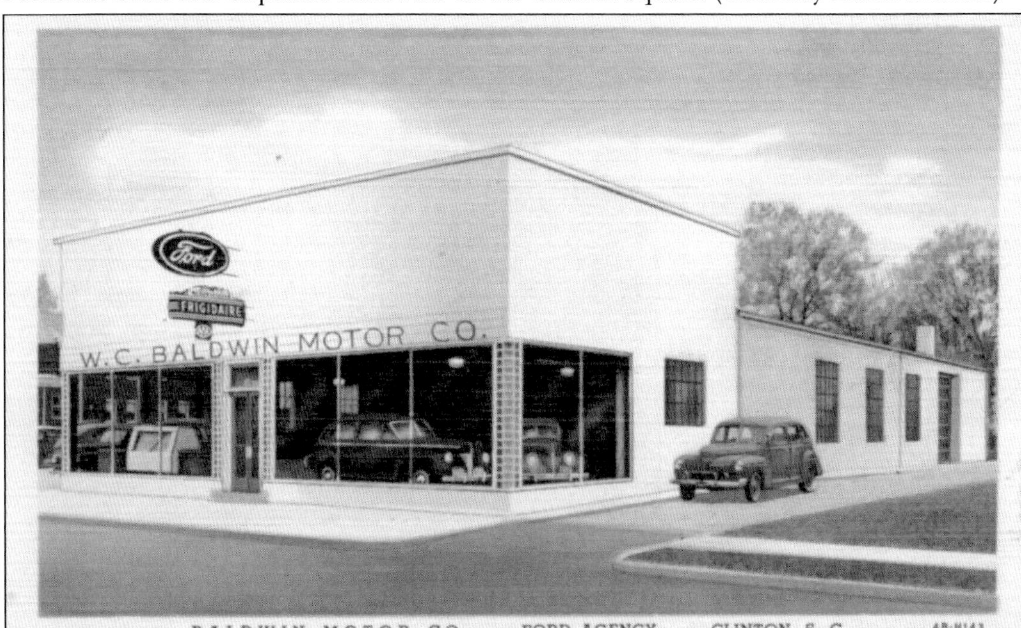

Located on North Broad Street in Clinton, the W. C. Baldwin Motor Company building was built in 1942 by W. C. Baldwin Sr. The Ford agency was located directly across from the old Clinton Post Office. In later years, the property was purchased by Broad Street Methodist Church and the building razed in order to make room for a church expansion. (Courtesy Clinton Museum.)

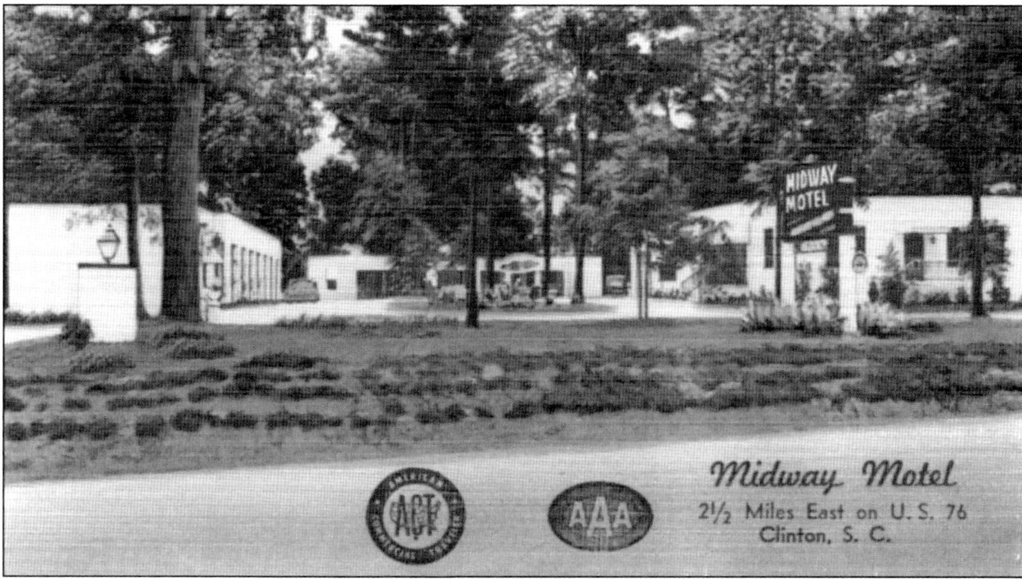

The Midway Motel was located two and a half miles east of Clinton on U.S. Highway 76, near Whitten Center and between Clinton and Joanna. It was advertised as being "the traveler's choice." A large sign advertised the motel, and a drive-in theater was located nearby. Mr. and Mrs. R. D. Nance were owners and managers of the motel. The motel was AAA approved. (Courtesy Elaine Martin.)

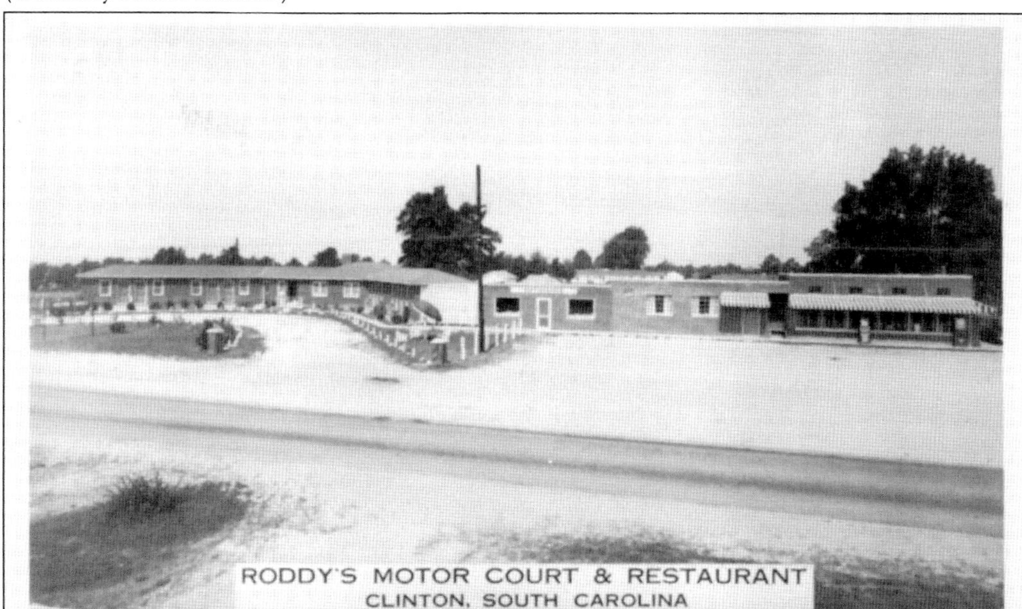

Located on Highway 72 South in Clinton, Roddy's Motor Court and Restaurant was owned and operated by Don Roddy. The modern court was AAA approved, and all eight units had tile baths and telephones and were heated with hot water heat. Ice, coffee, and newspapers were furnished at no charge. The air-conditioned dining room served delicious meals. The motel catered to tourist and commercial travelers. The brick motel and restaurant operated until the 1960s. (Courtesy Clinton Museum.)

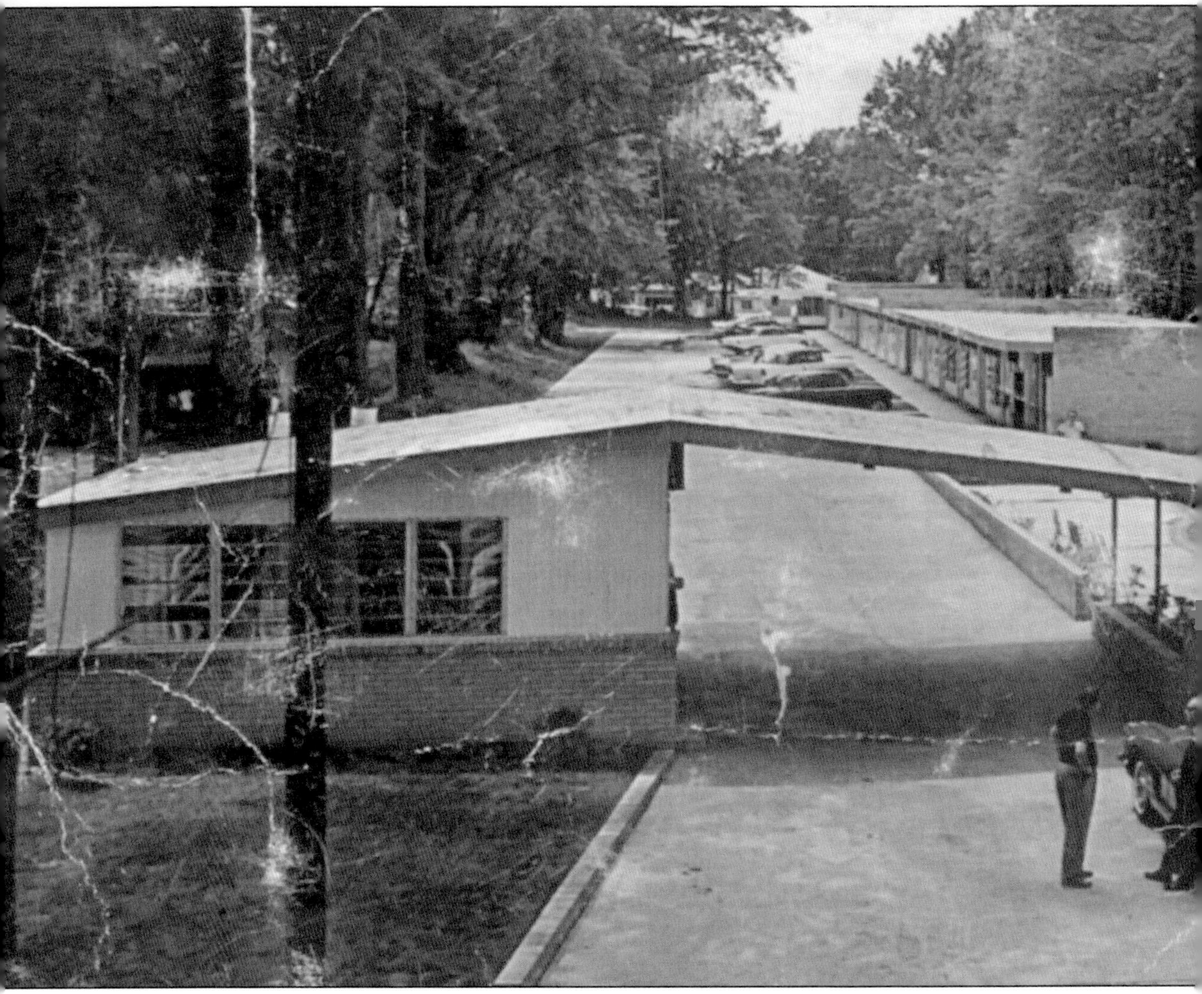

The Gala Motel was constructed in the 1950s on 407 North Broad Street in Clinton by Shelton Rimer, a mobile-home dealer and businessman. Rimer used mobile homes, along with fire walls, to construct the motel. The Gala was a popular motel in Clinton and was advertised as having 31 rooms, 24-hour telephone service, a swimming pool, music, and carpet. One

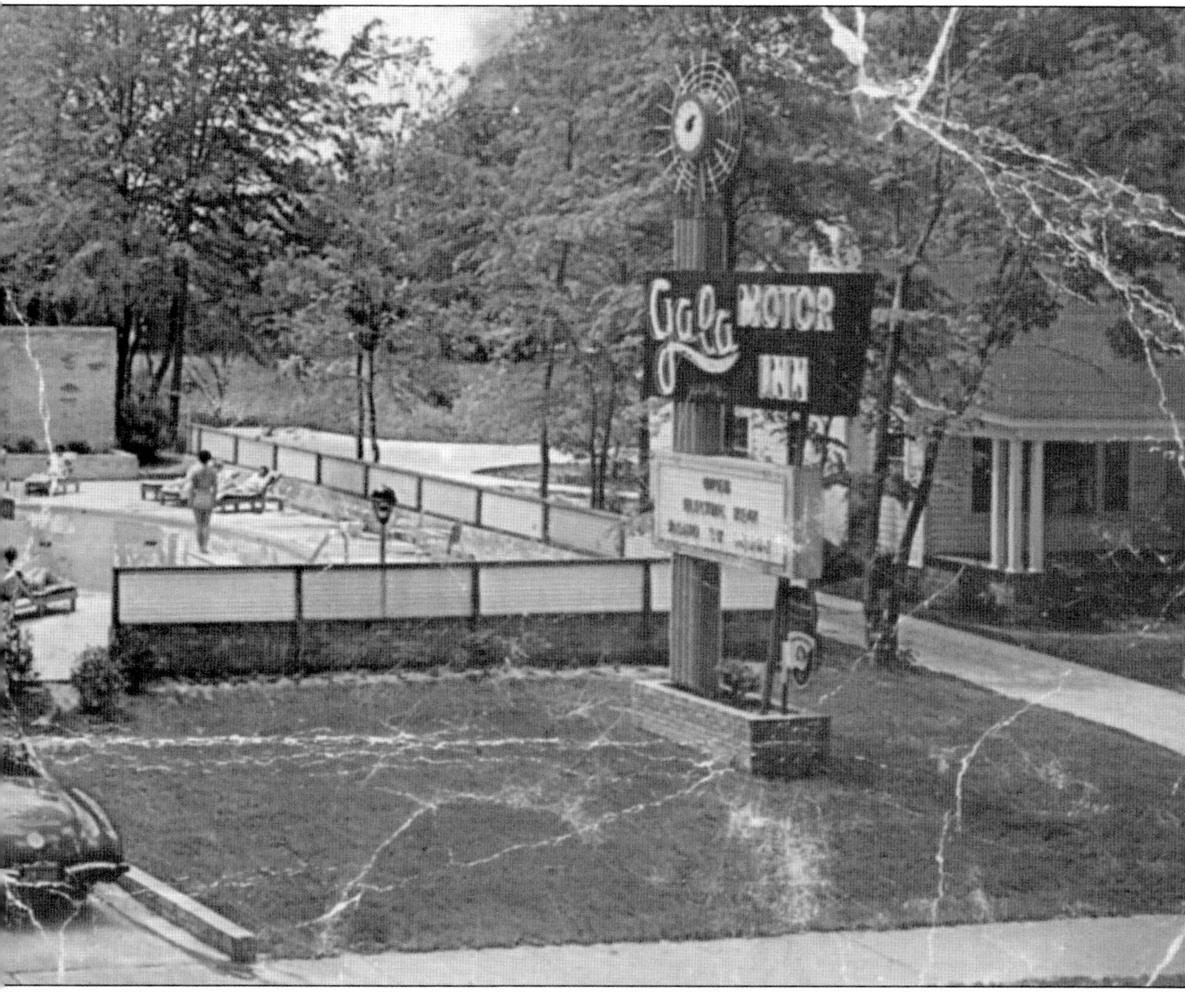

of the gentlemen pictured on the large postcard is believed to be Shelton Rimer. A Laurens man recalls serving on jury duty in 1958 and being sequestered in the Gala Motel. (Courtesy Deborah Deyton.)

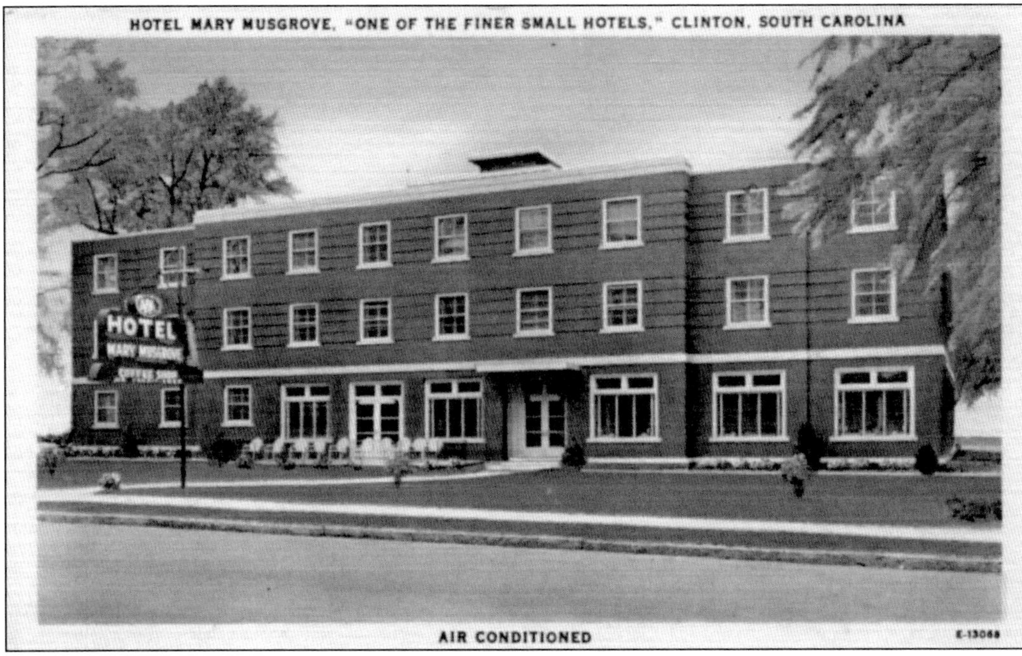

Mary Musgrove Hotel, located on Broad Street in Clinton, was constructed in 1951. The hotel had an AAA rating, 50 rooms, a delightful coffee shop serving excellent meals, tub and shower combination in every room, self-operated elevator, banquet space for 200, free parking for guests, and a television in the lobby. The hotel was headquarters for the Lions, Kiwanis, and Business and Professional Women's Clubs. (Courtesy Elaine Martin.)

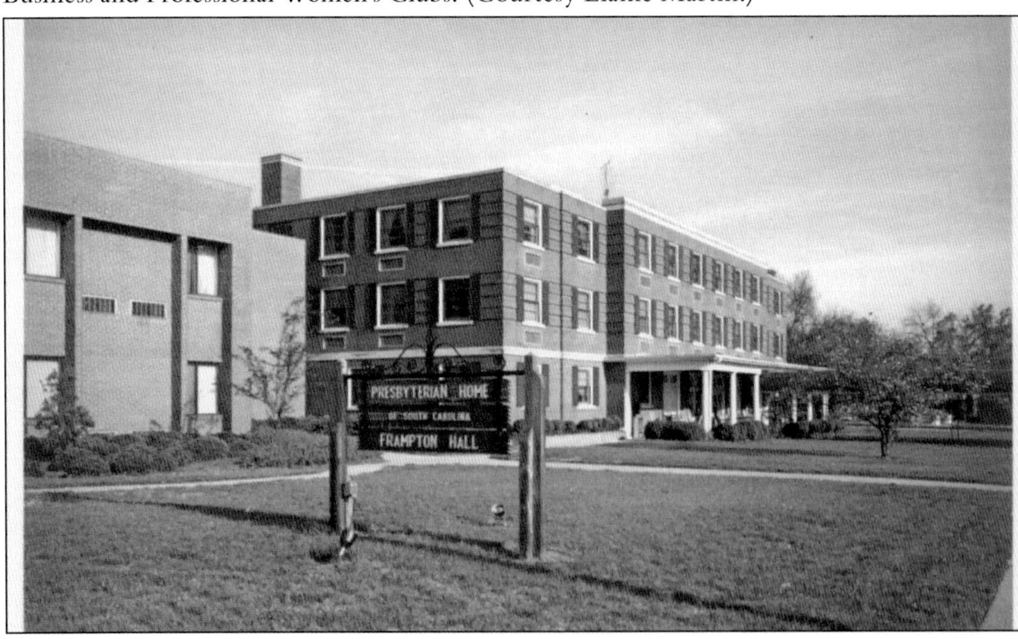

Frampton Hall is housed in the old Mary Musgrove Hotel on North Broad Street in Clinton. The facility houses senior citizens in both rooms and apartments. Frampton Hall is a part of the Presbyterian Home of South Carolina and was established in 1976. (Courtesy Lawrence E. Young.)

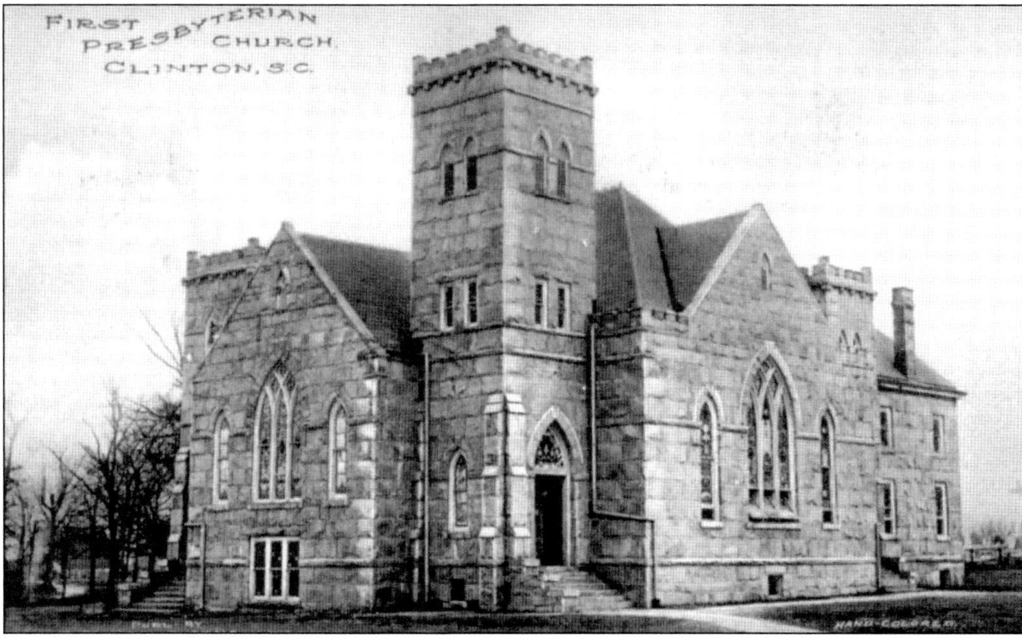

While serving Duncan's Creek Presbyterian Church in 1853, Rev. Zelotes Holmes believed that the village of Clinton was large enough to support a church. A committee was formed in 1855 to plan and organize a church. By 1863, the church had grown enough to have a full-time minister, and in 1864, William Plumer Jacobs, a young seminary student, was called to serve the congregation. Members of the First Presbyterian Church of Clinton have worshipped in three buildings—a wooden white frame church, a larger stone church built in 1904 (above), and the present stone church that was constructed in 1930 (below). The second church building was destroyed by fire in 1929. Dr. Jacobs penned these words: "Who can tell but that God has given us this thing to prove, that a little village church can become a tower of strength." (Above courtesy Richard Taylor Jr.; below courtesy Elaine Martin.)

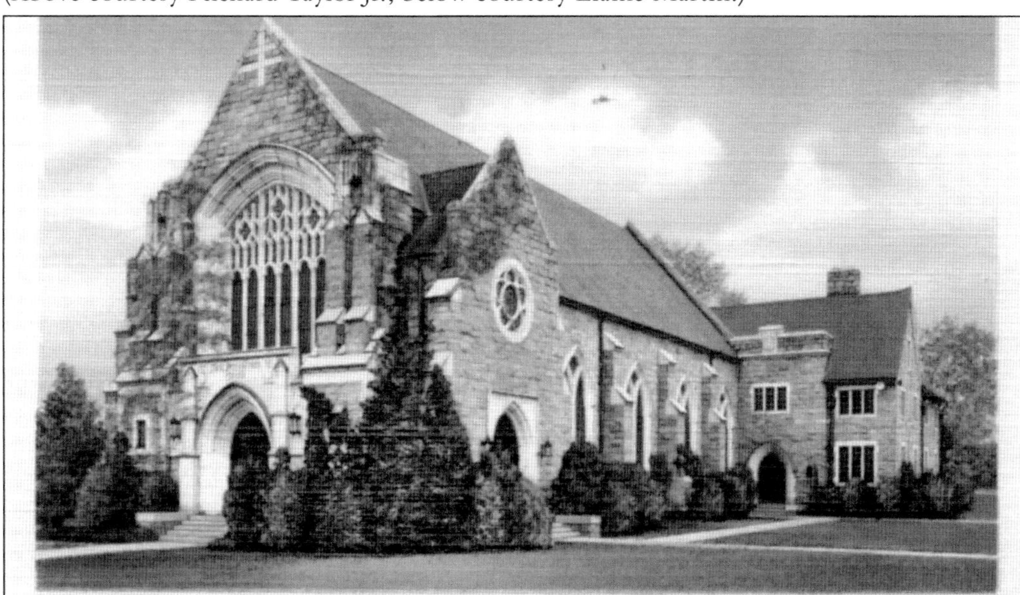

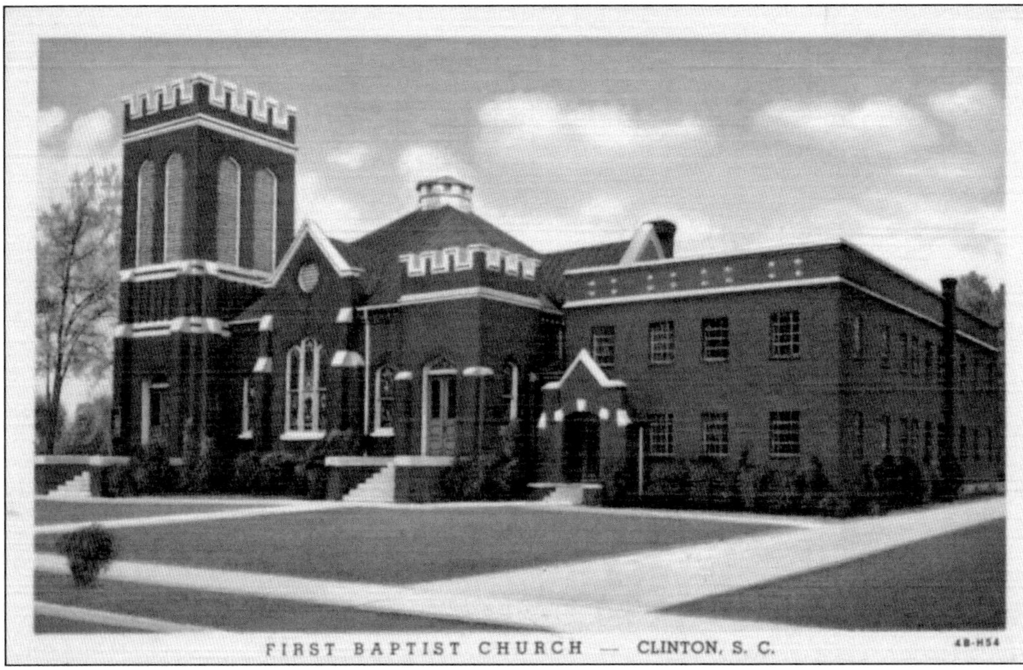

Clinton First Baptist Church was organized in 1881. The first church building was a wooden structure with a stately spire. The first Baptist service was held in the small Clinton church in 1882. Because of the rapid growth of the congregation, the building was demolished in 1908. The small frame church was then replaced by a brick structure, shown in this postcard. In an expansion program, an educational building was completed in 1938. The last service held in the old brick church was on August 9, 1964. The present sanctuary, located on South Broad Street, was constructed and dedicated in 1965. (Above courtesy Helen Phillips Dean; below courtesy South Caroliniana Library, University of South Carolina, Columbia.)

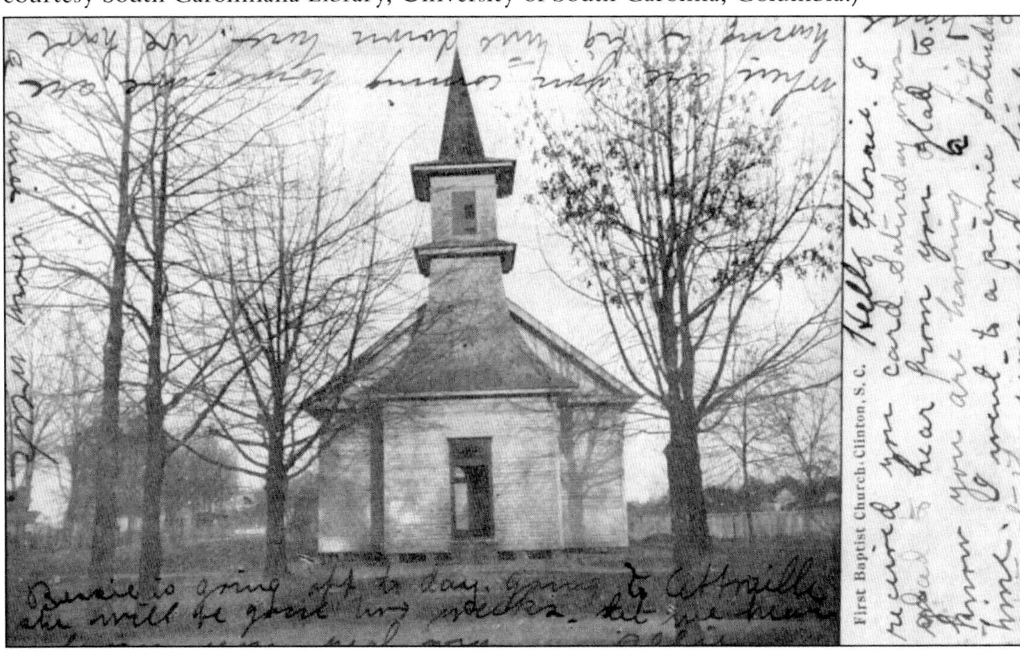

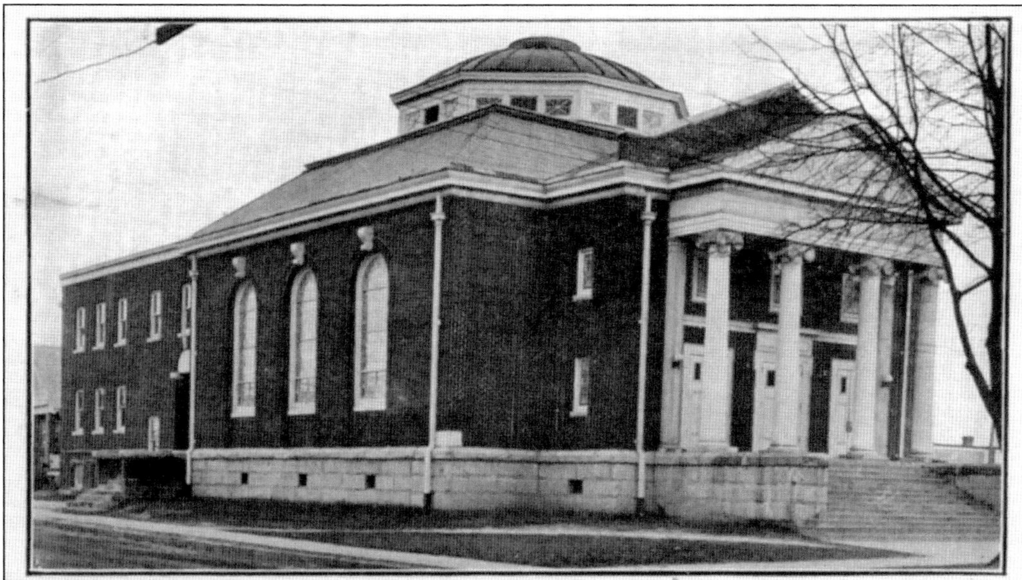

Broad Street Methodist Church, Clinton, S. C.

Methodism came to Clinton in 1854, and it was one of the first churches of any denomination to be established in the town. The roots of the first congregation are traced to the old Zion Church that was established in 1826. Clinton Methodists have erected four buildings. The first small building, located at the corner of West Main and Laurens Streets, was replaced in 1880 by a larger frame structure. By 1904, the congregation had grown, and a larger brick church was erected. In 1914, a modern well-equipped church was built on the corner of North Broad and Ferguson Streets. The present church was constructed in 1970, and on Palm Sunday of that year, the first service of worship was held in the new sanctuary. (Above courtesy Elaine Martin; below courtesy Clinton Museum.)

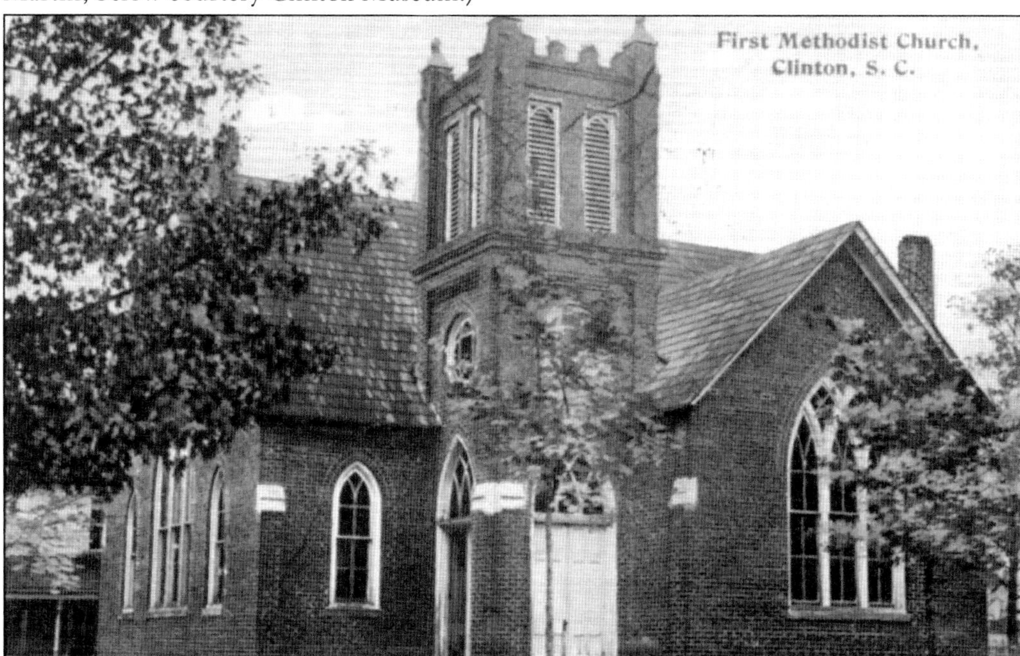

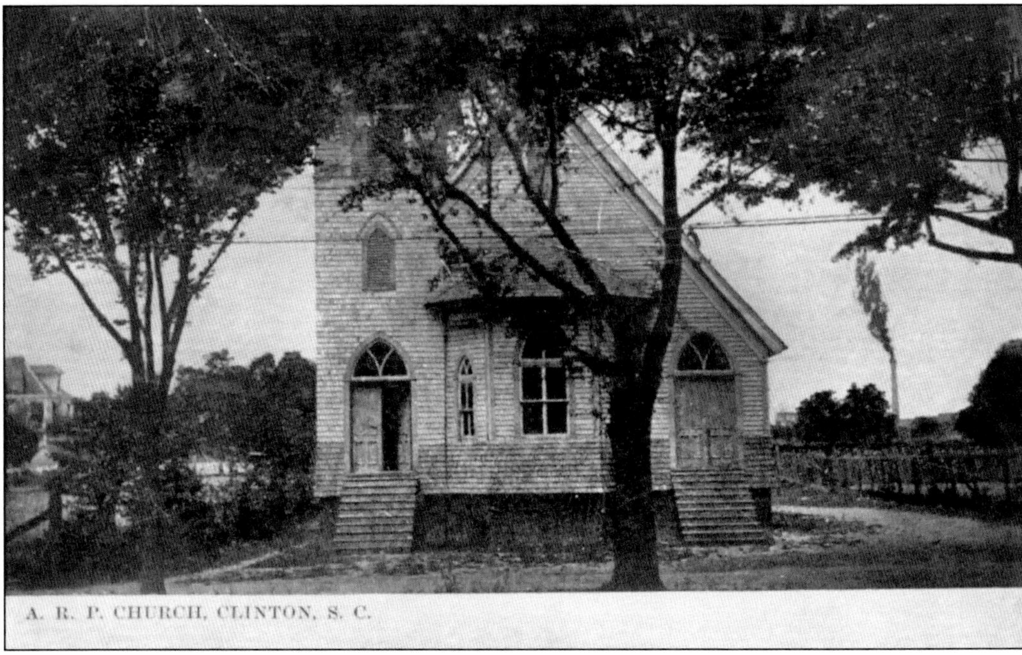

The Associate Reformed Presbyterian (A.R.P.) Church of Clinton was located on the corner of Florida and North Broad Streets. All Saints Episcopal Church purchased the wooden frame building *c.* 1955 and moved it to its present location on the corner of Calvert and Holland Streets. All Saints Episcopal Church continues to hold services in the quaint little church. The A.R.P. Church of Clinton is pictured on an advertising card for Sadler-Owens Pharmacy. The advertising card was mailed to L. M. D. Young of Clinton and reads, "You are cordially invited to come and inspect our newly arrived fixtures and get what you need in our line. . . . We are as near you as your phone." (Courtesy Lawrence E. Young.)

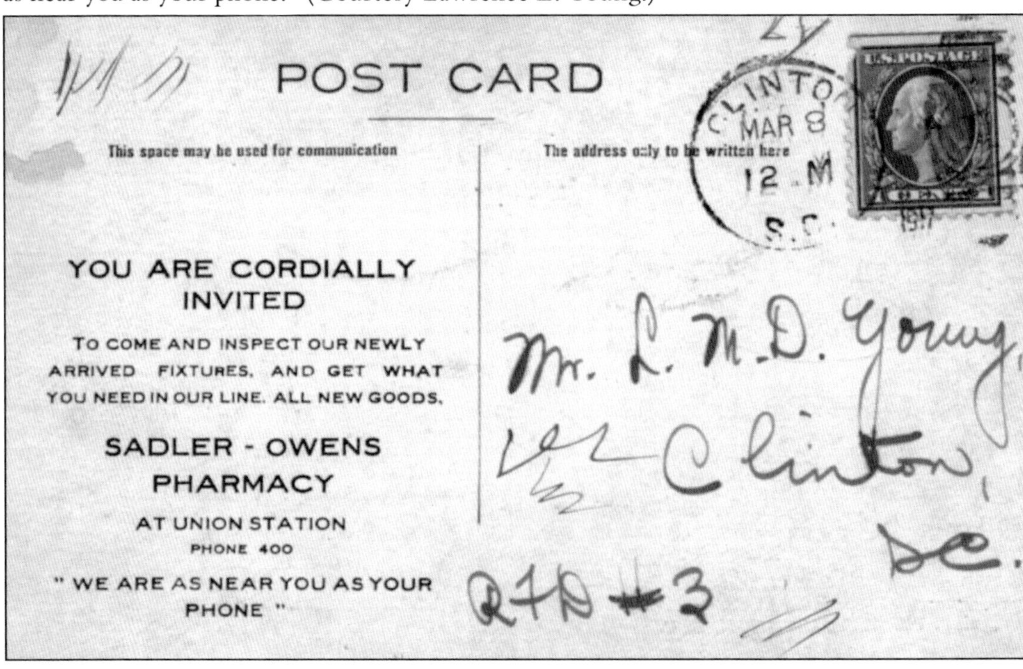

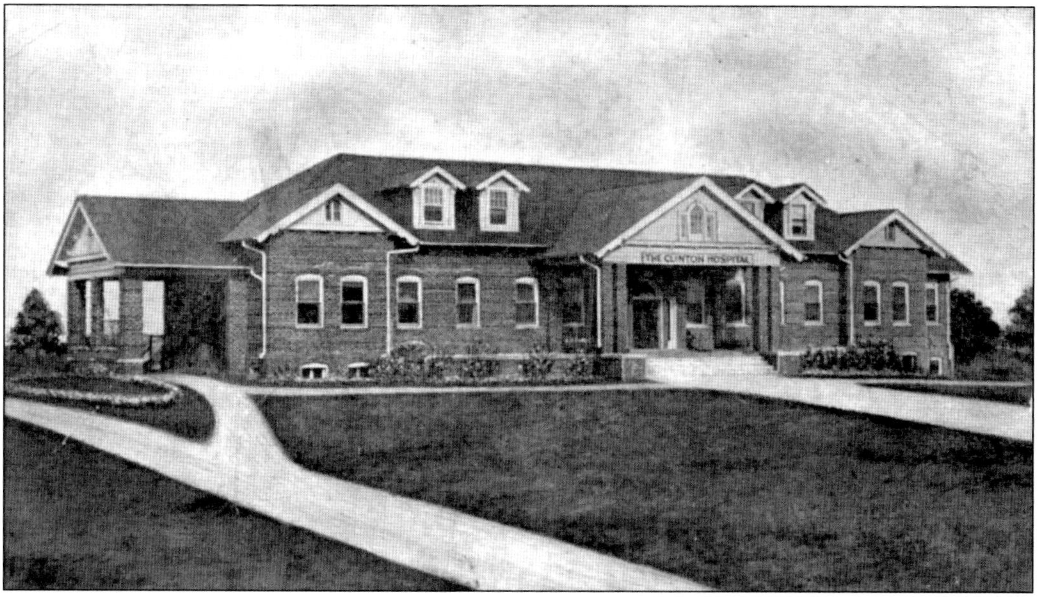

The Clinton Hospital, often called Hays Hospital, was erected in 1917 on East Main Street in Clinton. The brick hospital was a modern steam-heated facility, fully equipped with X-ray equipment, clinical laboratory facilities, and graduate nurses. The hospital was organized by Dr. S. C. Hays, C. W. Stone, J. D. Bell, and J. I. Copeland. The hospital burned in 1926. After the fire, Hays Hospital moved to the J. W. Copeland residence on the corner of Woodrow and Hampton Streets in Clinton. The Copeland House was converted into a hospital. (Above courtesy Lawrence E. Young; below courtesy Regan and Riley Freeman.)

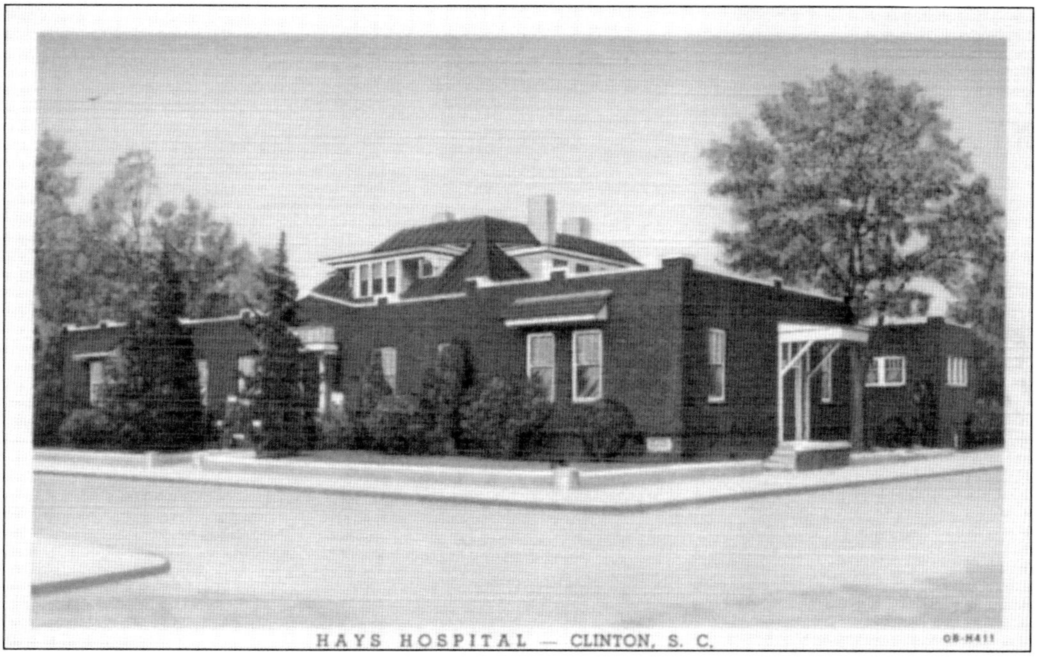

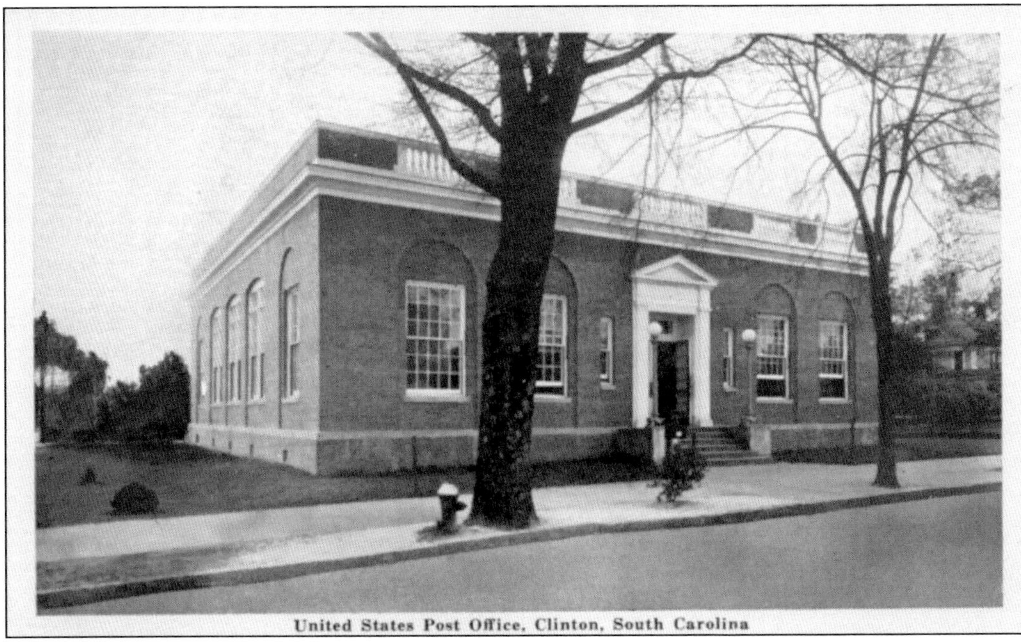

The U.S. Post Office in Clinton was constructed in 1925. The brick structure, located on North Broad Street, served Clinton residents until 1971, when a new post office was built on Elizabeth Street. The building was later turned into a banking facility and currently houses Sun Trust Bank. (Courtesy Clinton Museum.)

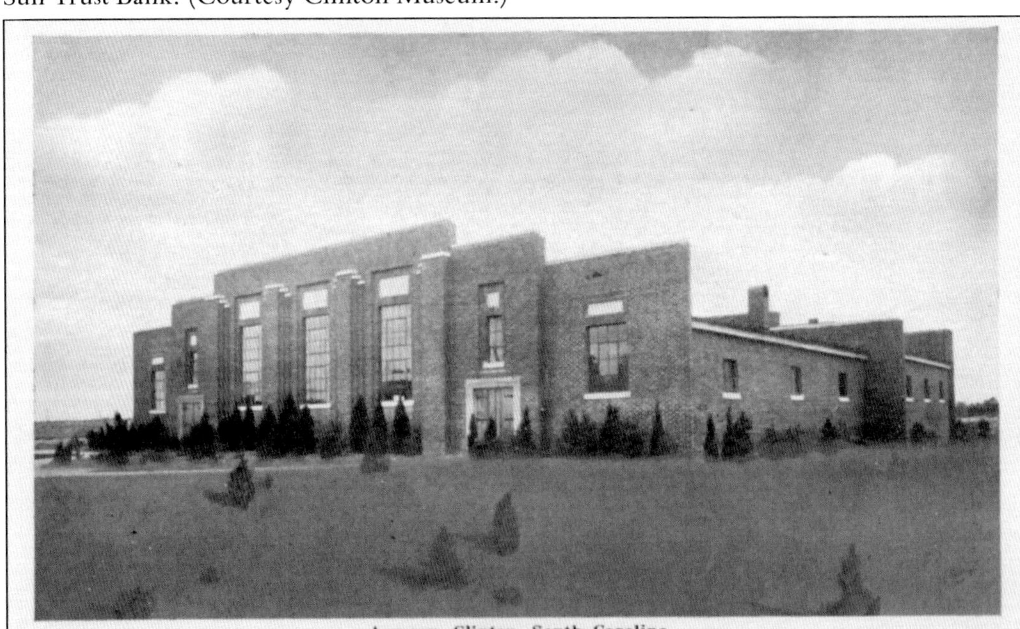

The Clinton Armory, once a Clinton landmark, housed Battery B of the South Carolina National Guard. The armory was located on South Broad Street. The brick military building was constructed in 1937. Before the building was demolished, numerous clubs and organizations from Clinton used the old armory for recreational and social events. (Courtesy Regan and Riley Freeman.)

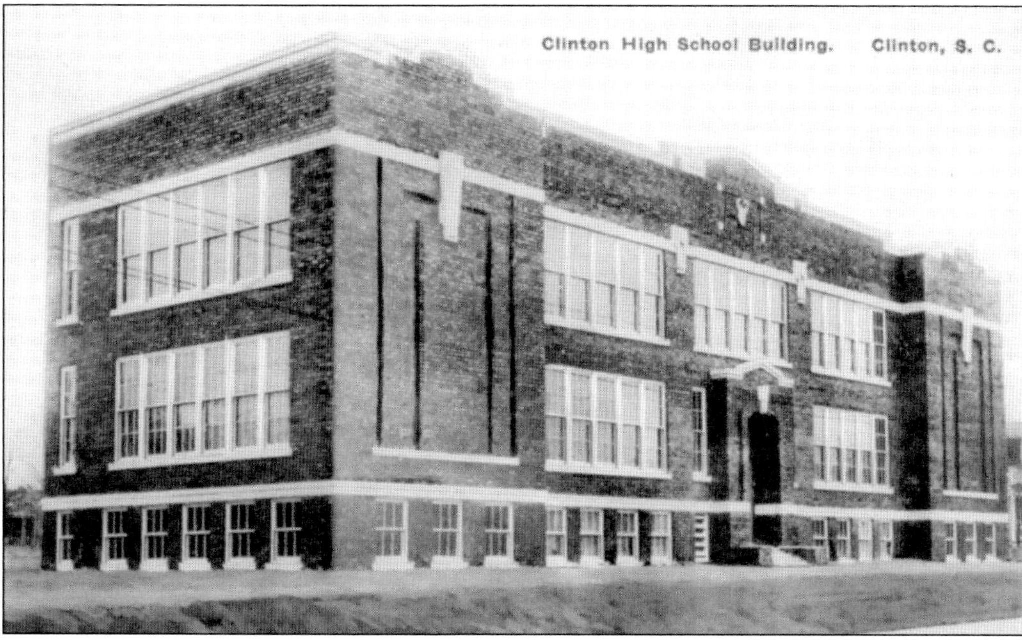

State-supported high schools were first established in South Carolina in 1907. Laurens County became one of the first rural counties to have public high schools. Hampton Avenue High School opened in Clinton in 1917. Later the building served as an elementary school and then housed the administrative offices for Clinton School District 56. In 1956, students moved into a new facility, Clinton High School, located on North Adair Street, and in 1957, the school celebrated its first graduation exercises. It continues to serve District 56 students as a high school. (Above courtesy Kathryn W. Johnson; below courtesy Lawrence E. Young.)

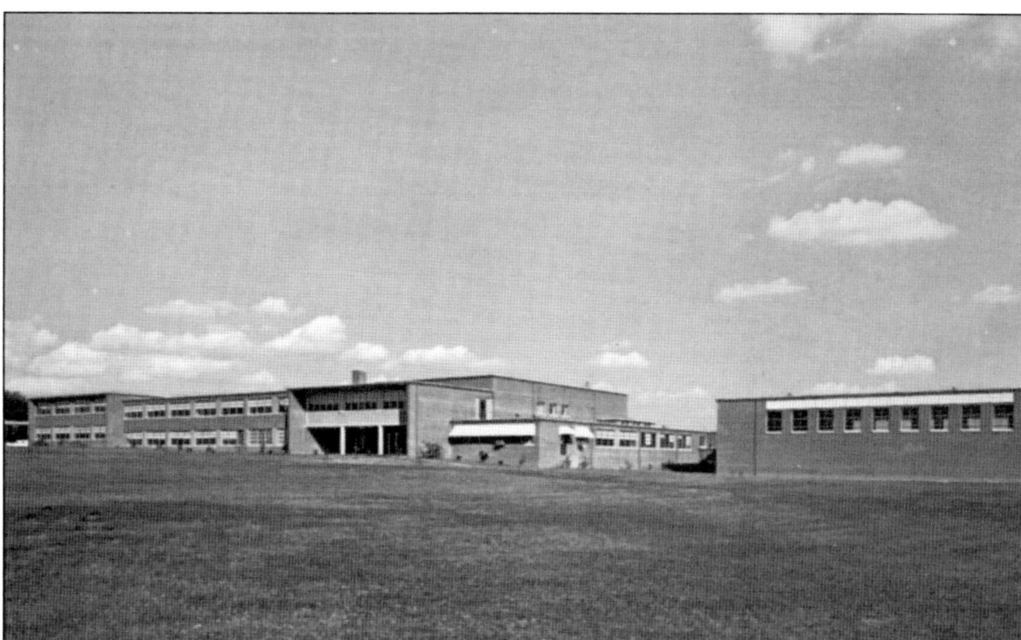

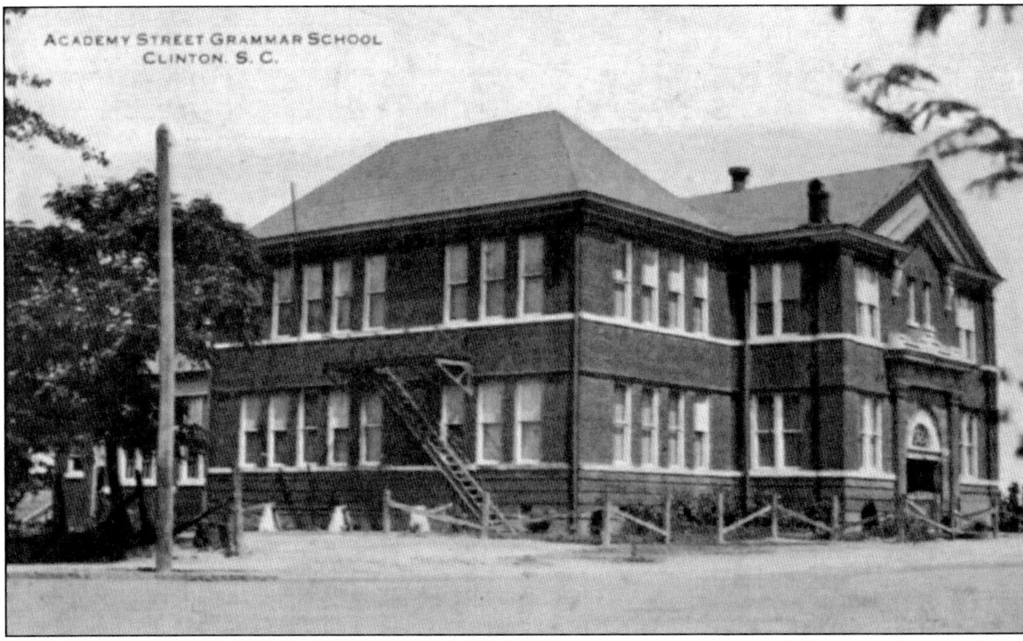

Through the years, Academy Street School in Clinton served students of all ages. The Academy Street School served as a high school prior to the construction of the Hampton Avenue High School in 1917. It later served as a grammar school. (Courtesy Clinton Museum.)

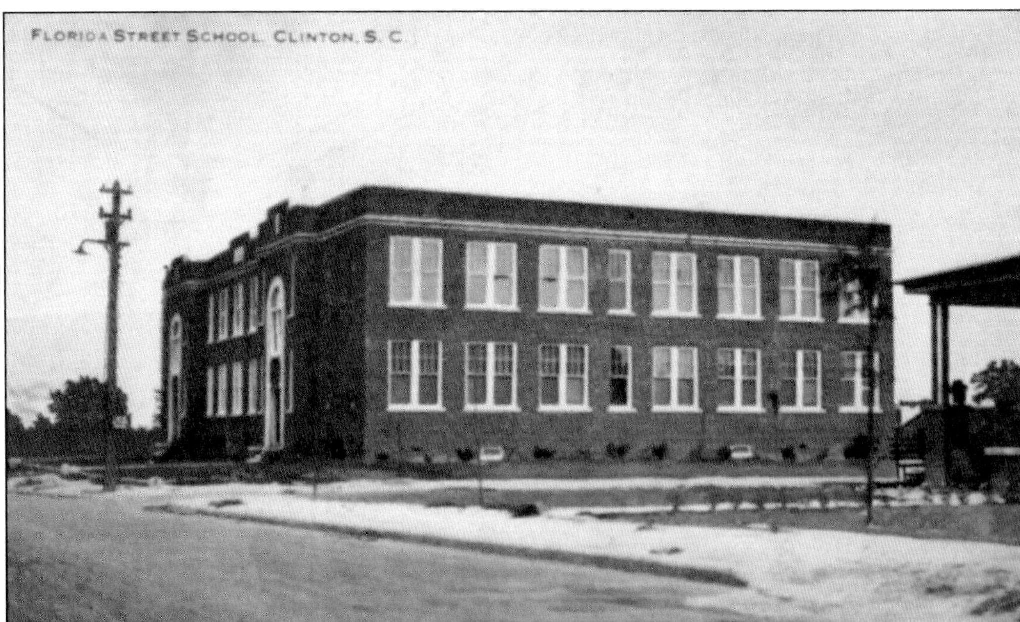

Florida Street School was built in 1924 on the corner of Florida and Jones Streets in Clinton. Through the years, it has served as an elementary school and junior high school. Currently Clinton School District 56 administrative offices are housed in the two-story brick school. (Courtesy Clinton Museum.)

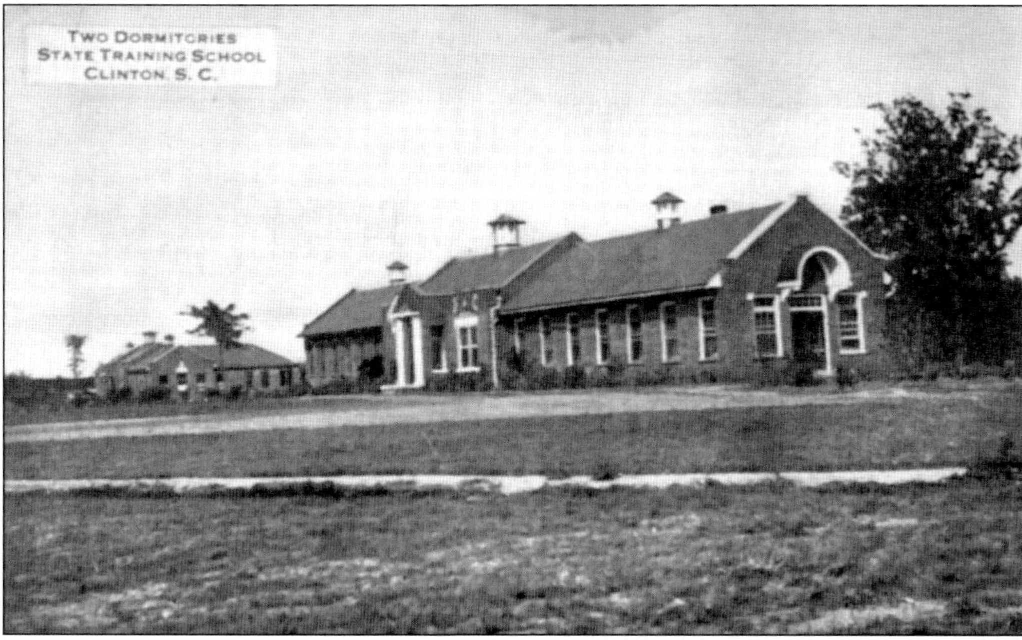

South Carolina passed a bill in 1918 to provide a training school for mentally handicapped persons. In 1920, the State Training School opened in Clinton under the direction of Dr. Benjamin Otis Whitten. In the beginning, there were two dormitories, a wooden dining hall, an old farmhouse that served as an office and staff quarters, and a wooden water tank. Dr. Whitten's staff consisted of a psychologist, Dr. Grace Kent; a supervisor; and an attendant. In later years, an administration building was constructed and named in honor of R. L. Plaxico, a Clinton businessman and friend of the school. (Courtesy Elaine Martin.)

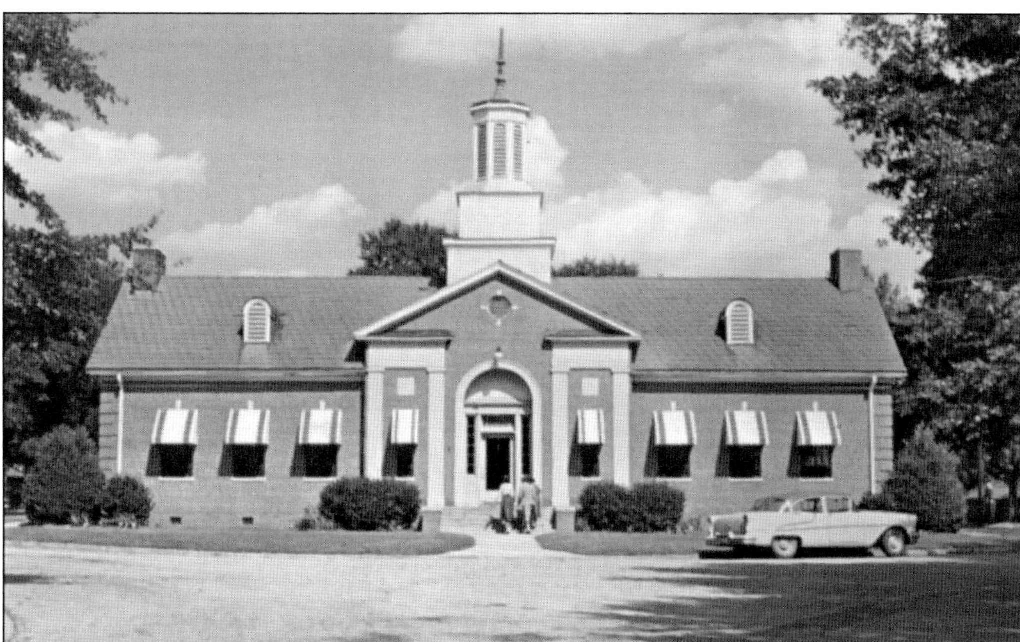

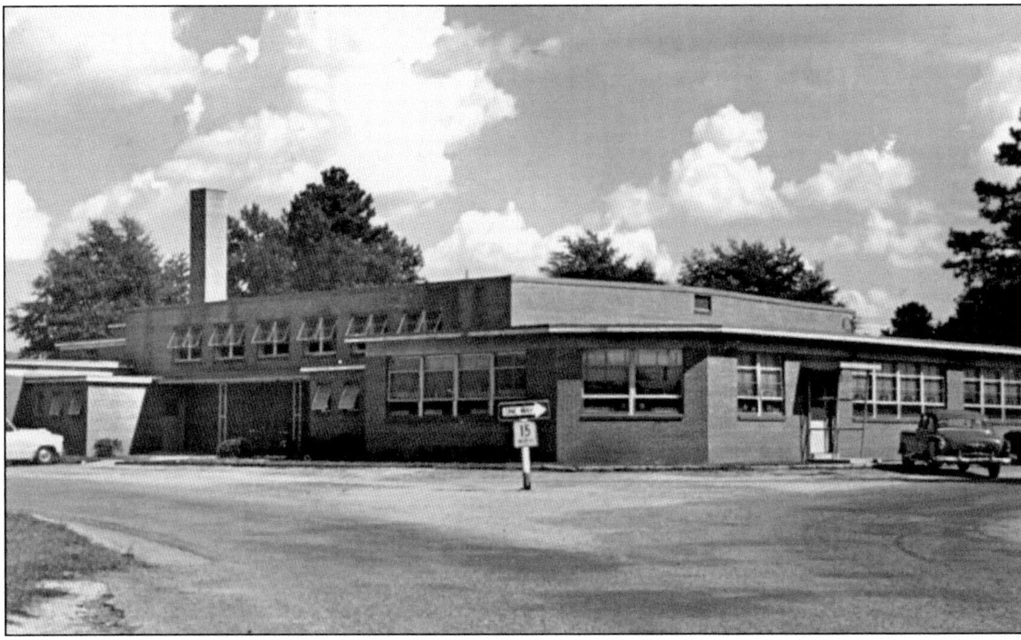

In 1954, the State Training School was an achievement, and Dr. B. O. Whitten was widely recognized as the force behind its success. The General Assembly of South Carolina passed legislation changing the school's name to Whitten Village. In 1979, the name was changed to Whitten Center. Over the years, more than 50 buildings were constructed on the campus, including the pictured Circle School. (Courtesy Elaine Martin.)

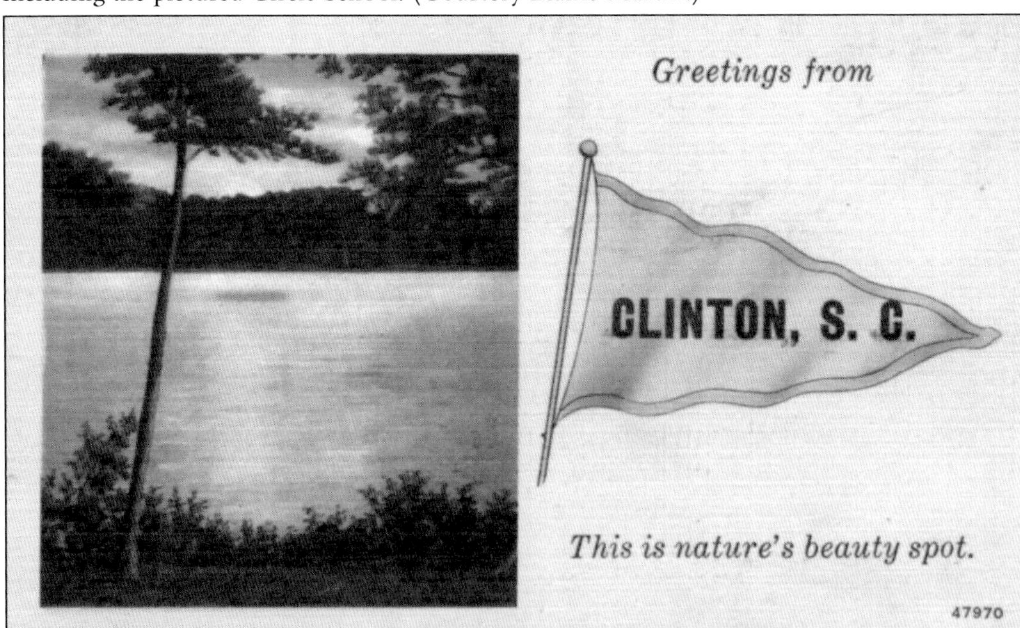

The Asheville Post Card Company printed this pennant Clinton postcard. The pennant landscape series came in an assortment of six different designs. They were priced $6 for 1,000 postcards. Clinton, like most small towns, was featured on a pennant postcard. (Courtesy Clinton Museum.)

The Battle of Musgrove's Mill, August 18, 1780, was one of the epic and classic battles of the American Revolution. It was a battle in which 300 American volunteers rode 30 miles at night to attack a British outpost. Today the battlefield and mill, located on the Enoree River, are a part of the Musgrove Mill Historic Site. Edward Musgrove's house and mill, where the British garrison was located, was on the south side of the ford, opposite the battlefield. The postcard shows a bird's-eye view of the site. (Courtesy Kathryn W. Johnson.)

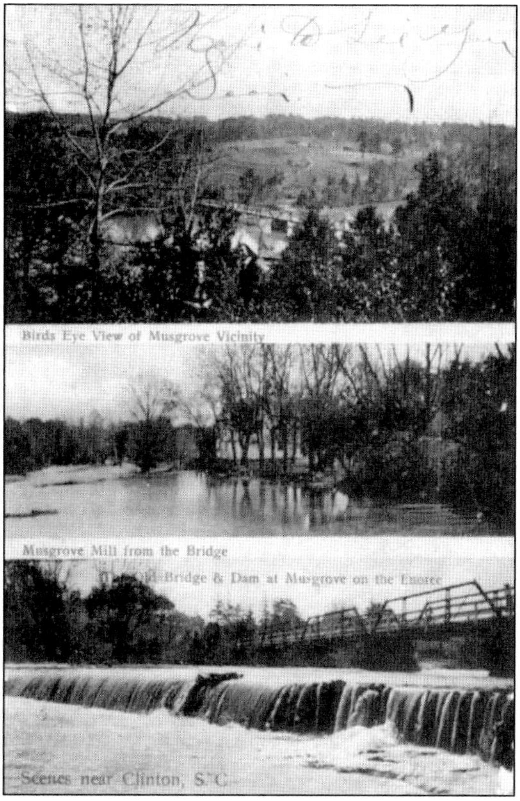

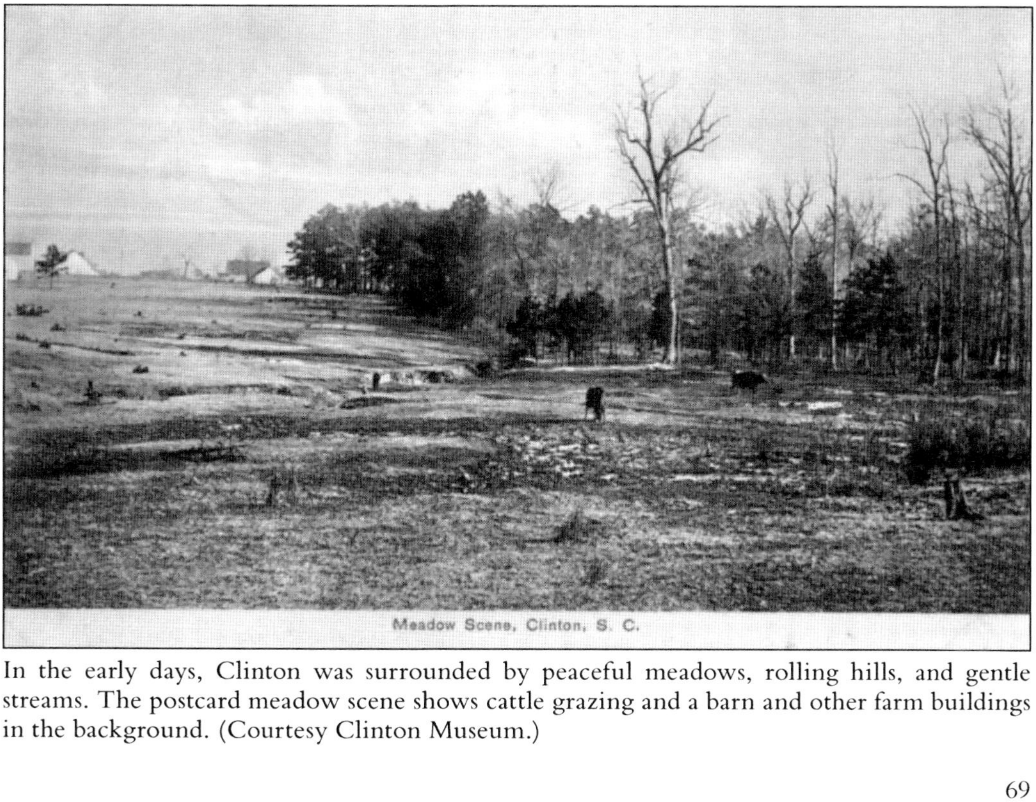

In the early days, Clinton was surrounded by peaceful meadows, rolling hills, and gentle streams. The postcard meadow scene shows cattle grazing and a barn and other farm buildings in the background. (Courtesy Clinton Museum.)

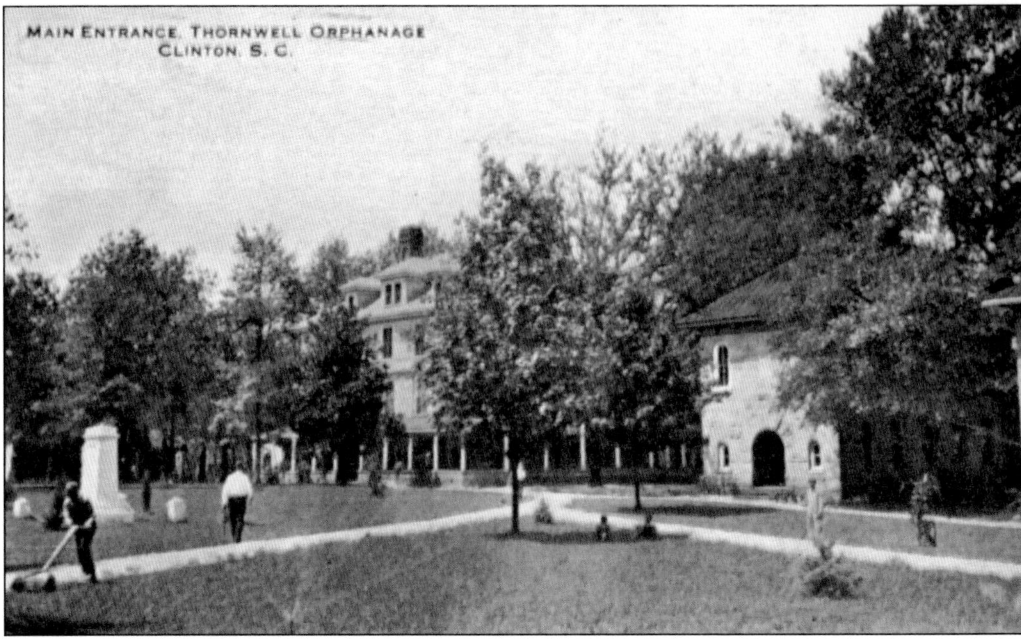

Thornwell Orphanage was organized in 1872 by Dr. William Plumer Jacobs, pastor of Clinton's First Presbyterian Church. Dr. Jacobs drafted plans for the home, and by 1873, land was purchased and a site chosen for the orphanage. The first donation to Thornwell came from a 10-year-old orphan, William P. Anderson, in the form of 50¢. The second gift came from Dr. Jacobs's daughter, Florence Jacobs. The name was later changed to Thornwell Home for Children. Thornwell's main entrance from Broad Street and a 1907 view of the campus are pictured. (Courtesy Elaine Martin and Robert W. Stansell.)

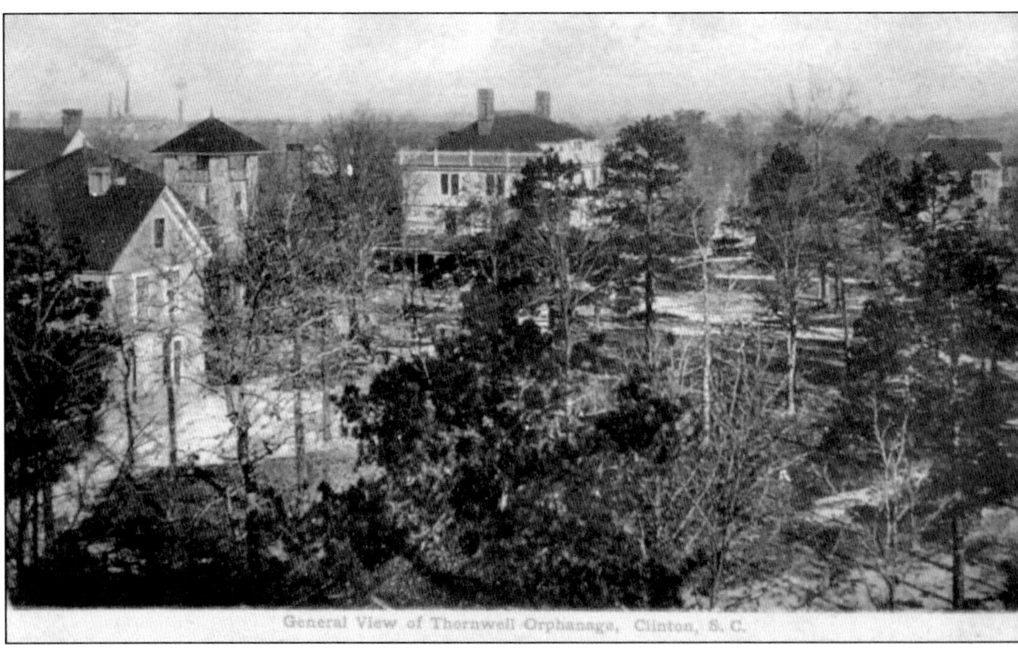

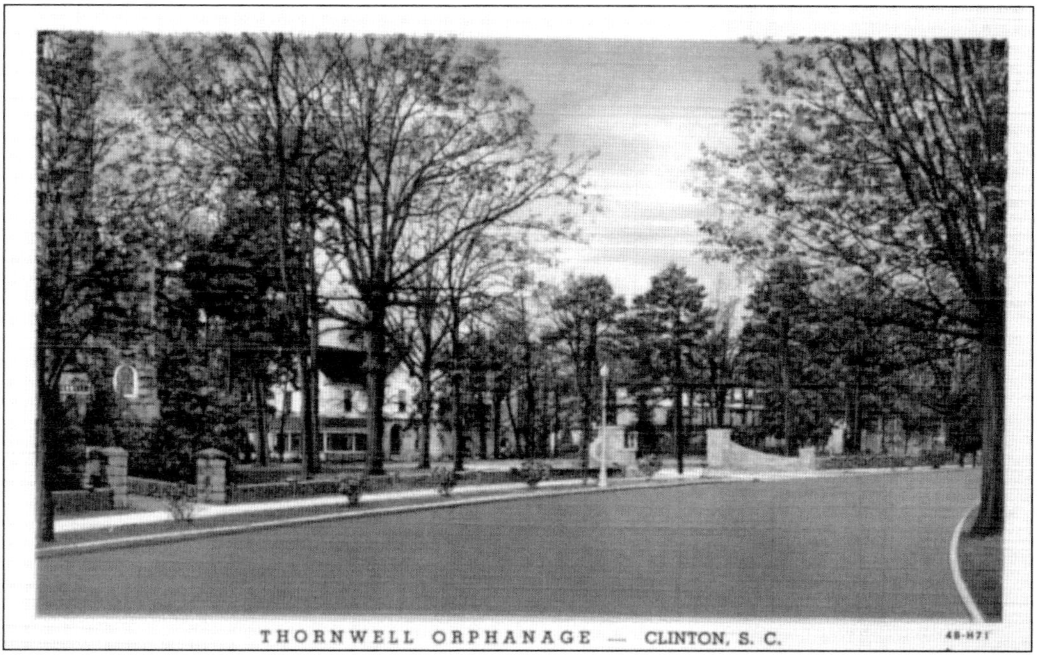

Dr. William Plumer Jacobs dreamed of a home for destitute children, and his dream became a reality when, as pastor of the First Presbyterian Church in Clinton, he built a home with the unswerving belief that God so willed and would support such a work. He named the home Thornwell for the great theologian Dr. James Henley Thornwell. Dr. Jacobs was married to Mary Jane Dillard, daughter of Dr. and Mrs. James H. Dillard. Dr. and Mrs. Jacobs became the director and housemother of Thornwell. Mary Jacobs gave herself totally to whatever work her husband undertook. (Courtesy Mary Alice Mundy.)

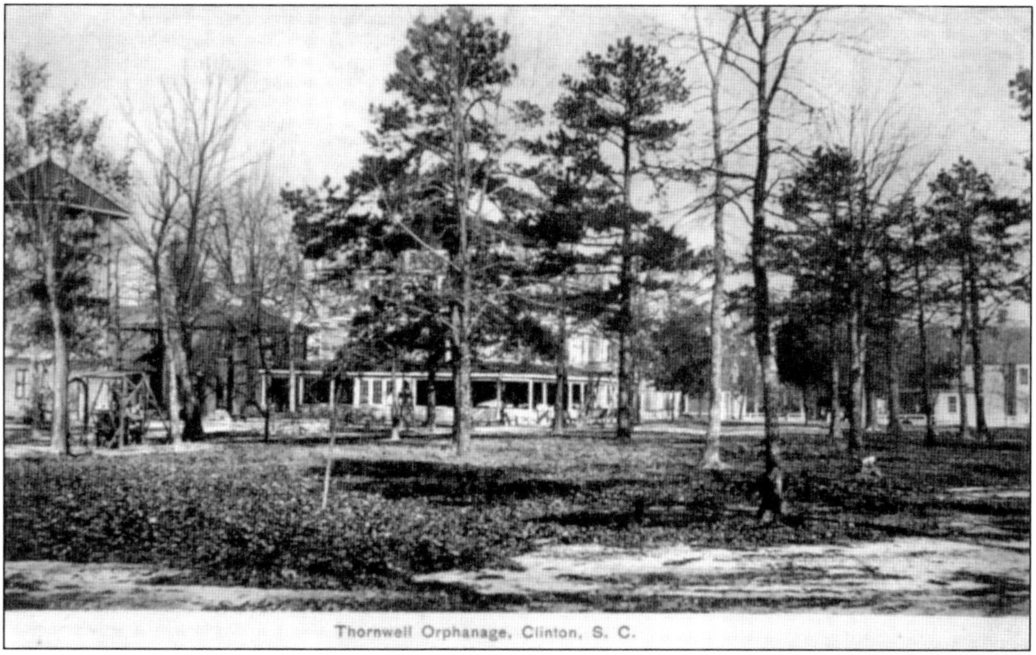

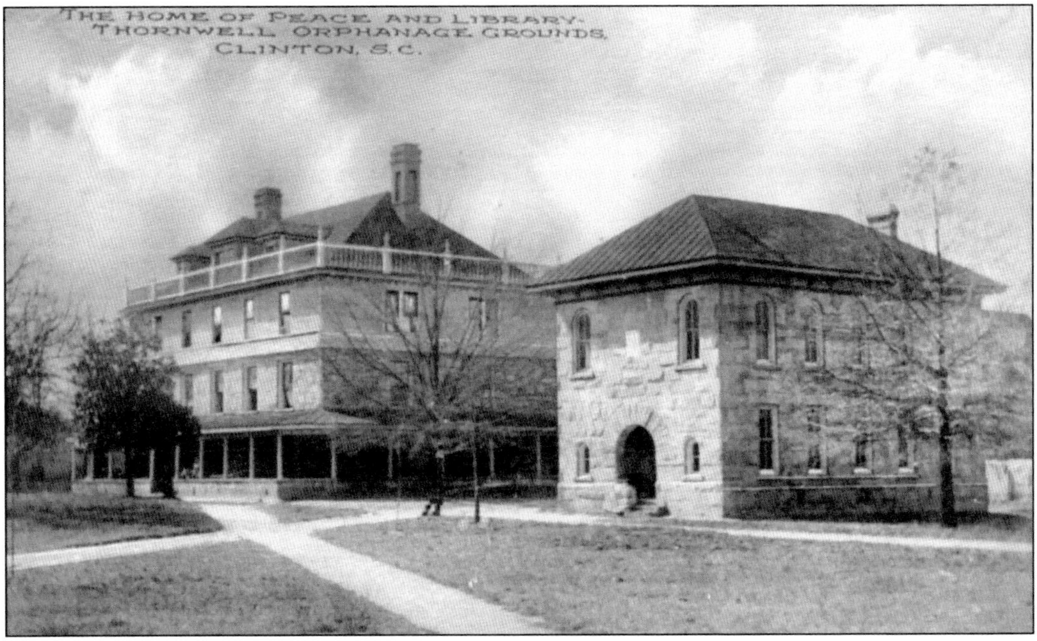

On October 1, 1875, despite adversities such as lack of money, opposition of church members, runaway laborers, and the rebuilding of part of the front wall because of faulty mortar, the doors of the Home of Peace were opened to eight children, all South Carolinians and orphaned by the War Between the States. Friends from Laurens, Clinton, Cross Hill, and neighboring communities were present for opening day. They arrived bringing gifts of food and household equipment. Women of Second Presbyterian Church in Charleston furnished the school room, and the Glebe Street Presbyterian Church in Charleston furnished the room for girls. The Nellie Scott Library is shown beside the Home of Peace. (Above courtesy Mary Alice Mundy; below courtesy Elaine Martin.)

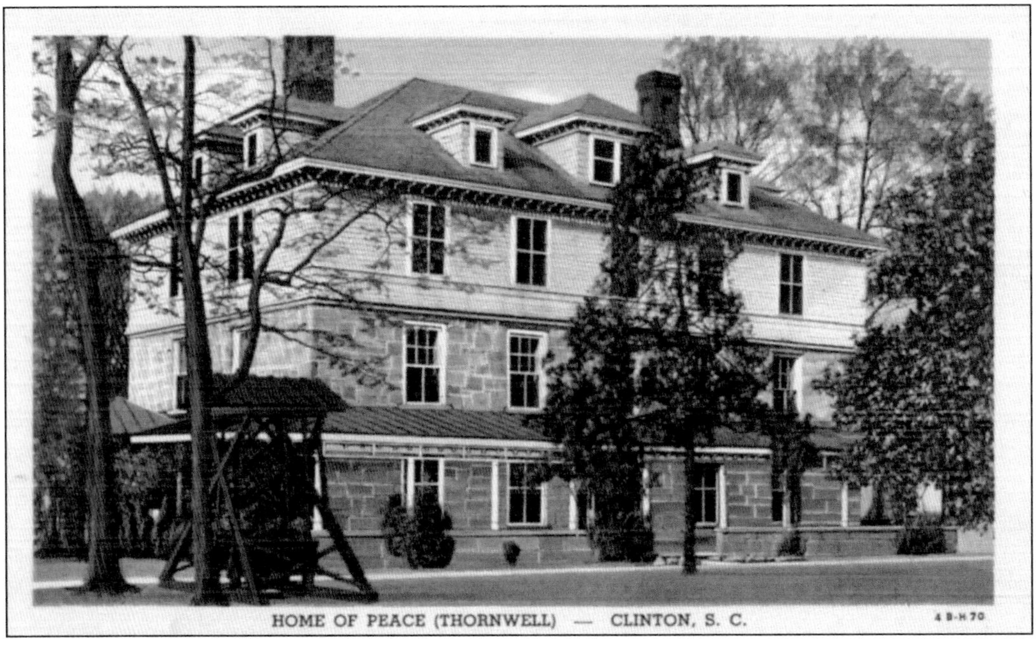

Presbyterian churches throughout Georgia raised funds to build the brick Georgia Home on the Thornwell campus. The construction cost was $6,000. The home was dedicated October 1, 1906, and occupied by young boys. Mrs. Lydia D. Brown was housemother. The home was destroyed by fire in 1936. It was rebuilt at a cost of $16,000 in 1939 as a gift of W. D. Beatie of Atlanta, Georgia, in memory of his mother, Mary L. Beatie. The new granite cottage was renamed the Georgia-Beatie Home. (Above courtesy Robert W. Stansell; below courtesy Elaine Martin.)

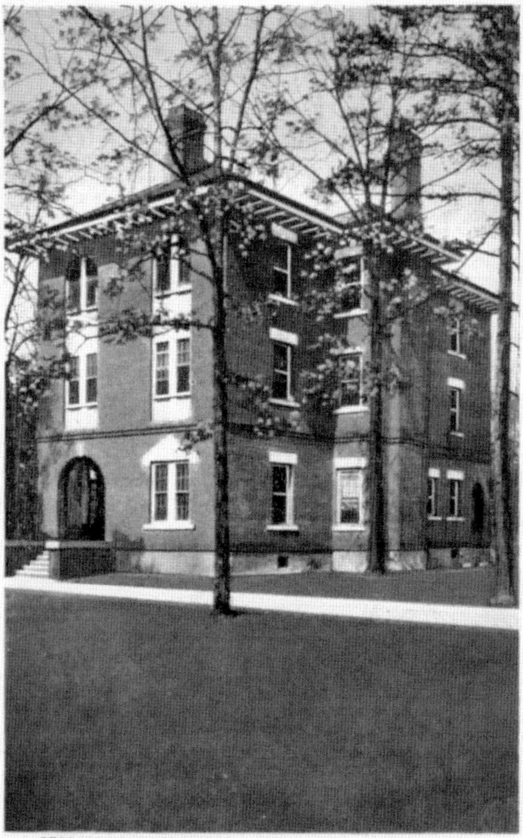

GEORGIA HOME. THORNWELL ORPHANAGE. CLINTON, S. C.

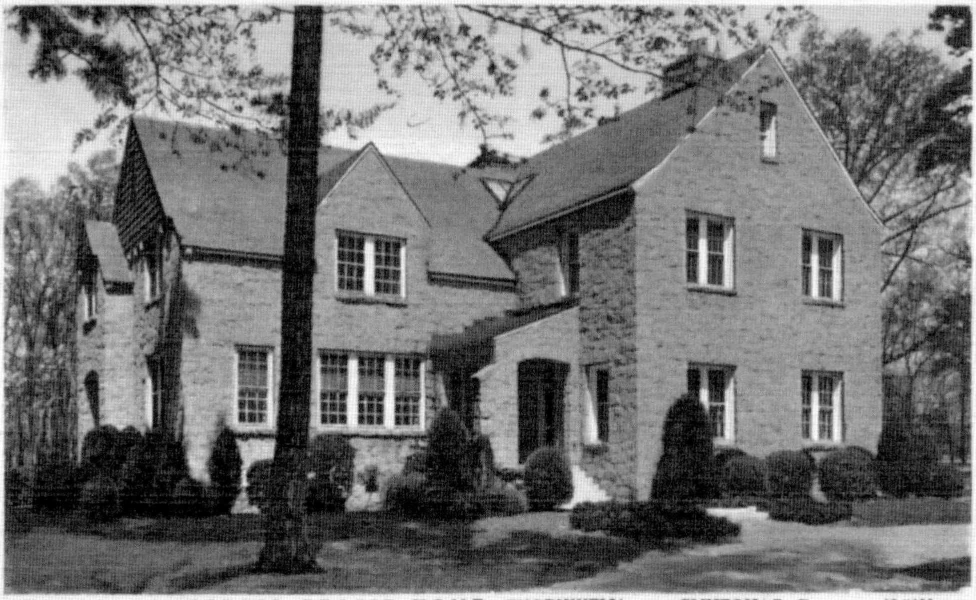

GEORGIA-BEATIE HOME (THORNWELL) — CLINTON, S. C. 4B-H432

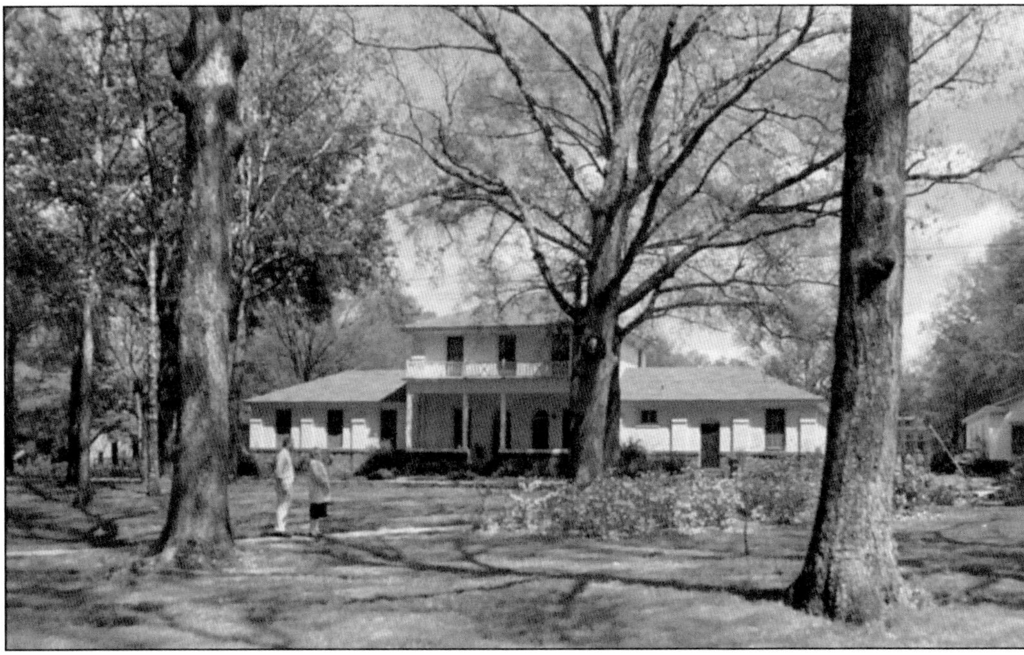

The Fowler Cottage on the Thornwell campus once served as a kitchen, classrooms, and home for boys. It was constructed in 1905 and was one of eight buildings erected by Nettie Fowler McCormick of Chicago, Illinois. (Courtesy Elaine Martin.)

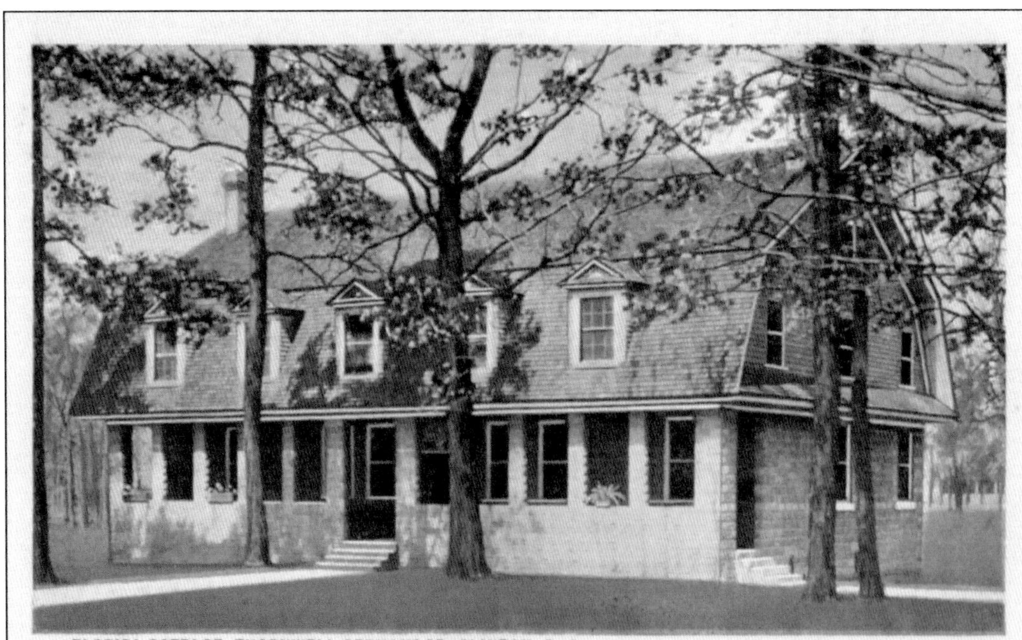

The Florida Home on the Thornwell campus was constructed with contributions given by churches in the Synod of Florida. Rev. J. B. Branch, assistant to Dr. Jacobs, was instrumental in raising the funds for this cottage, which was begun in 1912 and occupied in the fall of 1913. The building housed boys, and Kitty Norris was the housemother. (Courtesy Robert W. Stansell.)

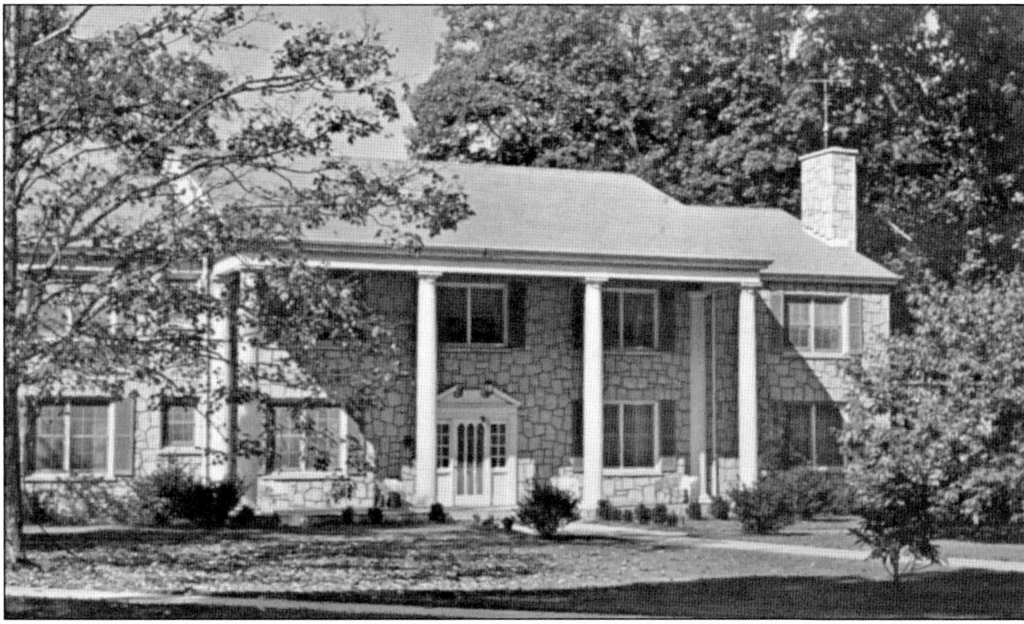

Mrs. Tom P. Hartness of Spartanburg designed the Sara Jo Hartness Hall to be a model home for older girls. It was constructed in 1954. Here girls were taught cultural qualities of gracious living and good housekeeping in an atmosphere of happiness, friendship, and security. Mrs. Mary Armstrong was the first housemother of the Colonial home for 16 girls. (Courtesy Elaine Martin.)

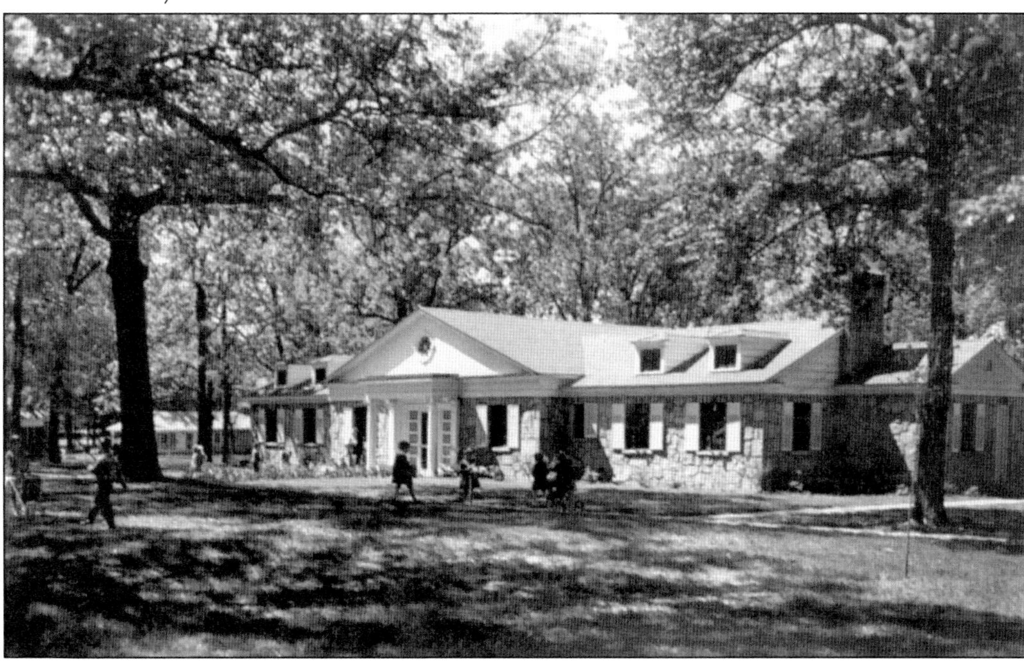

Located on the Thornwell campus, the granite Stewart Cottage was constructed in 1950. It was a gift of J. W. Stewart of Fountain Inn and Greenville. The Stewart Cottage was a home for kindergarten-age children. Mrs. Carrie Atkinson was the first housemother. (Courtesy Elaine Martin.)

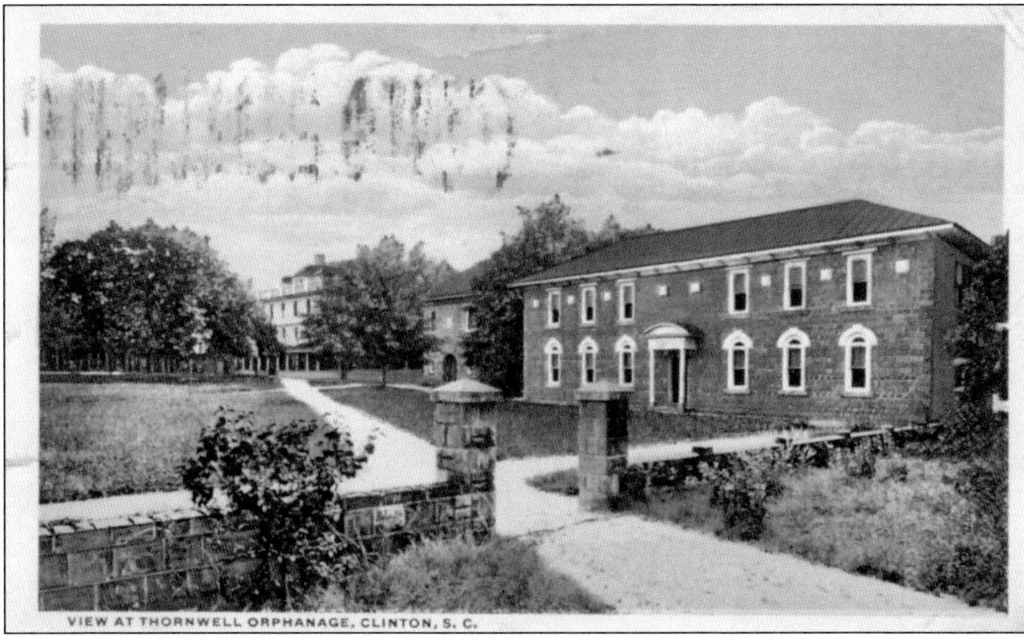

The brick building originally served as the Thornwell Museum. A varied and unique collection was accumulated over the years. Donations from the Smithsonian, federal government, private individuals, and other sources created much interest for Thornwell children as well as the Clinton community. The building was razed for the Sara Jo Hartness Hall, at which time the artifacts were removed to the Nellie Scott Library. (Courtesy Mary Alice Mundy.)

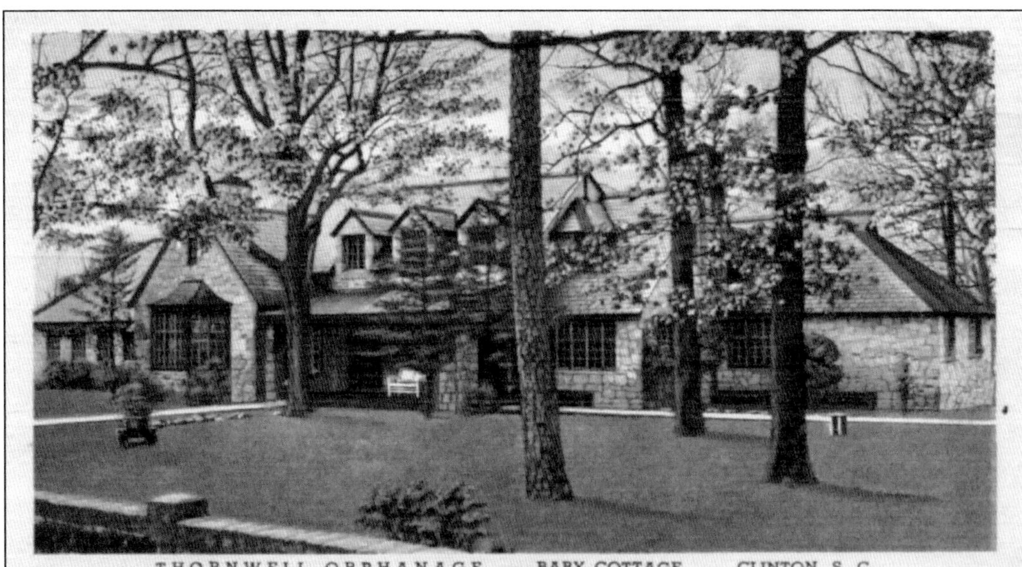

Louise F. Mayes of Greenville, while president of South Carolina Synodical in 1923, approached Presbyterian women from South Carolina, Georgia, and Florida Synodicals in an effort to build a cottage for preschool children on the Thornwell campus. Louise Mayes passed away before the cottage was completed. In 1925, the Louise F. Mayes Baby Cottage opened and was named in her honor. (Courtesy Elaine Martin.)

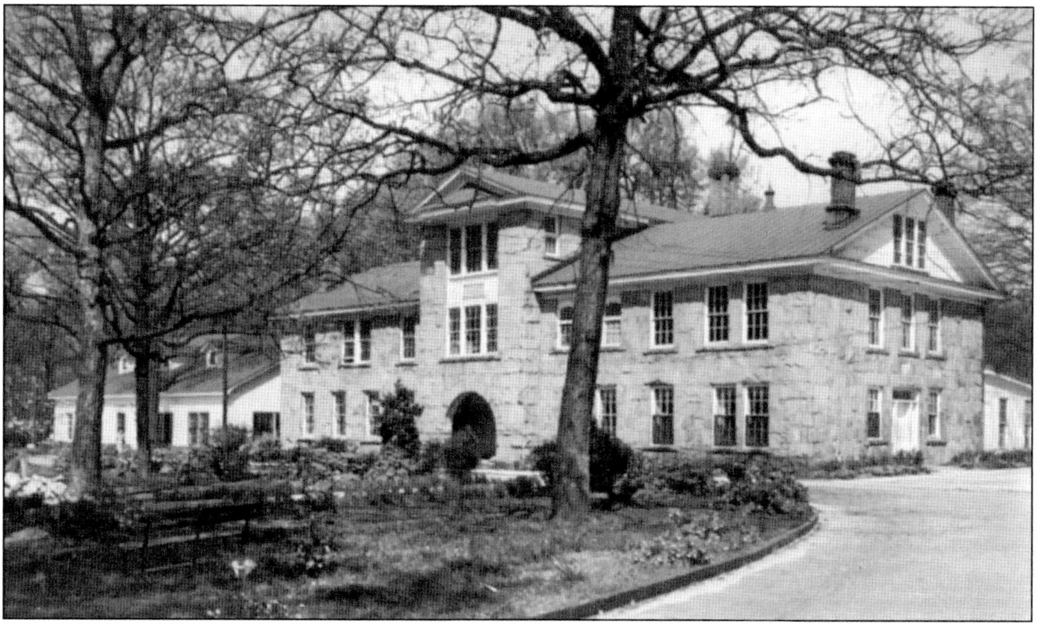

Thornwell's Technical School was the first facility of its kind for dependant children in the South. In earlier days, the building housed a print shop, a binding and electroplating operation, and sewing room, and it also provided classrooms for typewriting, shorthand, chemistry, mineralogy, and photography courses. The program was self-supporting. In later years, the building became the Student Activities Center. (Courtesy Mary Alice Mundy.)

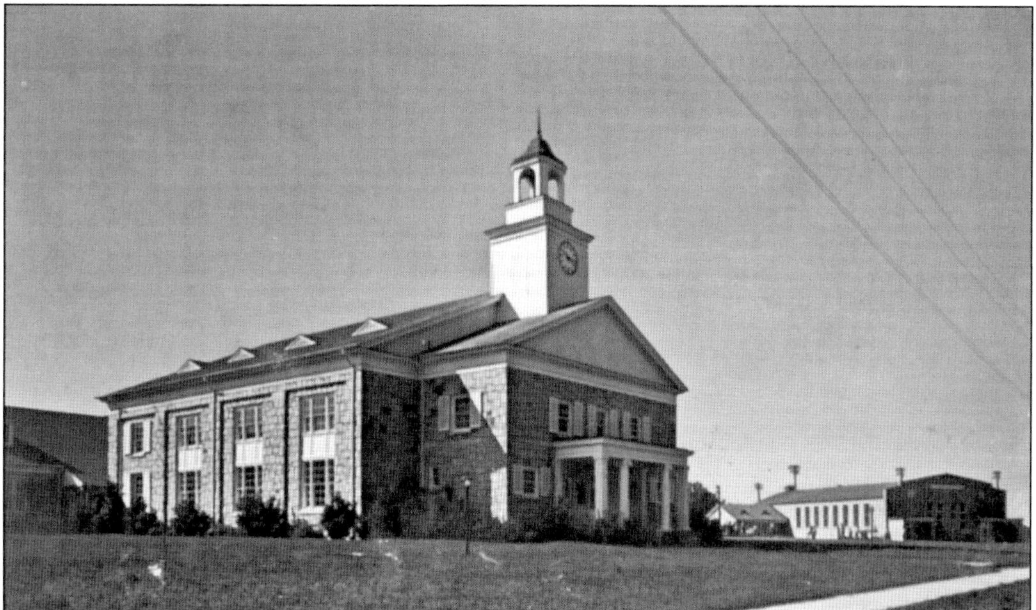

The Hartness Gymnasium was built in 1950 from funds given by Mr. and Mrs. T. P. Hartness of Spartanburg. Other contributions allowed the completion in 1952 of an educational complex, which included Coffin Memorial High School, Montgomery Memorial Hall, and Mary Schane Grammar School. (Courtesy Elaine Martin.)

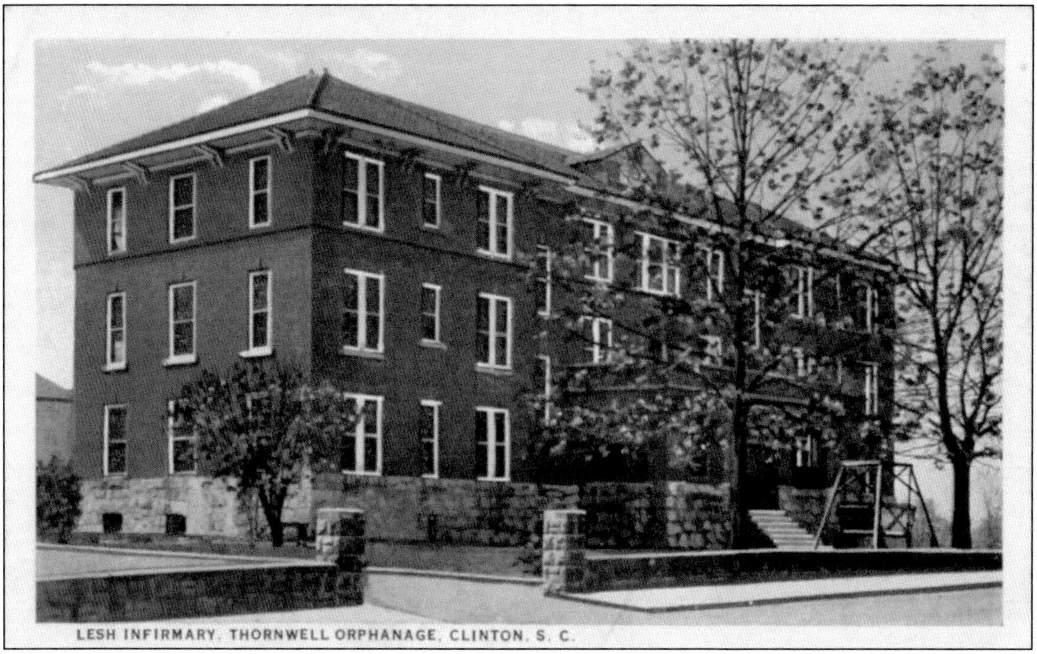

In 1913, Thornwell received a gift from Mrs. John H. Lesh of Newton Center, Massachusetts, for the erection of a new infirmary. The Mary Lesh Infirmary, complete with elevators, steam furnace, and operating room, opened in 1914. Carrie Lee Oliver, a Thornwell graduate, served as head nurse. The infirmary was razed in 1974 when the new Tom and Joe Infirmary was opened. (Courtesy Elaine Martin.)

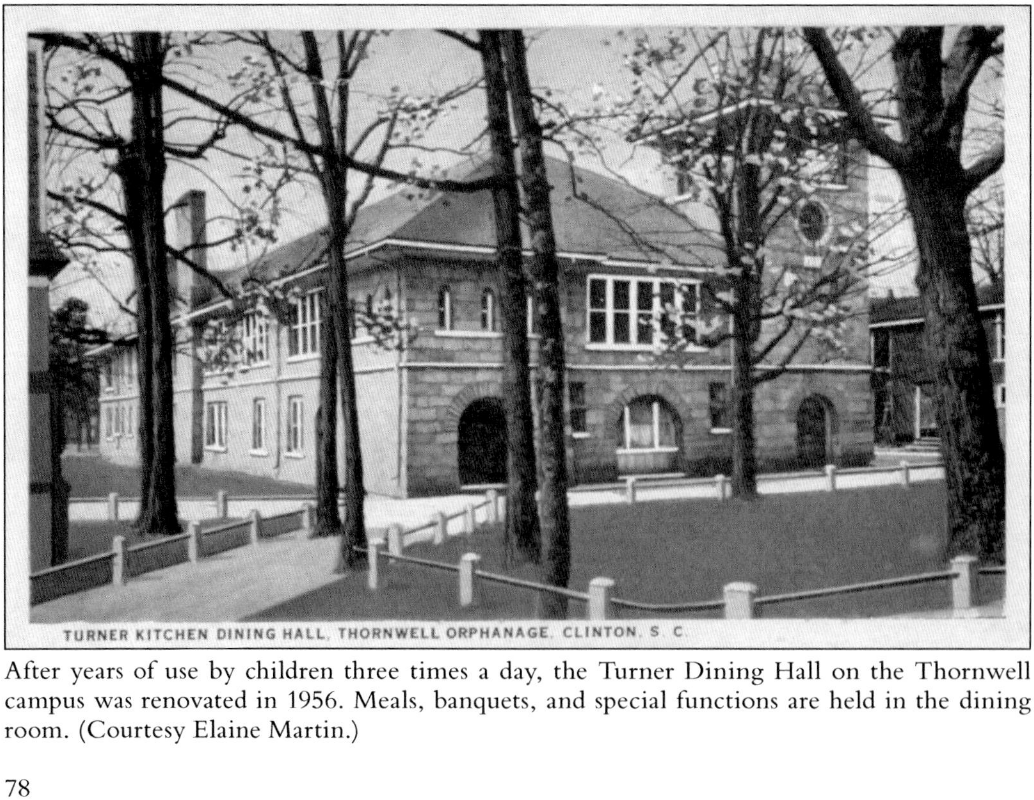

After years of use by children three times a day, the Turner Dining Hall on the Thornwell campus was renovated in 1956. Meals, banquets, and special functions are held in the dining room. (Courtesy Elaine Martin.)

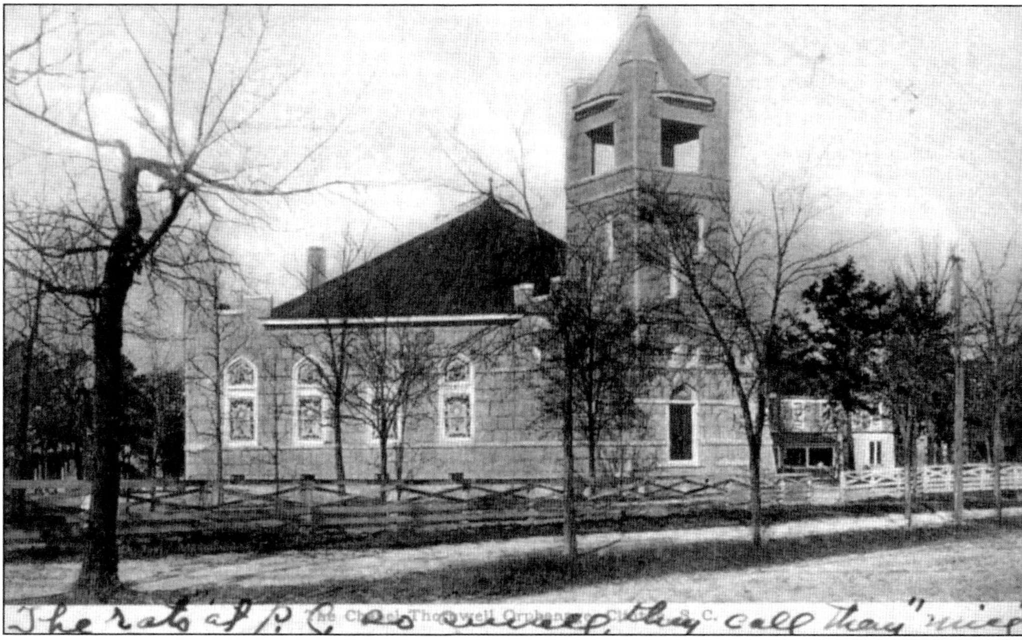

In 1906, the Carolina Memorial Chapel was erected at Thornwell. It was used as a meeting hall until 1909, when the Thornwell family was organized by the Enoree Presbytery into a church. The name Thornwell Memorial was chosen and 163 members enrolled. Two elders, Dr. A. J. Briggs and Thomas Scott, and two deacons, Johnson Kilgore and H. J. Brissenden, were elected. The Thornwell Memorial Church was replaced in 1966 by the Hartness-Thornwell Memorial Presbyterian Church. (Above courtesy Mary Alice Mundy; below courtesy Elaine Martin.)

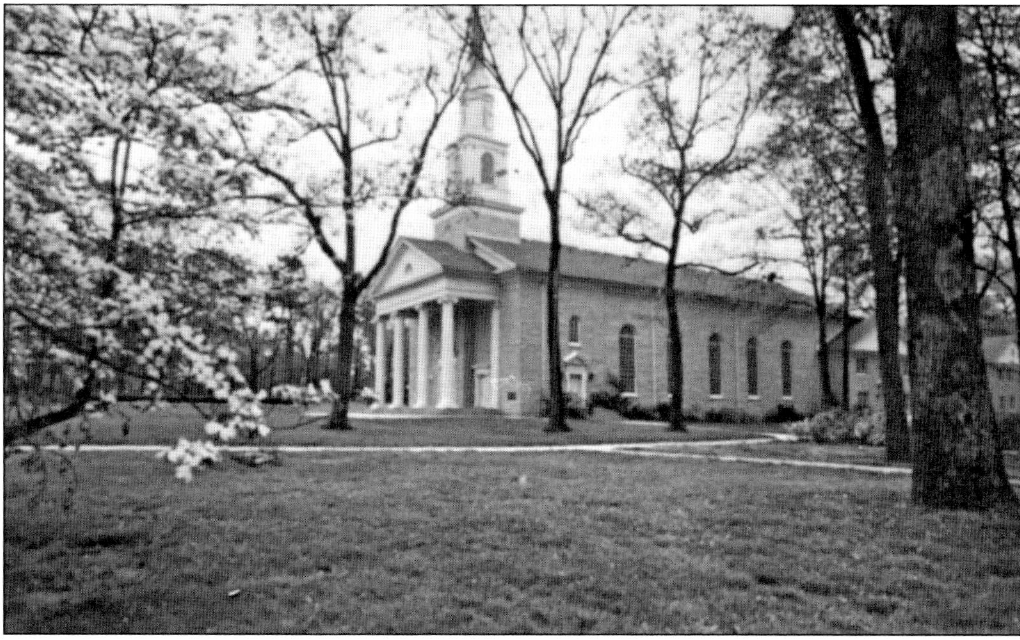

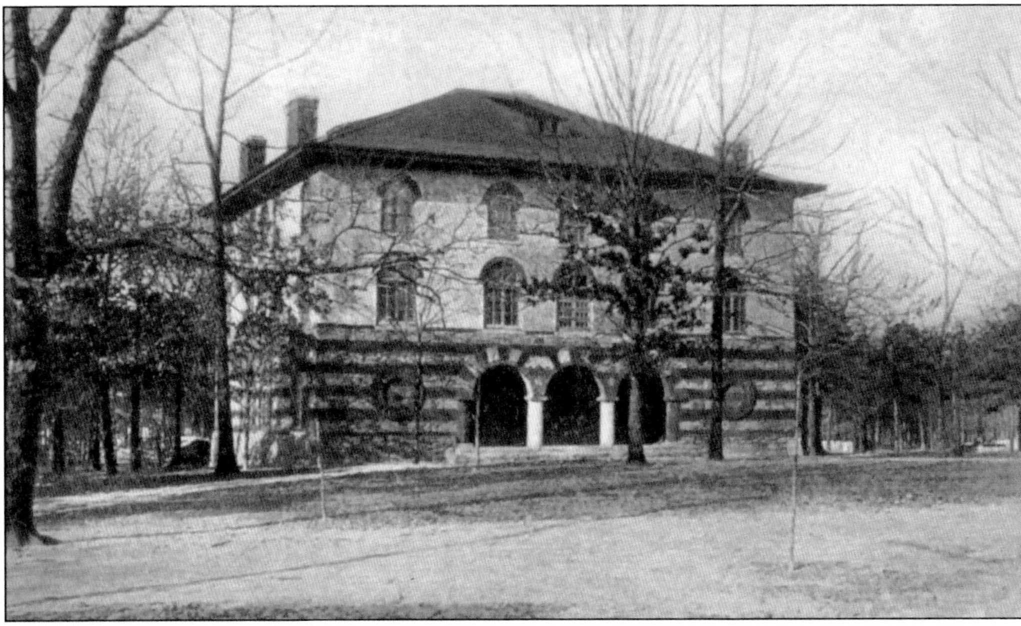

The Recitation Hall was erected in 1886 and was a part of Clinton College, which later became Presbyterian College. Dr. William P. Jacobs was largely responsible for establishing the college. When the decision was made to move Presbyterian College to a new location, the old college building was purchased by Thornwell in 1906 and named McCall Building. The McCall building burned in 1943. (Courtesy Robert W. Stansell.)

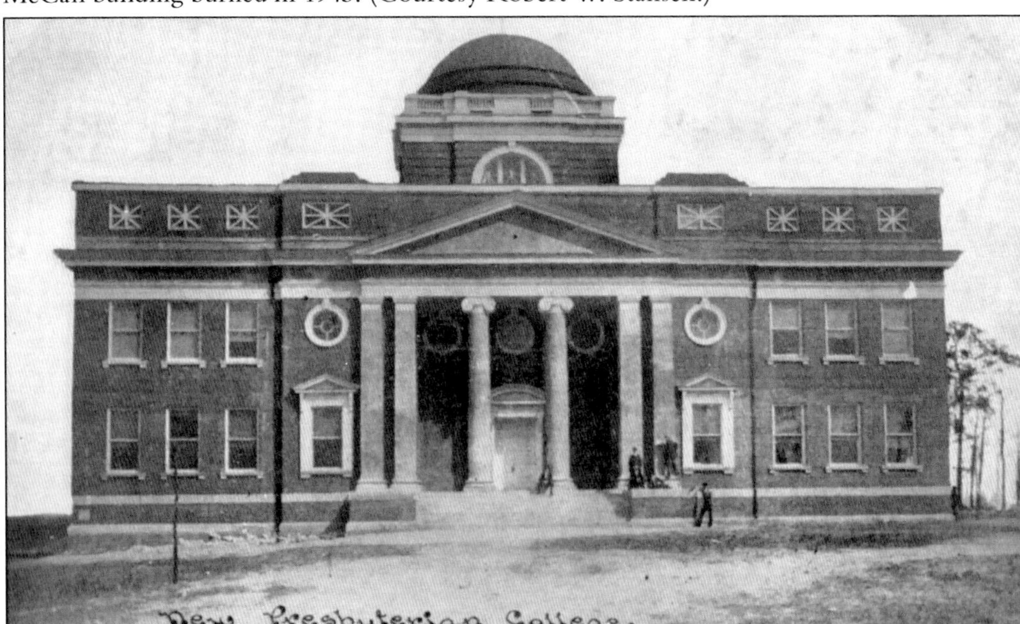

Neville Hall was completed in 1907 in a field that later became the Presbyterian College Campus. Its Colonial-styled Georgian Revival architecture set the pattern for future buildings. Through the years, the hall has served as classrooms, administrative offices, and fraternity suites. It remains the focal point of Presbyterian College. (Courtesy Presbyterian College Archives.)

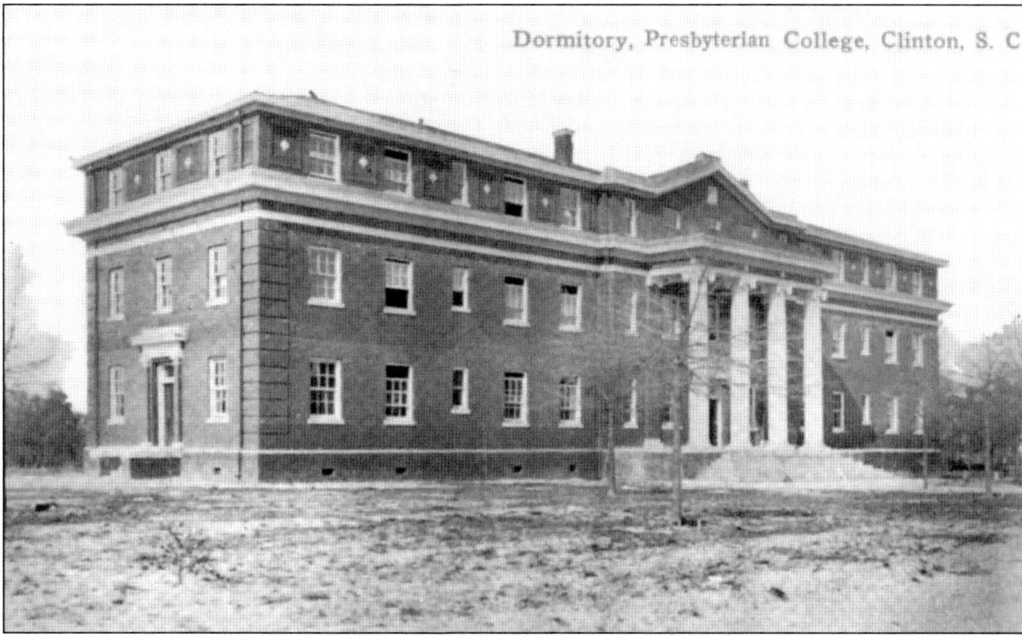

The Spencer Hall Dormitory, located on the West Plaza of Presbyterian College, opened in 1912. The building was razed in 1995 and replaced by the Harrington-Peachtree Building. The original columns from Spencer Hall were used in constructing the new facility. (Courtesy Lawrence E. Young.)

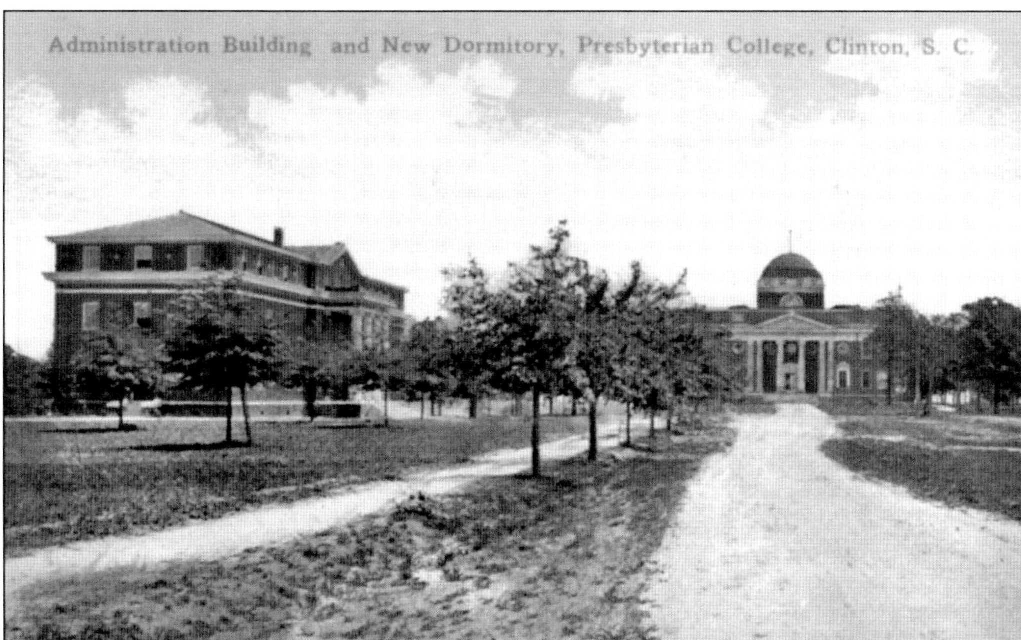

Neville Hall, named for former president Dr. William Gordon Neville, and Spencer Hall are pictured in an early postcard of the Presbyterian College campus. Spencer Hall, a dormitory, was named for Dr. A. E. Spencer, who served as a professor and president of the college. A dirt walk and drive were a part of the campus. (Courtesy Presbyterian College Archives.)

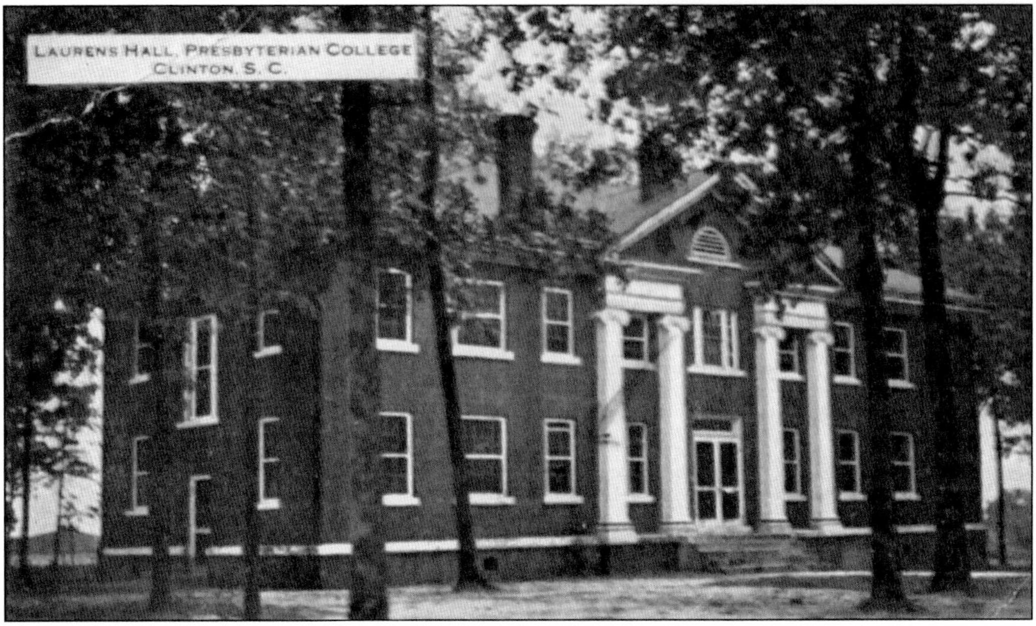

Laurens Hall, a Presbyterian College dormitory, was built in 1908. It housed 24 male students. The dormitory was constructed with funds raised by Presbyterians throughout Laurens County. The cost of the dormitory was $7,000. (Courtesy Lawrence E. Young.)

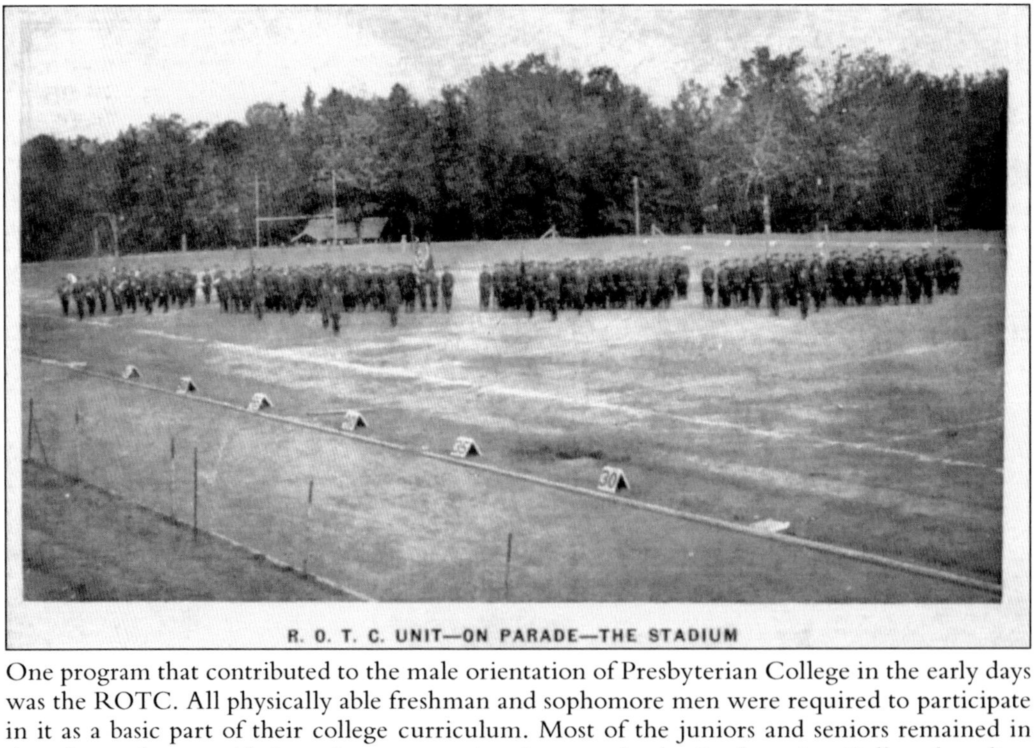

R. O. T. C. UNIT—ON PARADE—THE STADIUM

One program that contributed to the male orientation of Presbyterian College in the early days was the ROTC. All physically able freshman and sophomore men were required to participate in it as a basic part of their college curriculum. Most of the juniors and seniors remained in the advanced course if given the opportunity. As a result, the Presbyterian College battalion numbered around 300, and the position of cadet commander was among the highest campus honors. (Courtesy Lawrence E. Young.)

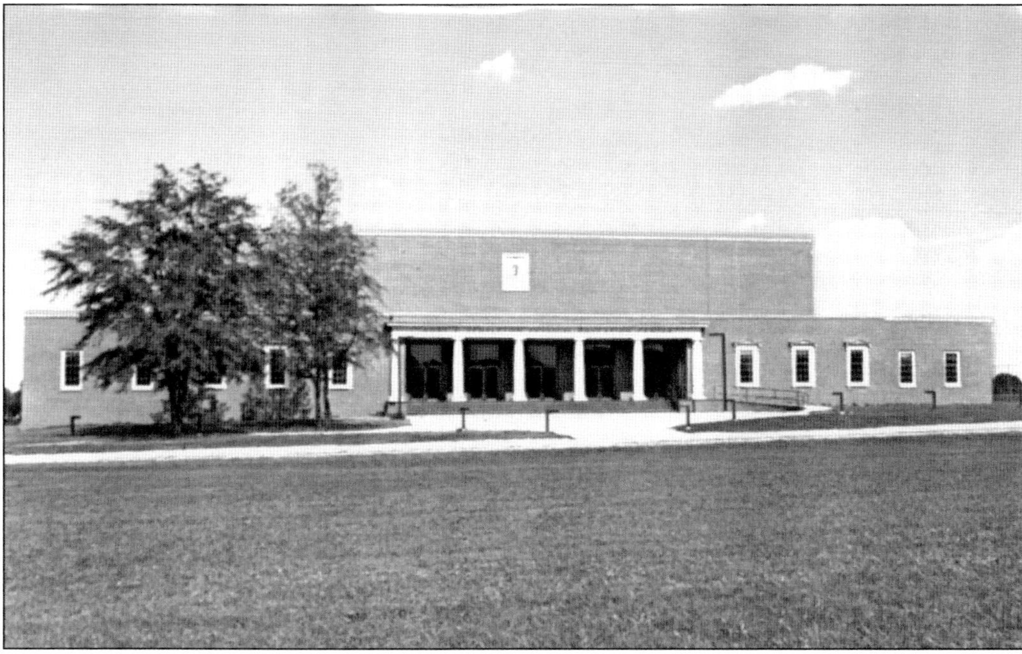

The Ross E. Templeton Physical Education Center is named for a distinguished alumnus and benefactor of Presbyterian College. The facility is the home of the Blue Hose athletic teams and provides classrooms and multi-purpose rooms for physical education and recreation. The Furman B. Pinson basketball area seats approximately 3,000. (Courtesy Lawrence E. Young.)

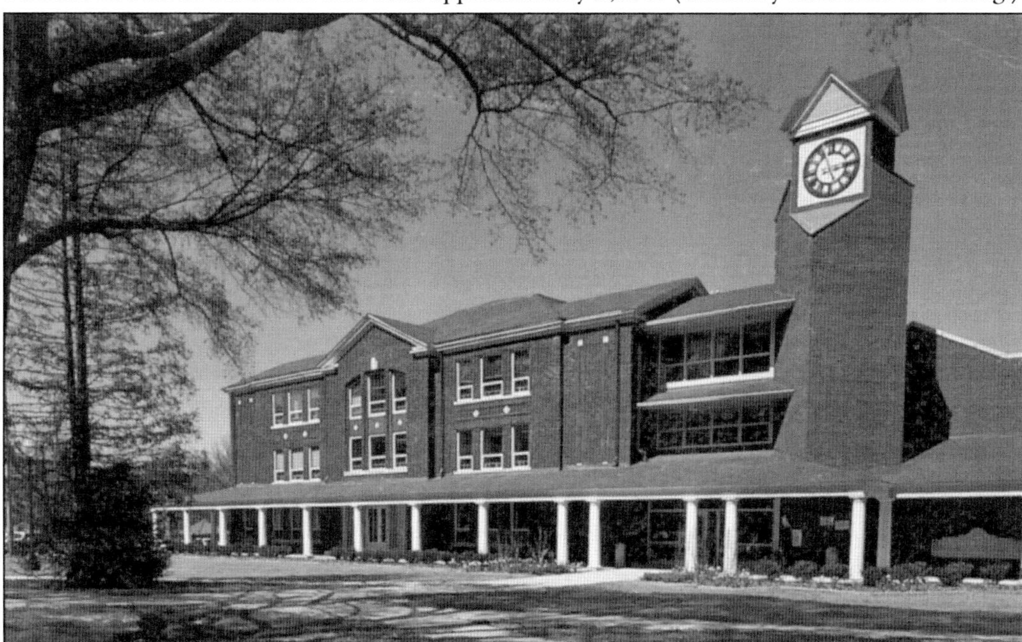

The Springs Campus Center is the hub of student life at Presbyterian College. The original building, built in 1924 with an indoor swimming pool added in 1929, underwent a renovation in 1985. Today it houses the campus store and canteen, student government and publications offices, and fitness and intramural facilities. (Courtesy Lawrence E. Young.)

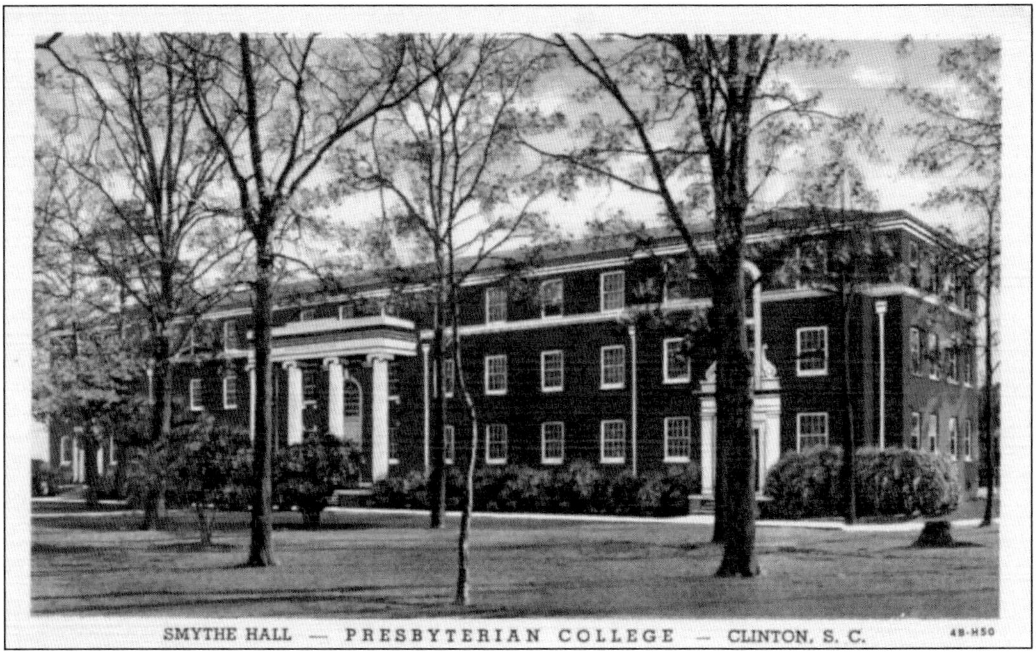

At a cost of $95,000, Smyth Hall, with space for 72 students, was added to the Presbyterian College campus in 1924. Continuing the Georgian Revival style, it featured a central Ionic portico and flanking end pavilions. (Courtesy Elaine Martin.)

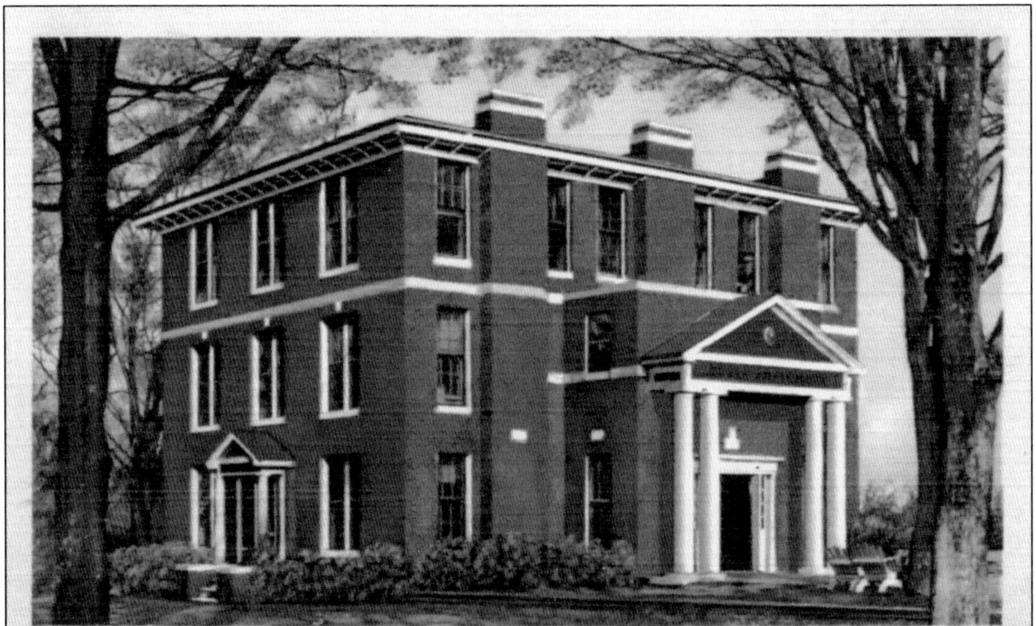

Alumni Hall dormitory had changed little in appearance since its erection in 1891. However, in 1942, Alumni Hall was renovated completely into Doyle Infirmary. The stucco exterior was covered by brick and the main entrance moved from side to front, creating a new facade. (Courtesy Elaine Martin.)

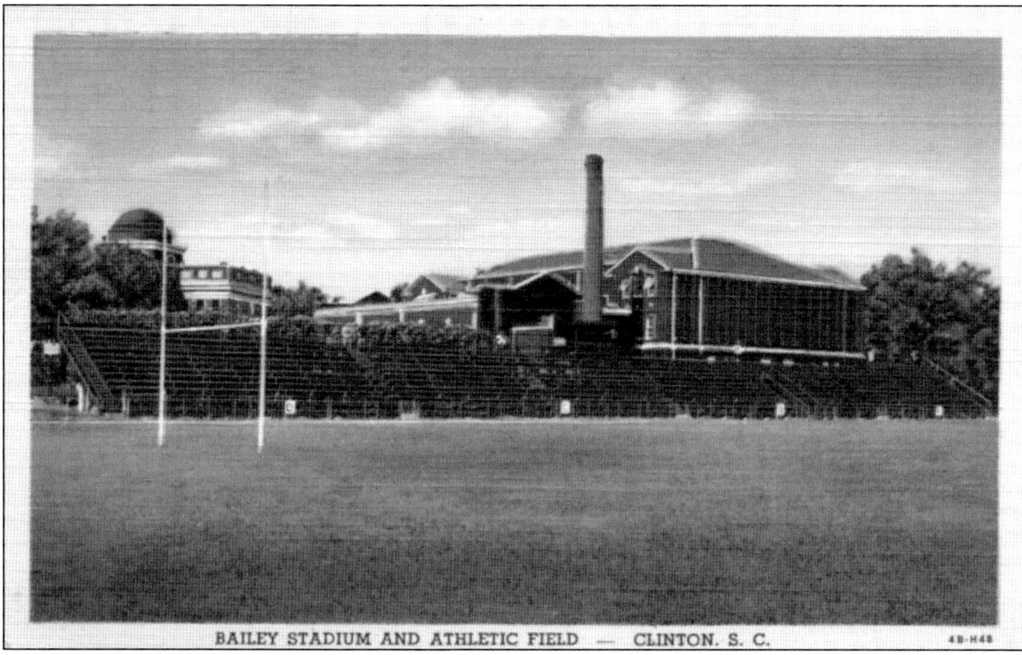

An athletic center became a reality for Presbyterian College in 1924 with the erection of Leroy Springs Gymnasium. Col. Leroy Springs of Lancaster, South Carolina, contributed funds for the building, which was planned by gymnasium experts to include the latest design concepts of a sports facility. The gym housed the first indoor college swimming pool in the state. Built to encircle the football field behind the gymnasium was a track modeled after a Harvard track. The track proved so superior that every state meet was held at Presbyterian College between 1925 and 1958. Only limited stands were available for football seating during that era. (Courtesy Elaine Martin.)

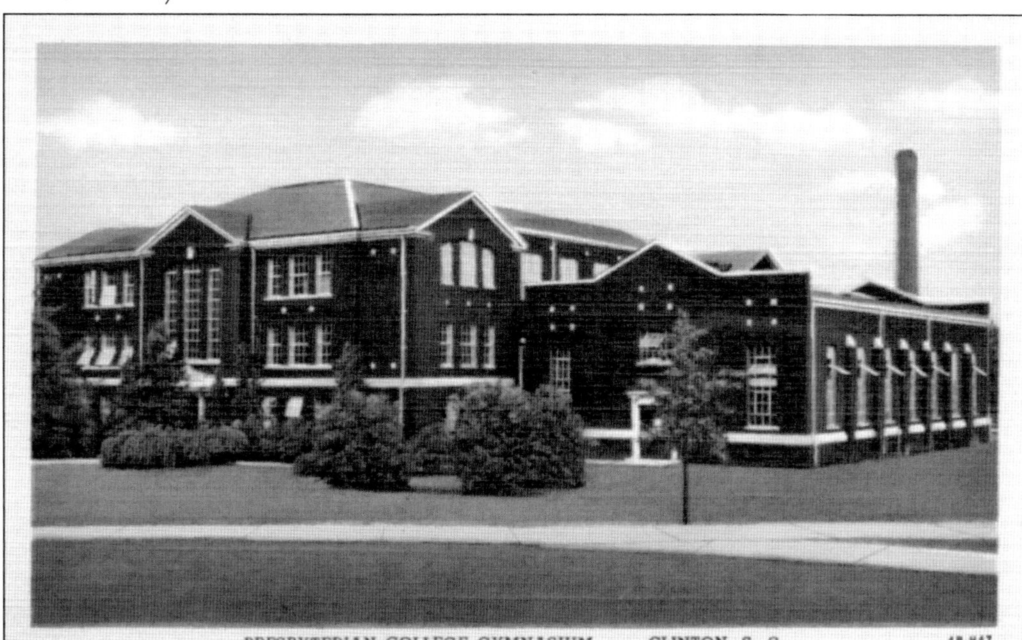

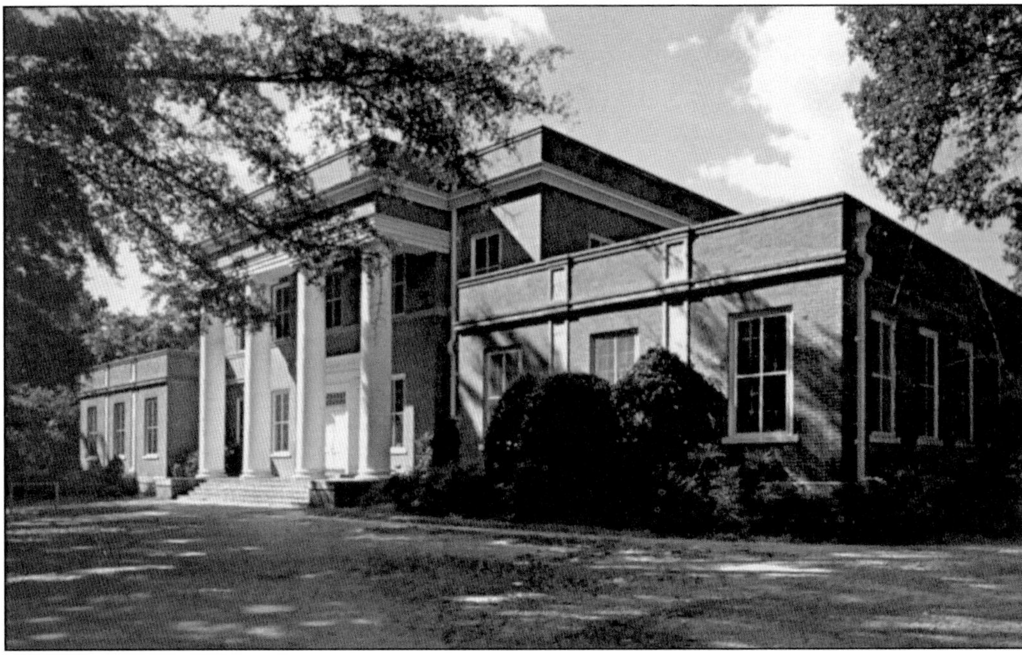

This building once served as the Presbyterian College Library. It was constructed in 1942 with a capacity of 90,000 volumes. It is currently used as the Smyth Administration Building. (Courtesy Elaine Martin.)

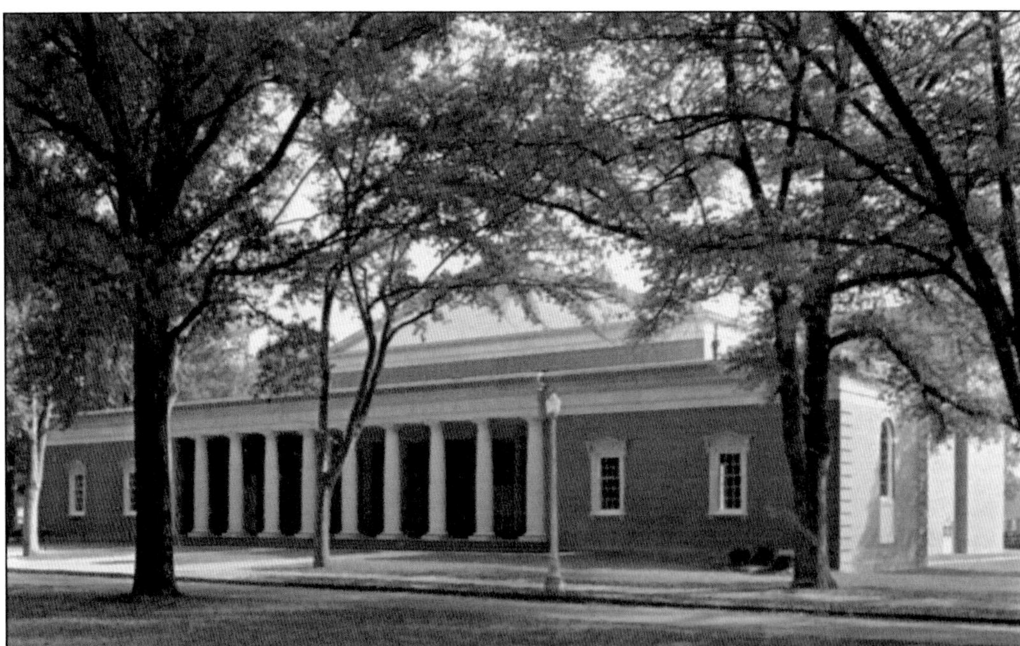

The William Henry Belk Auditorium was constructed on the Presbyterian College campus in 1960 and named for the late "Merchant Prince of the South," William Henry Belk. The building provides a 1,200-capacity auditorium, chapel, and fine arts facility. The chapel is named in honor of Mrs. May Wyatt of Chickamauga, Georgia. (Courtesy Elaine Martin.)

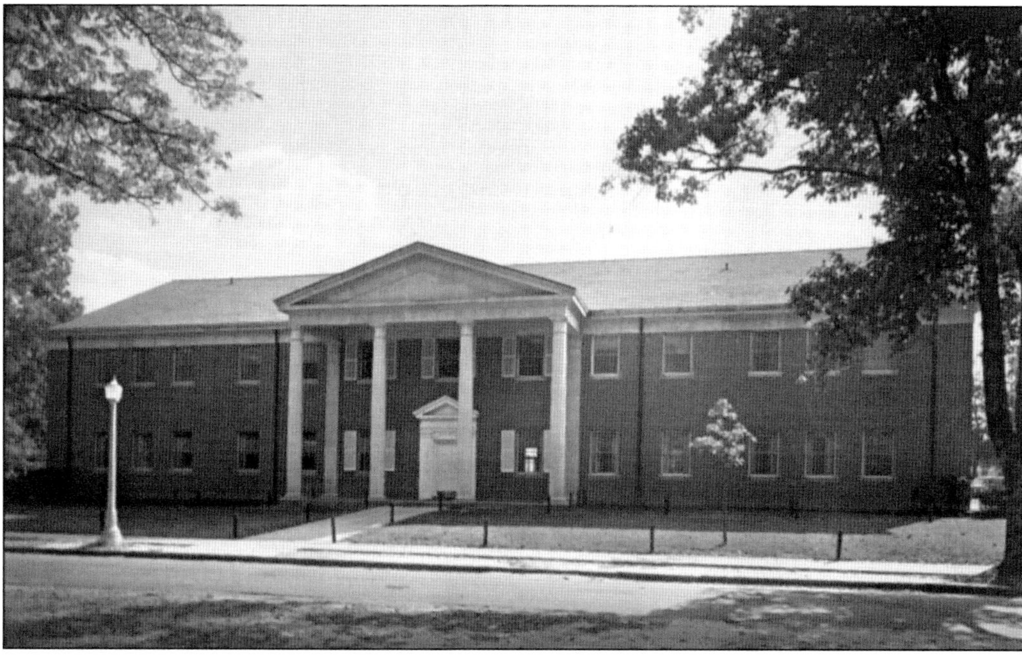

The Douglas House of Presbyterian College was erected in 1958 to honor former Presbyterian College president Davidson McDowell Douglas. It also stood as a memorial to alumni killed in World War II and the Korean War. The Douglas House was built to serve as a student center and contained lounges, a snack shop, a post office, recreational facilities, and a guidance center. (Courtesy Elaine Martin.)

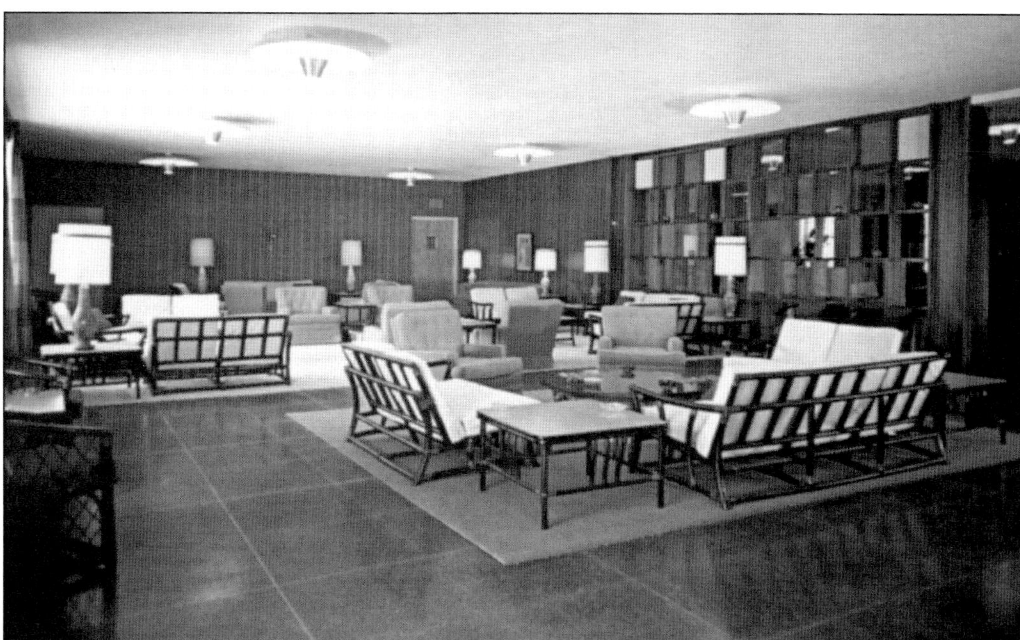

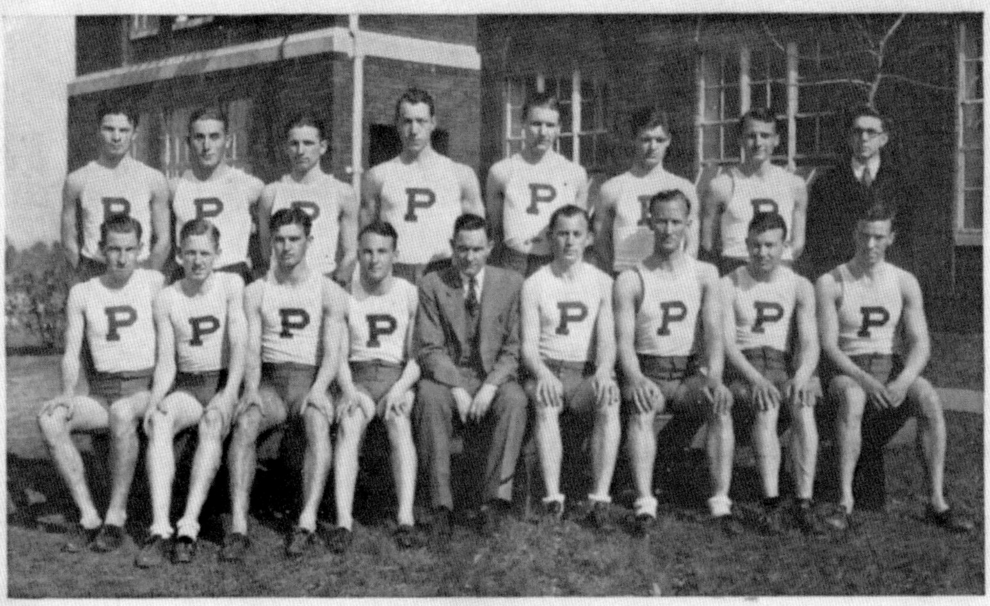

THE VARSITY TRACK TEAM—1928

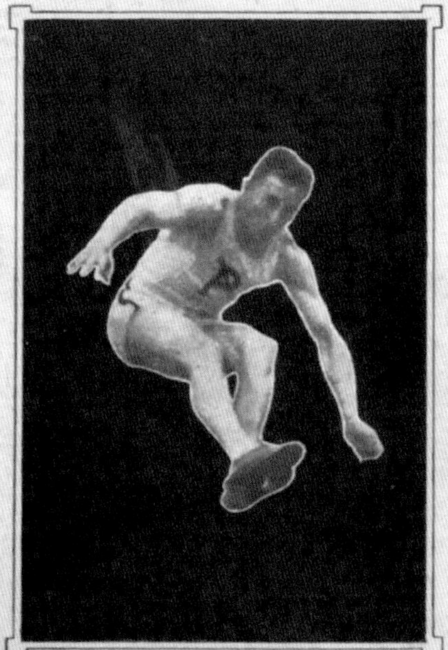

CHARLIE WILSON IN MID AIR
WINNER LAVAL MEDAL FOR 1927-1928
P. C.'s GREATEST ALL-ROUND ATHLETE

In 1928, Presbyterian College was advertised as a man's college. "Where Men are Made" became the motto and reflected justified pride in a well-balanced program of high quality designed to develop the whole person. There was a 10-year period, from 1921 until 1931, when girls were not enrolled in the college. Postcards of the varsity track team of 1928 and Charlie Wilson, who was the winner of the Laval Medal for 1927–1928 and was once crowned as Presbyterian College's greatest athlete, indicate the male dominance of the college. Wilson was a Thornwell student and brother-in-law to the late C. W. Anderson of Clinton. (Above courtesy Presbyterian College Archives; below courtesy Lawrence E. Young.)

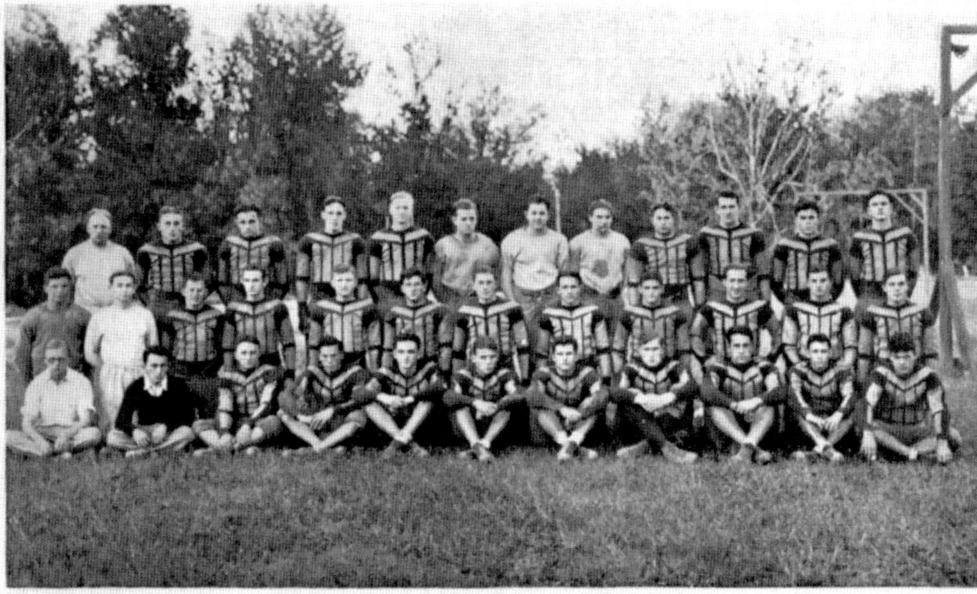

THE VARSITY FOOT BALL SQUAD—1927

Football promptly became the most popular campus sport. Presbyterian College students, in addition to their spectator interest in varsity contests, formed teams within each class and had hot competitions to decide non-varsity campus championships. Equipment was simple and basic in the 1920s, when Presbyterian College football teams gained stature for hard, fair play. At early games, cars parked close to the sidelines and small but enthusiastic crowds got close to the action on the field. An early postcard shows football star Jimmie Stamps racing around the end. (Above courtesy Presbyterian College Archives; below courtesy Lawrence E. Young.)

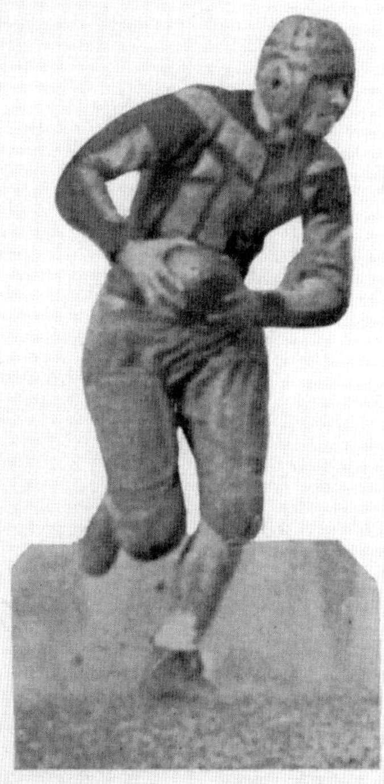

CAPT. JIMMIE STAMPS RACING AROUND END

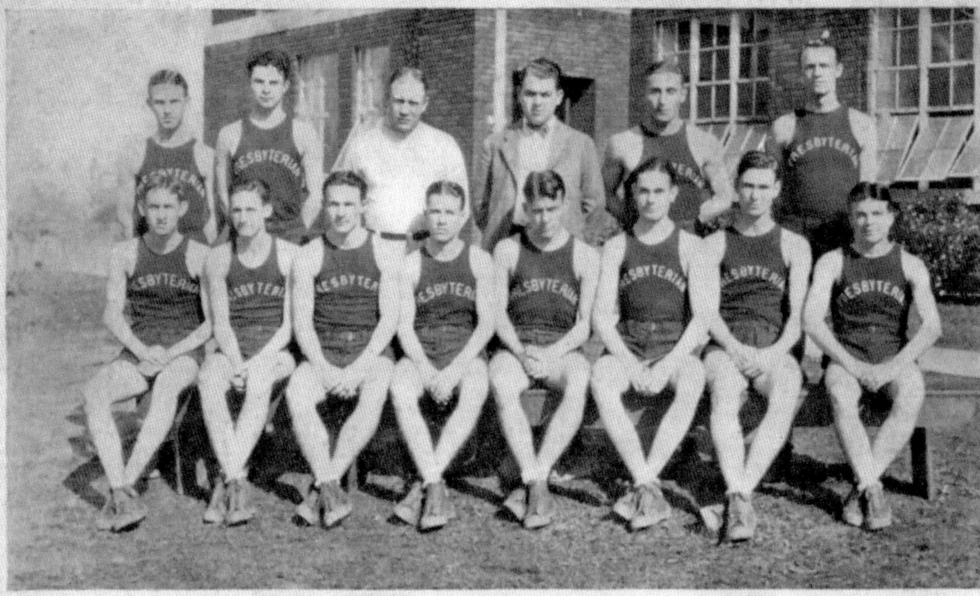

THE VARSITY BASKET BALL TEAM—1927-28

The varsity basketball team and the varsity baseball team for 1927–1928 are pictured on these postcards. The late William David Young of Clinton played on both teams. He also was the valedictorian of the Presbyterian College class of 1929. Following his college graduation, Young served as postmaster for Clinton for more than 25 years and was a prominent person in his community. (Courtesy Lawrence E. Young.)

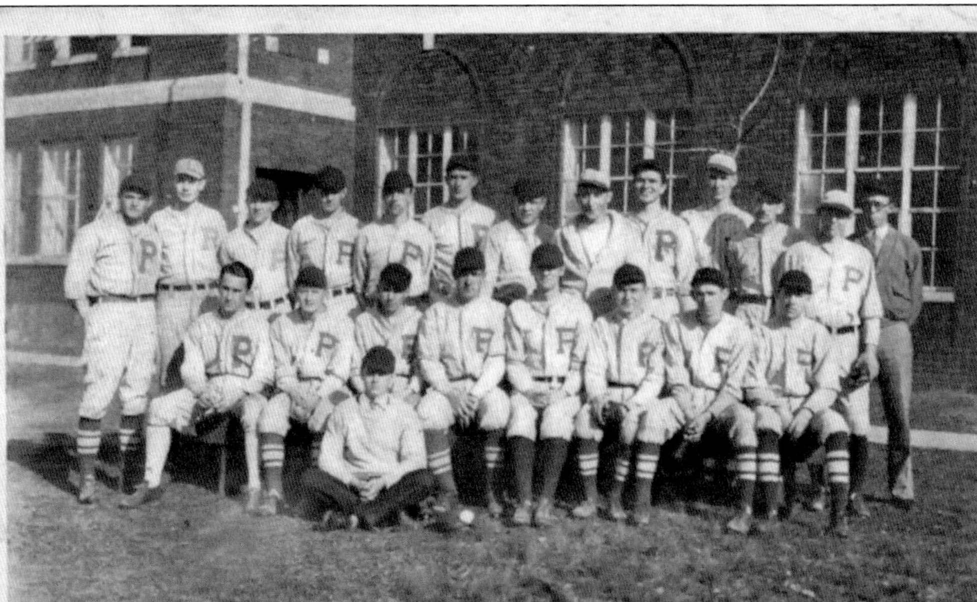

THE VARSITY BASE BALL TEAM—1928

Three

MILL VILLAGES
Whirring of Spindles and Beating of Looms

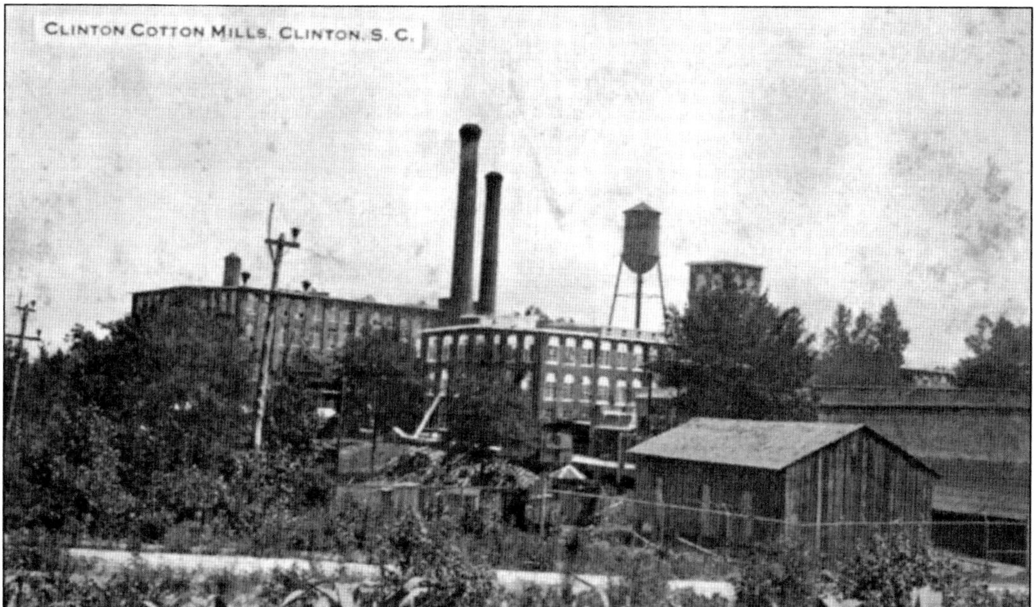

Textile mills shaped the New South. As the South emerged from the devastation of the War Between the States, business and professional men bound themselves to the humming of spindles and the thrashing of looms. From the late 1800s, when mill building began, well into the 1930s, men, women, and children from every walk of rural life beat a path to the mill gate. As in many other Southern towns, a new society rapidly took shape in Laurens County. (Frances C. Weathers.)

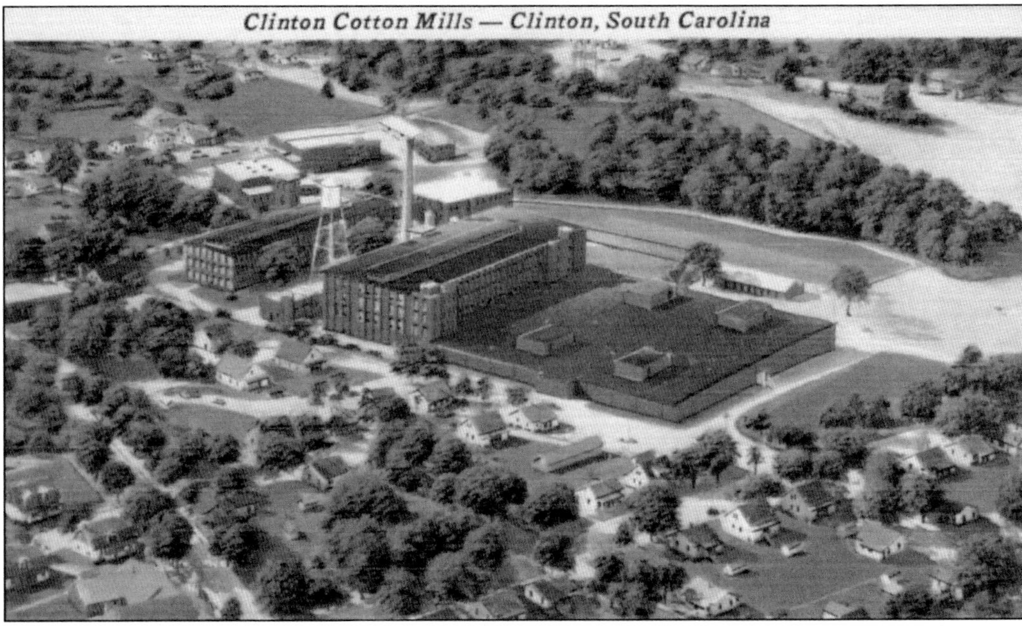

Clinton Mills was founded February 1, 1896, by Mercer Silas Bailey and a group of Clinton business people. Realizing the vast potential of the textile industry, the group initially invested $50,000 in the new manufacturing venture. The first operations consisted of 5,000 spindles and 150 looms. As successful merchants, bankers, educators, and civic and political leaders, in addition to their manufacturing abilities, the Bailey gentlemen played important roles in the development of Clinton from a small hamlet into a thriving city with a socioeconomic background well balanced among the educational, the institutional, and the industrial. The organization produced superior-quality print cloths, broad cloths, twills, blended voiles, and batistes. Bailey Memorial Church was located in the Clinton Mills village. (Above courtesy Presbyterian College Archives; below courtesy Elaine Martin.)

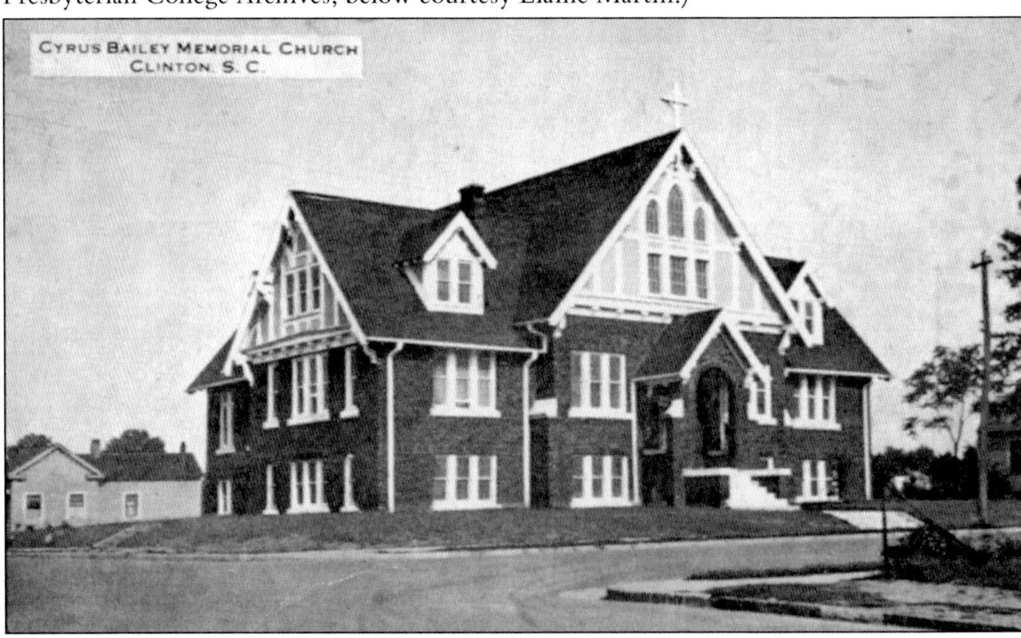

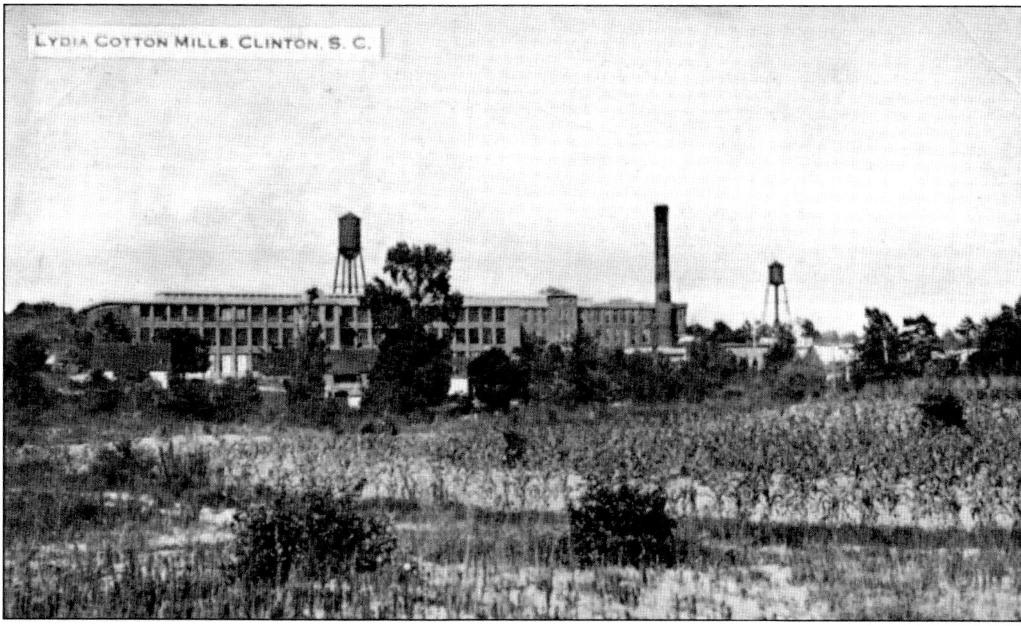

Located in Clinton, Lydia Cotton Mills was founded in 1902 with 40 employees, 4,000 spindles, and 150 looms. Mercer Silas Bailey, a pioneer banker, merchant, and industrialist, served as president until his death in 1926. Cassius Mercer Bailey became the next president and served until his death in 1935. When C. M. Bailey died, William James "W. J." Bailey assumed the presidency of both the Lydia and Clinton Cotton Mills. He headed the two textile firms until his death in 1948. W. J. was succeeded by Putsy S. Bailey as president of the textile organization. During Putsy's tenure, the company expanded its production facilities and improved the company benefits program, making it one of the most competitive in the industry. He was succeeded in 1958 by Robert Vance and, later, George Cornelson. (Above courtesy Clinton Museum; below courtesy Laurens County Library.)

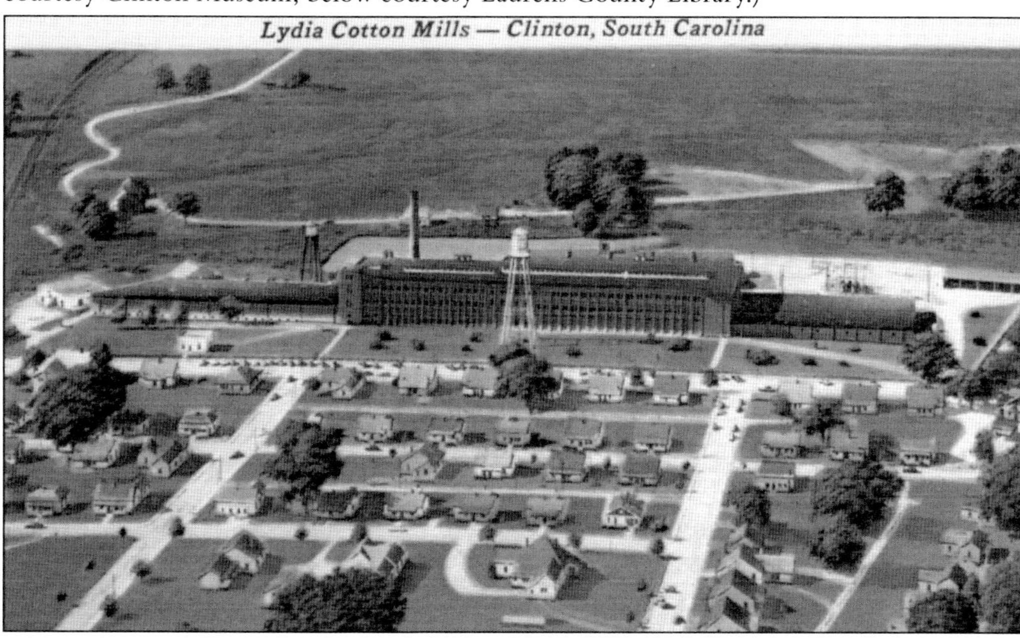

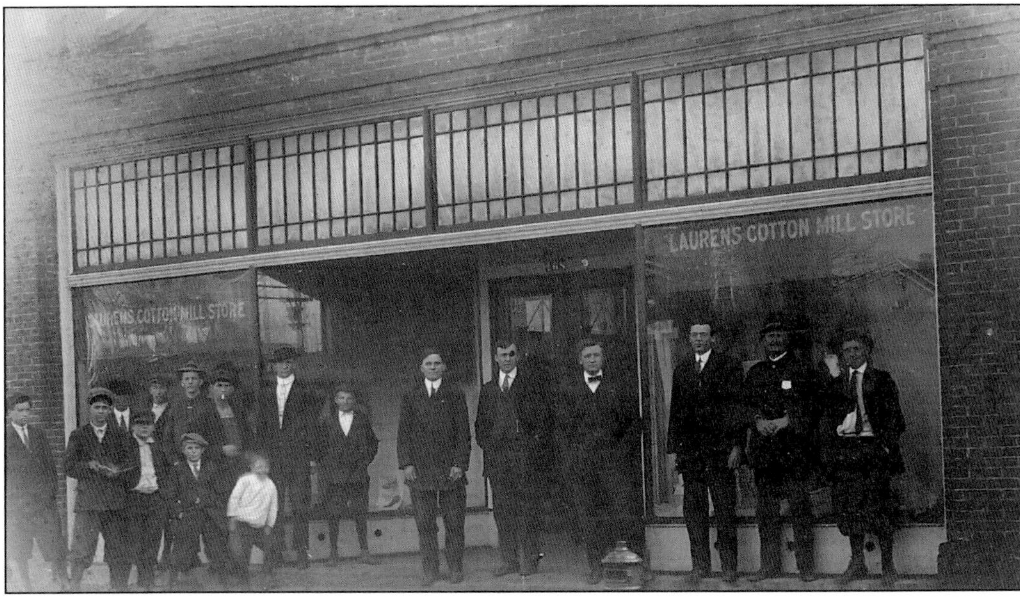

Laurens Cotton Mills, or "The Old Mill," was organized in 1895. John Ferguson, N. B. Dial, and W. H. Martin incorporated the mill. W. E. Lucas, Dr. J. P. Simpson, J. W. Todd, Capt. Albert Dial, Col. J. O. Fleming, J. W. Ferguson, and M. V. Montgomery made up the board of directors. W. E. Lucas, instrumental in organizing and building the mill, was elected president and treasurer. From the start of operation until 1926, the machinery was driven by a Corless steam engine, one of the largest in the country. The flywheel on the engine had a diameter of 27 feet, and its rim surface was about 10 feet wide. There were three main drives, one for the card room and one for each of the two weave rooms. The Laurens Mill Company Store, located on Fleming Street, sold a variety of items and served the needs of mill workers. (Above courtesy South Caroliniana Library, University of South Carolina, Columbia; below courtesy Richard B. Taylor Jr.)

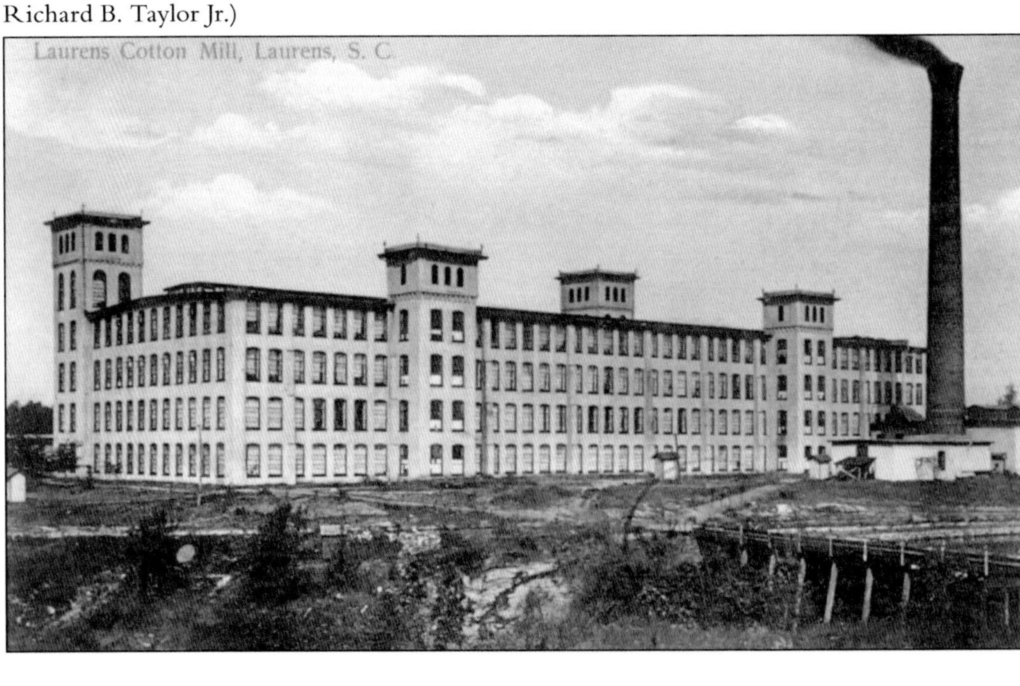

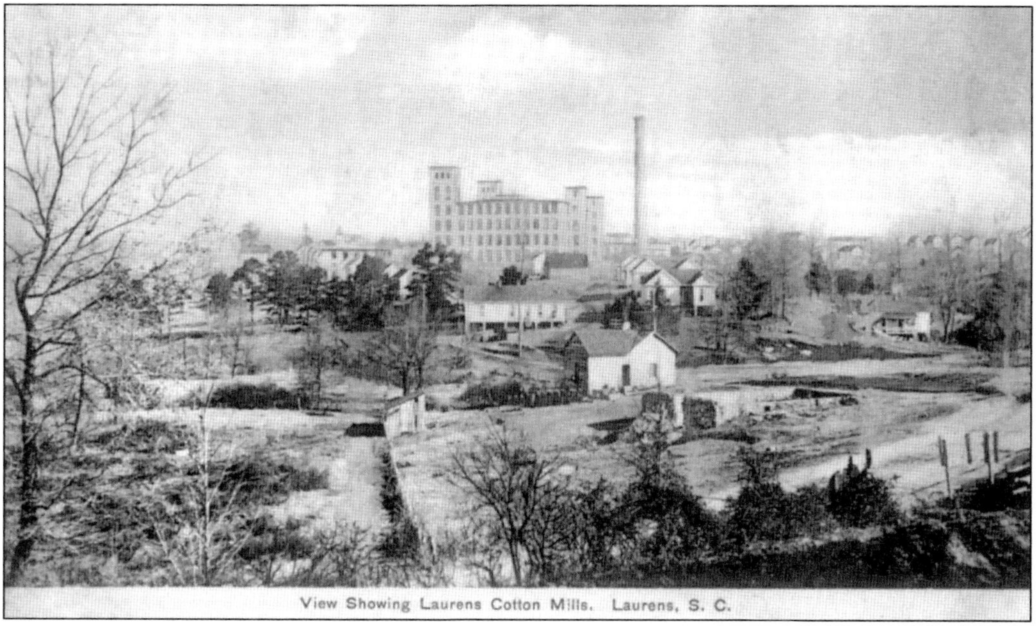

Constructed on a hill overlooking Little River on the east side of Laurens, Laurens Cotton Mills was the center of a once-thriving textile village. Families moved from rural Laurens County and other towns and states, especially Tennessee, to seek employment in the mill. Laurens residents have fond memories of a lighted Christmas tree that was placed atop the mill's tower each Christmas season. (Courtesy Richard B. Taylor Jr.)

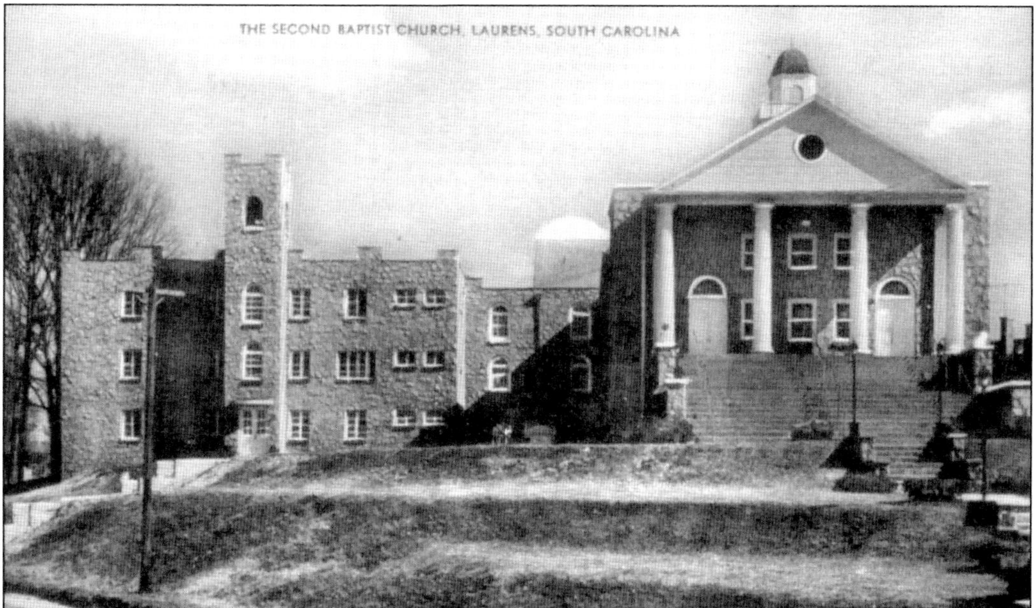

In 1898, a church was constructed on Holmes Street in the Laurens Mills village and was referred to as the "Second Baptist Church of Laurens." The new name was officially listed in an annual report to the Laurens Baptist Association in a September 1902 session. Some years later, a granite church was built on Fleming Street to serve the needs of the Second Baptist Church congregation. (Courtesy Ellen D. Simpson.)

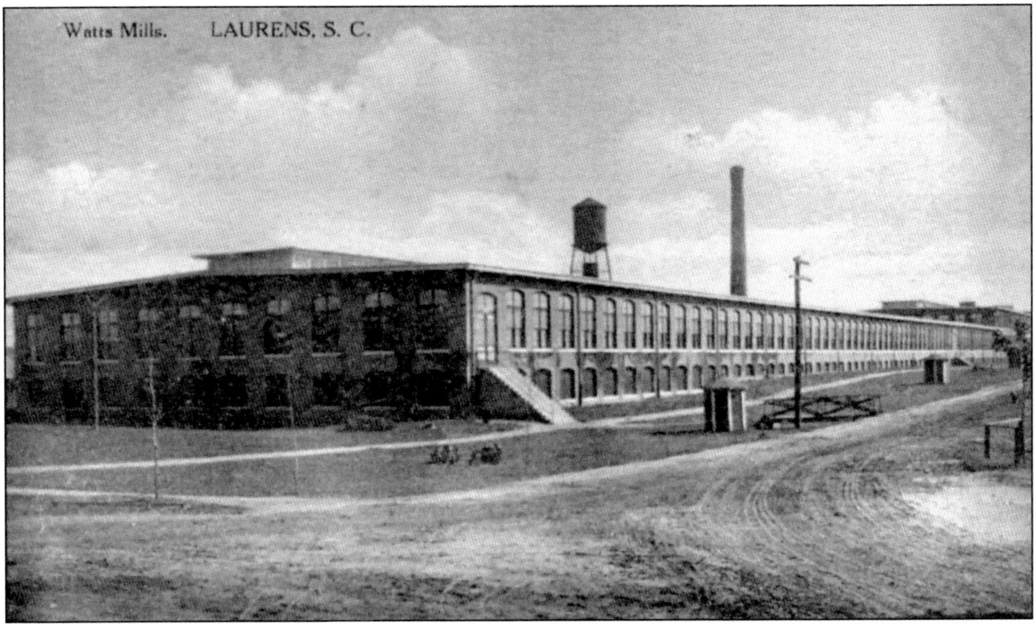

A group of Laurens businessmen met in 1902 and officially organized Watts Mills. At the meeting, W. E. Lucas was elected president and treasurer. The mill was constructed on what was once a part of the Watts Plantation. Production began in 1904. The mill was originally housed in a two-story building and wove strictly cotton cloth, making "fancies," including ginghams and handkerchiefs. Watts Mill continued to produce cotton cloth until the 1930s and the advent of rayon. At this time, the mill produced synthetic fibers as well as some cotton. During World War II, Watts Mills produced parachute fabric. After it became a part of the war effort, a fence was placed around the mill and employees were required to have identification badges to enter the workplace. (Courtesy Frances C. Weathers.)

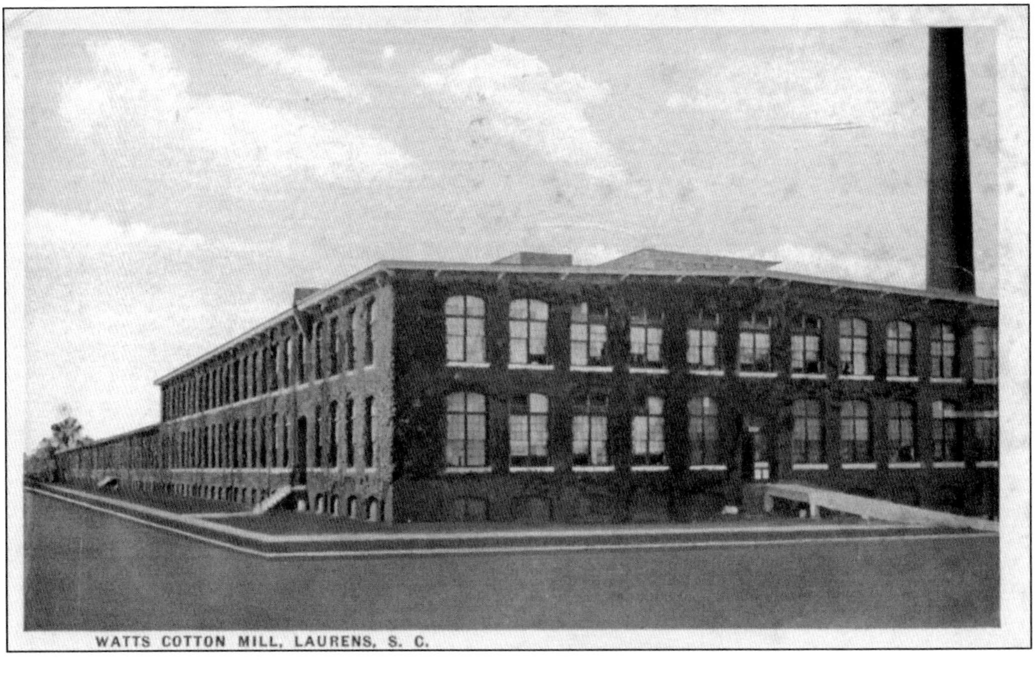

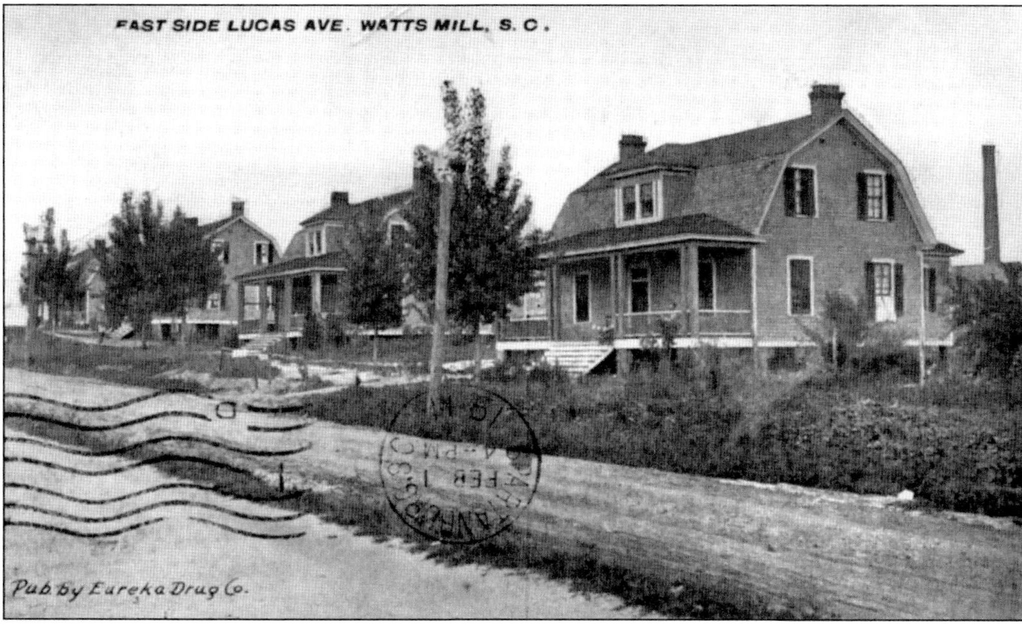

Adjoining Watts Mill on the east side of Lucas Avenue was a row of houses occupied by mill overseers. Printed on a pamphlet called "Instructions Governing Watts Mill Property," which was passed out when the mill began operation in 1904, were rules for tenants. A section of the pamphlet read, "See your overseer if you are bothered with stray chickens or dogs or if you want screen doors hung." (Courtesy Kathryn W. Johnson.)

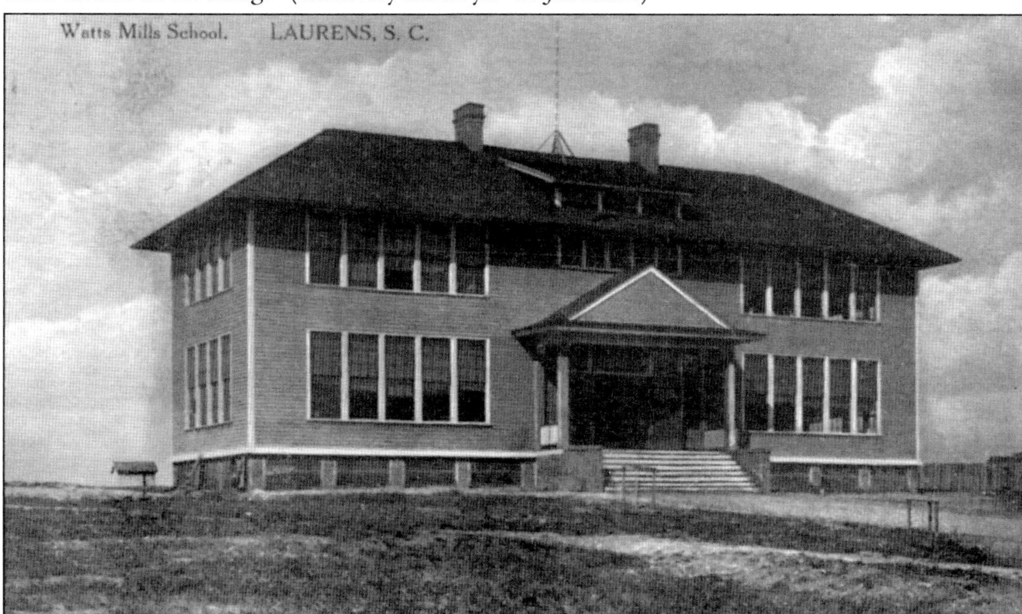

Watts Mill School was constructed in the early 1900s and was an integral part of the Watts Mill textile village. The two-story frame school stood on Lucas Avenue, a street that was named for W. E. Lucas, one of the mill's founders. At the closing of the Watts Mill Old School, teachers and students marched from the old school to the new brick Ford School, located a few blocks away. (Courtesy Frances C. Weathers.)

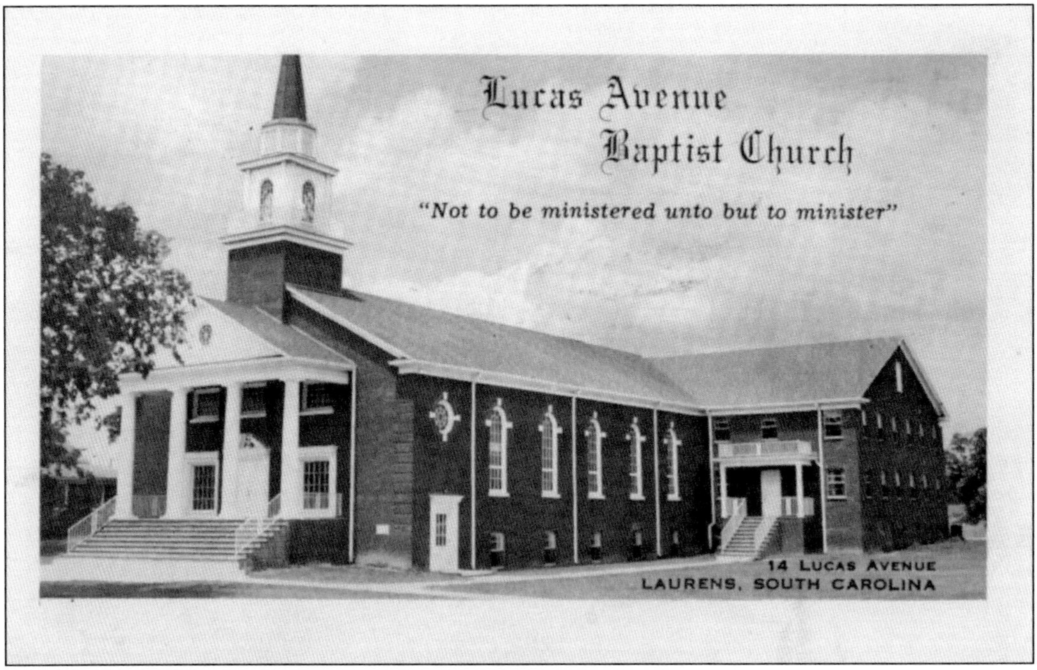

Watts Mill Baptist Church first met in a house provided by the mill company at 63 Lucas Avenue. There were 21 charter members. The church was accepted into the Laurens Baptist Association in 1904, and in 1911, the name was changed to Lucas Avenue Baptist Church. Construction was started on the present brick structure in 1950. (Courtesy Frances Weathers.)

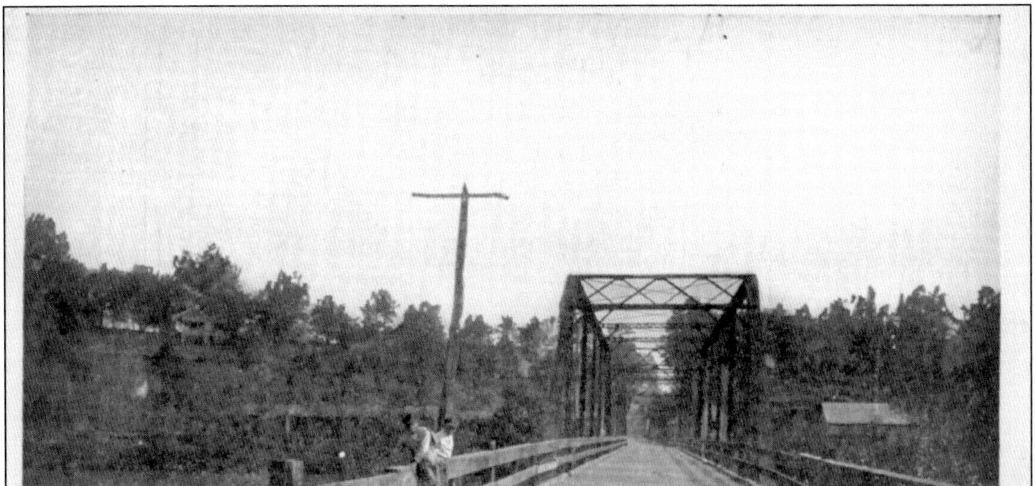

Upon Leaving Watts Mill, travelers often followed the Old Spartanburg Road and crossed the Enoree River on their way to Enoree or Spartanburg. Often people from Laurens sought employment in the Enoree Mill. Yarborough's Mill, located on the Enoree River, was a favorite site for swimming, fishing, and picnics. (Courtesy Frances C. Weathers.)

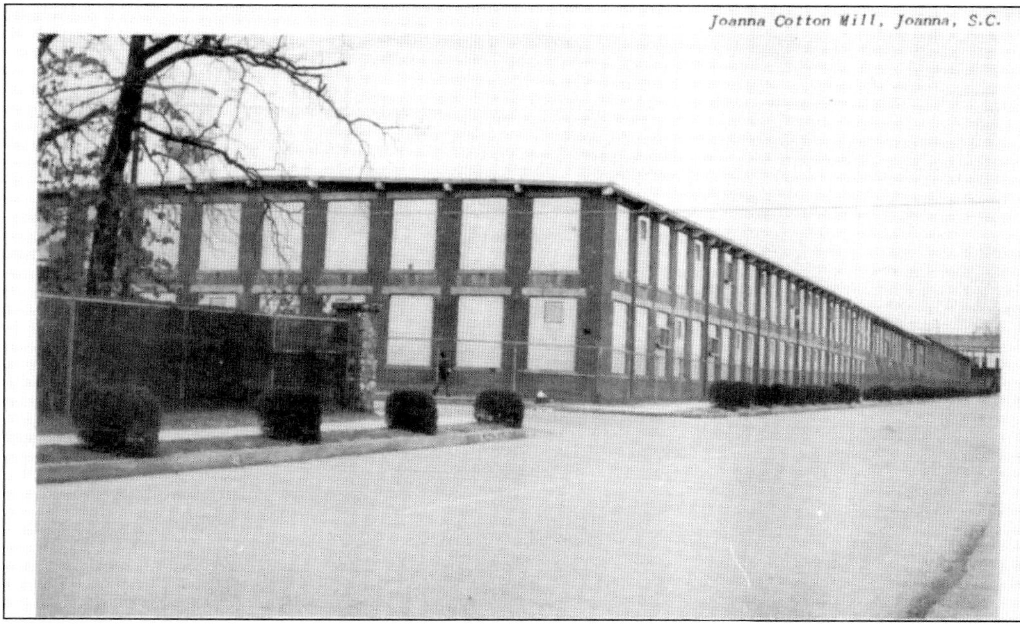

Two pioneers in the development of the textile industry in lower Laurens County were James S. Blalock and his son, Leumas William Calhoun Blalock. In 1872, James Blalock purchased 7,000 acres at Martin's Depot with gold. The community then became known as Goldville. The Blalocks built a small yarn mill, gin, and oil mill, all known as Goldville Manufacturing. Later the yarn mill was called Banna Cotton Mills, having been named for the wife of L. W. C. Blalock, who, before her marriage, was Banna Piester of Newberry. In 1924, Banna Manufacturing Company was sold to Hartshorn Interests of New York and became Joanna Manufacturing Company, named for Joanna Hartshorn Hack. The mill properties were purchased by Western Shade Cloth Company in 1927, and Greenwood Mills purchased the operation in 1965. (Courtesy Elaine Martin.)

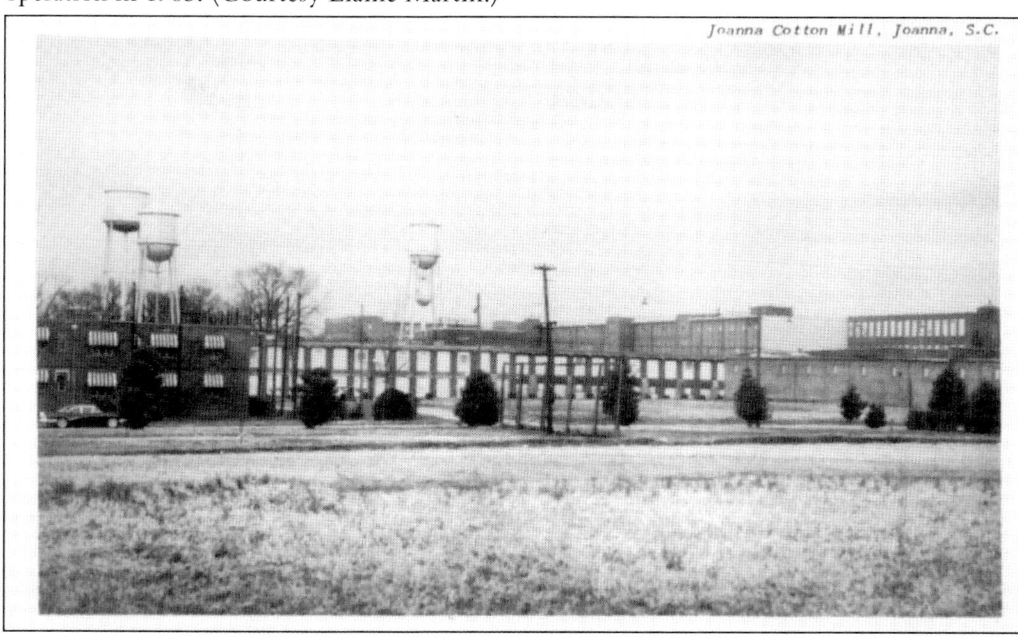

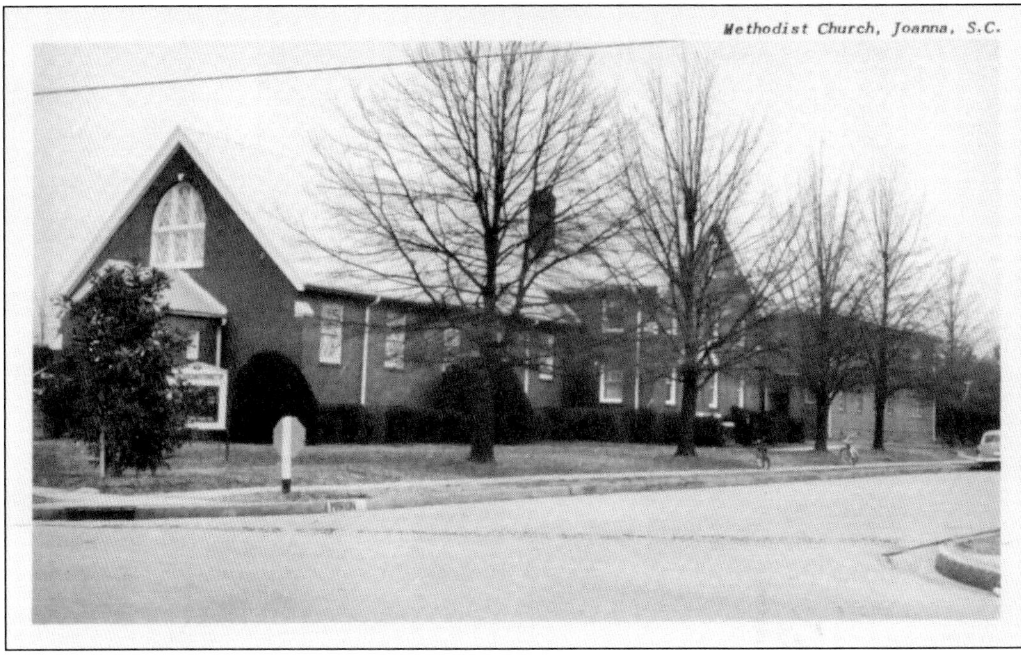

The Joanna Methodist Church was organized in 1911 with Rev. W. K. Bouknight as the first pastor. A frame church, built on Milton Road and known as Epworth Methodist Church, was made possible by gifts, including $600 contributed by Joanna Mill and framing materials by George W. Hopkins. In 1937, the Methodists, encouraged by a $10,000 gift from the mill, began construction on a new church that was dedicated in 1940. The Presbyterian congregation first occupied the frame church on Milton Road that had previously been used by the Methodists. In 1956, the Presbyterians constructed a new church on the site of the old frame church. (Courtesy Elaine Martin.)

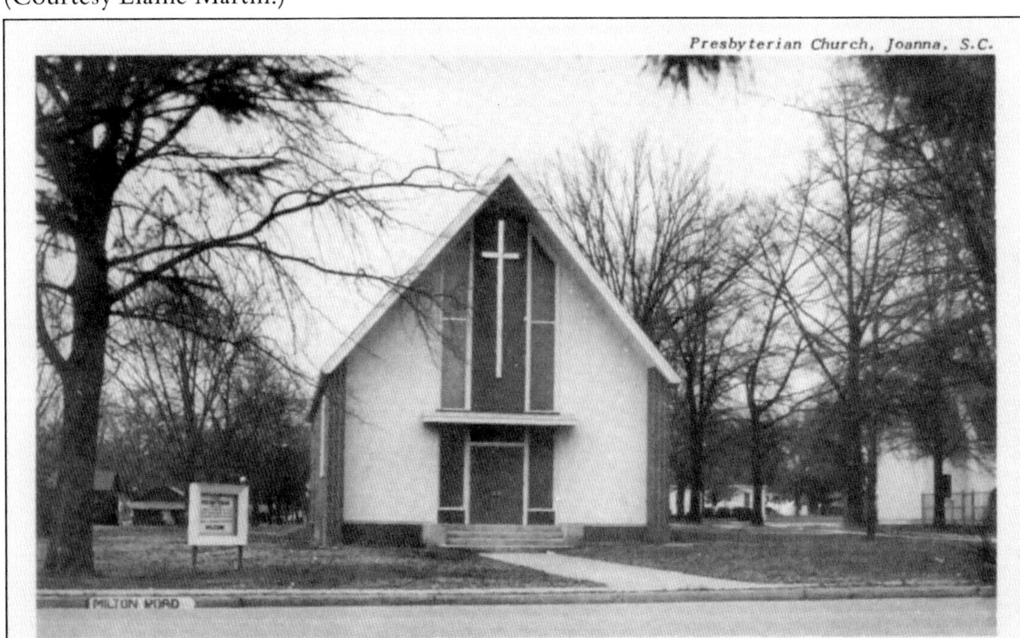

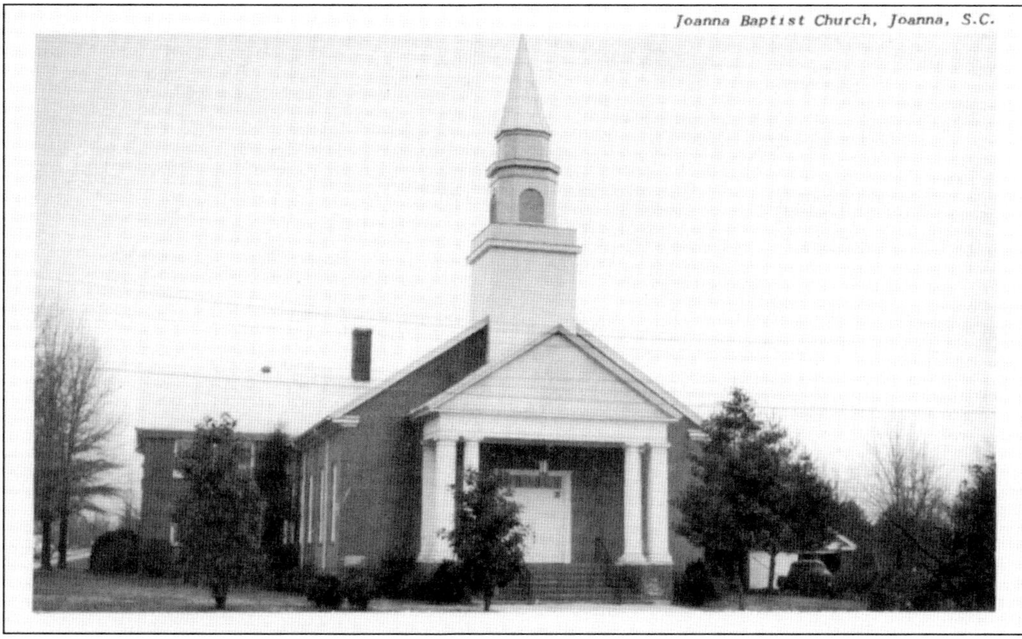

The Joanna Baptist Church was organized in 1913. The Baptist congregation met for several years in the old Union Church. In 1941, the $30,000 Goldville Baptist Church, to which Joanna Mills contributed $10,000, was dedicated. The church has undergone several expansions throughout the years and continues to serve members of the Joanna community. (Courtesy Elaine Martin.)

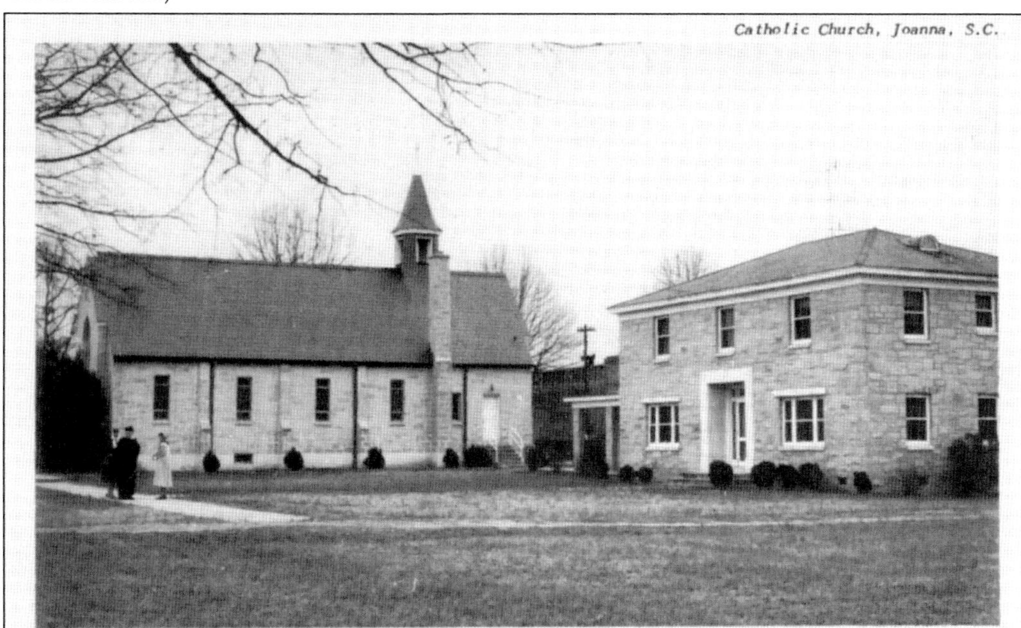

St. Boniface Roman Catholic Church, located in Joanna, was dedicated by Bishop Emment M. Walsh in honor of St. Boniface on March 20, 1949. The Catholic church continues to serve the spiritual needs of Joanna residents as well as persons from surrounding communities. (Courtesy Elaine Martin.)

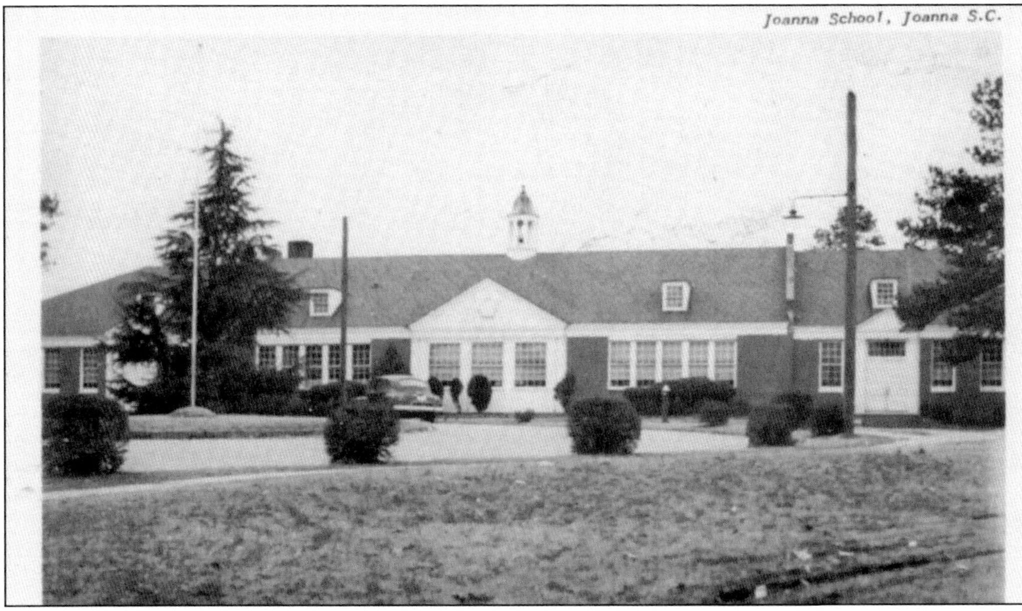

With the expansion of Joanna Mill and residential facilities in the mill village, it became necessary to erect a larger school building. On June 1, 1929, ground was broken for a new and modern school. Following a fire that destroyed the east wing of the building in 1937, rebuilding changes provided for 15 classrooms, a library, and a manual training shop. In 1942, a modern cannery was installed in the school's basement. (Courtesy Elaine Martin.)

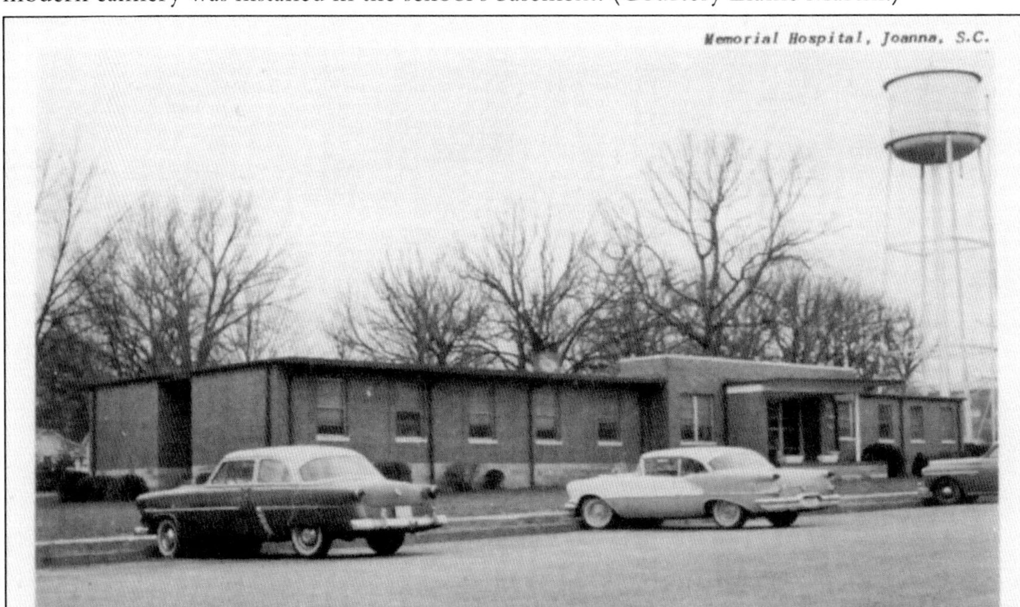

The Joanna Memorial Hospital was dedicated in 1949 to servicemen of Joanna who served in World War I and World War II and especially to the men who sacrificed their lives in World War II. The hospital was under the direction of Kittie Mae Mosley. The hospital discontinued operations at the time of the opening of Bailey Memorial Hospital in Clinton in 1962. A branch of the Laurens County Library once operated in the hospital building. (Courtesy Elaine Martin.)

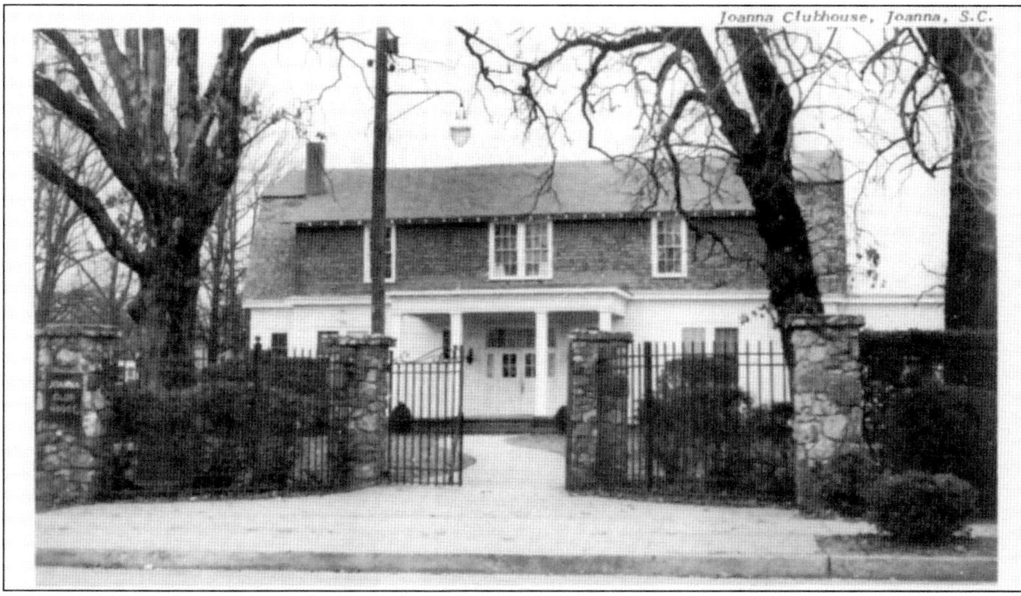

Sponsored by the Education Committee of Joanna Mills was a well-rounded, comprehensive program of activities under the supervision of a full-time director, including adult classes, arts and crafts classes, and sewing classes, as well as many other activities. Frances Warner rendered dedicated service as educational director and Joanna Club House hostess. (Courtesy Elaine Martin.)

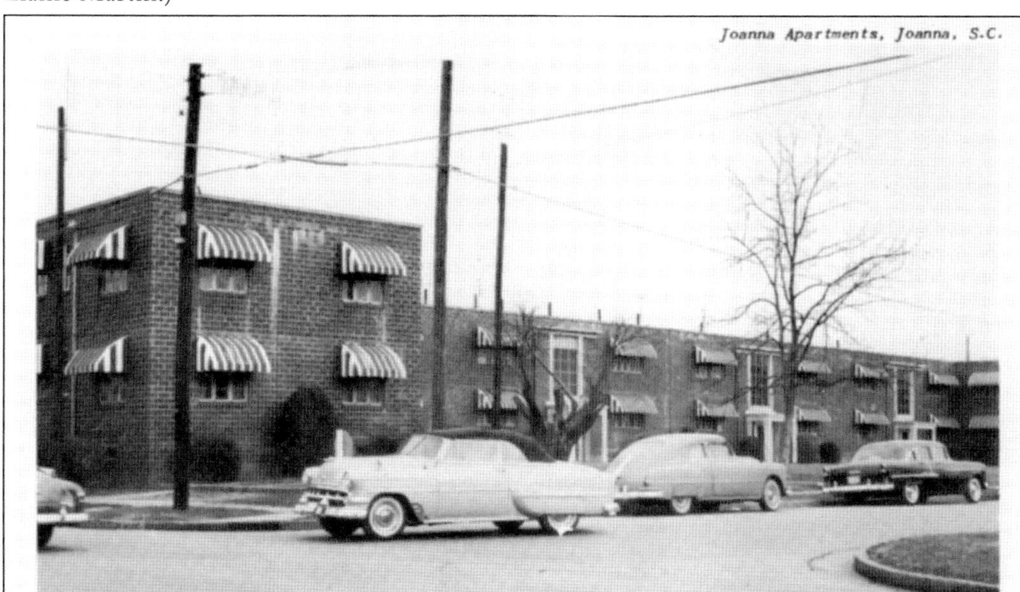

Joanna Mill village expanded from a small beginning and eventually encompassed 450 low-rent homes, many made of brick, and a 24-unit apartment building. Through the personal interest and leadership of the Hartshorns and later the Regnerys, who took pride in developing attractive homes for their employees, and with the oversight of such men as W. A. Moorhead, George H. Ellis, and Julian S. Bolick, the Joanna village became a model community. (Courtesy Elaine Martin.)

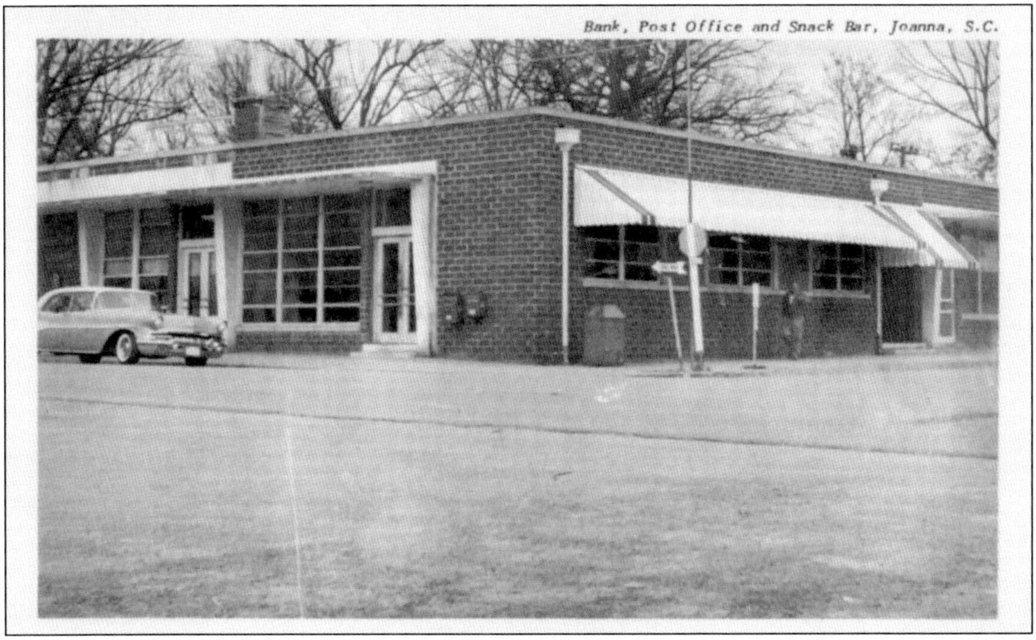

The bank, post office, and snack bar were a part of the Joanna village. Also in 1927, Joanna Mills printed a newspaper, the *Joanna News*, which was devoted exclusively to the activities of the people of the busy, beautiful, healthful town of Goldville. The paper served a positive role in cementing good human relations. Following the newspaper, a 16-page monthly employee magazine, the *Joanna Way*, served a useful purpose from 1950 through 1964. (Courtesy Elaine Martin.)

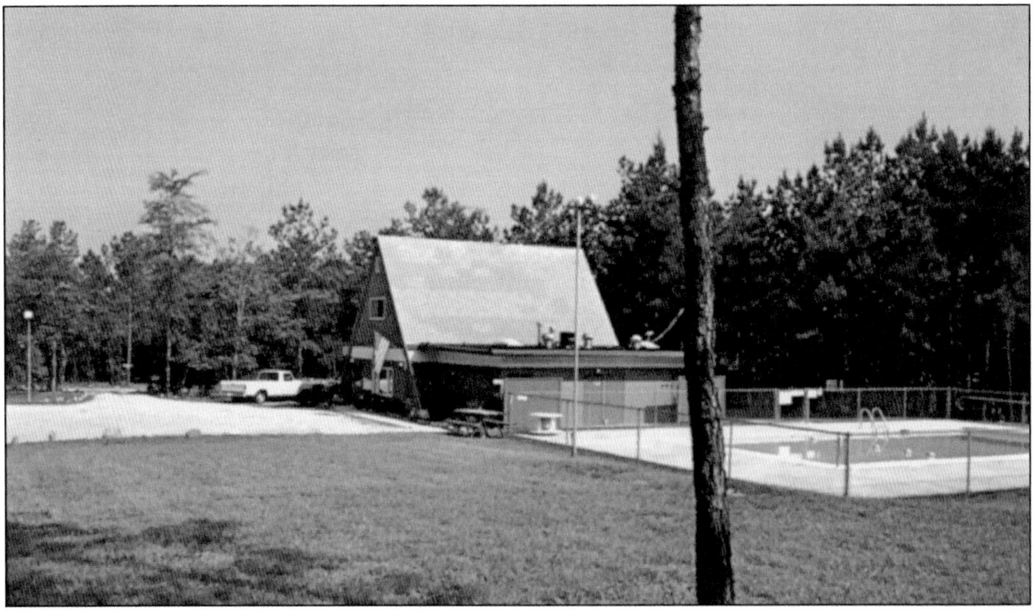

The Joanna KOA Campground is located in Kinards, South Carolina. It is nestled among pine trees and is surrounded by the Sumter National Forest. It received the KOA Award of Excellence. The campground is made up of shady camp sites for recreational vehicles and has camp sites for tents. It also has a swimming pool and unique woodland playground. (Courtesy Elaine Martin.)

Four

WHISTLE-STOPS
Railroad Tracks Crisscross Laurens County

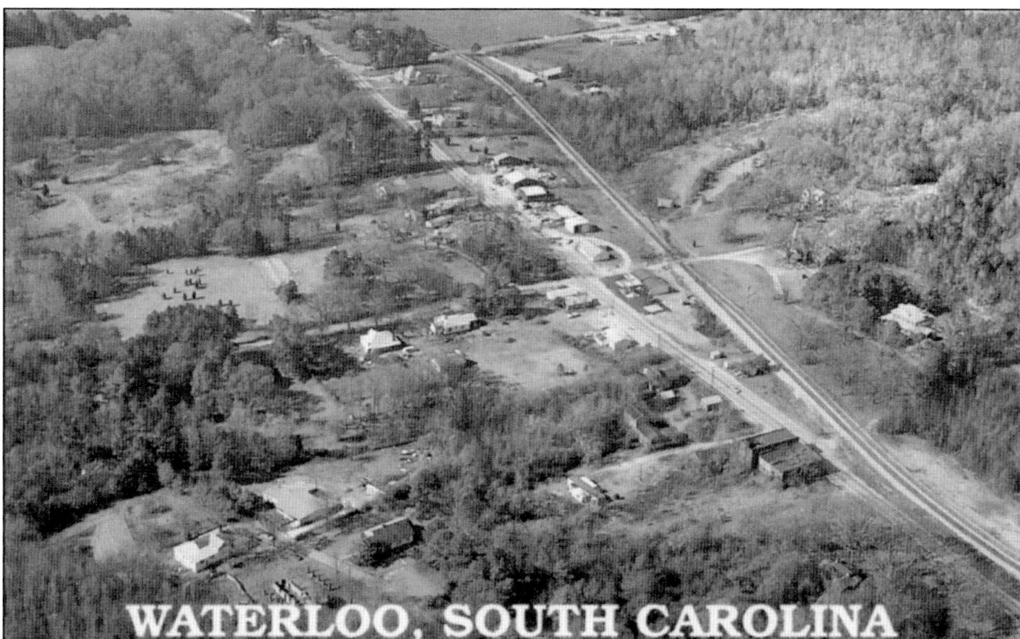

With the coming of the railroad, crossroads and communities throughout Laurens County quickly turned into thriving little towns. Waterloo, Renno, Gray Court, Martin's Depot, Owings, Cross Hill, and Mountville were a few of the small hamlets that dotted Laurens County. Trains carried passengers from whistle-stop to whistle-stop. The rails provided transportation to the Laurens Court House and county seat for court, sales, elections, and other special events. The railroad carried goods to market for farmers and delivered goods and supplies to the all-important general stores in each little community. Cotton was the primary crop; thus cotton gins and oil mills were located in the small towns. Banks, schools, churches, drugstores, doctors' offices, and a variety of small businesses made up the agricultural towns. Improved roads and automobiles caused the small towns to wane. Today most of these towns are filled with empty buildings and memories of another era, a time when life was simpler. (Courtesy Elaine Martin.)

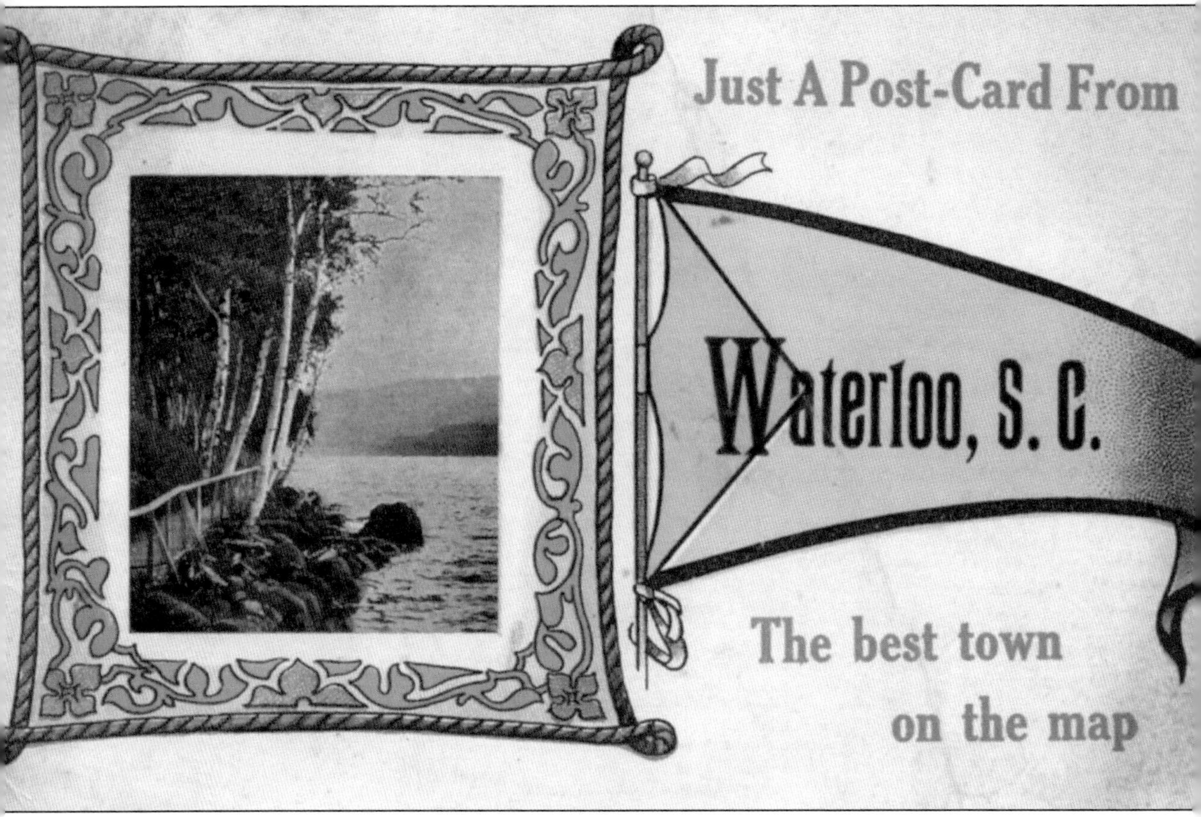

Located 12 miles south of Laurens on Highway 221, the town of Waterloo received a charter on December 4, 1885. The date of the original settlement is not known, but the census of 1790 indicates that there were several families already living in the area. Waterloo Township, located in Laurens County, covers approximately 90 square miles. When the railroad was built, Waterloo, like other townships in Laurens County, became a thriving town to and from which passengers and freight were carried. The community, as with most small towns, was primarily agricultural, with cotton being the money crop. Farms ranged in size from 5 acres (a one-horse farm) to 1,000 acres. In the early days, Waterloo claimed three hotels, a bank, a general store, a drugstore, a cotton gin, a furniture store, a blacksmith shop, a Methodist church, a Baptist church, and schools. (Courtesy Libby C. Rhodes.)

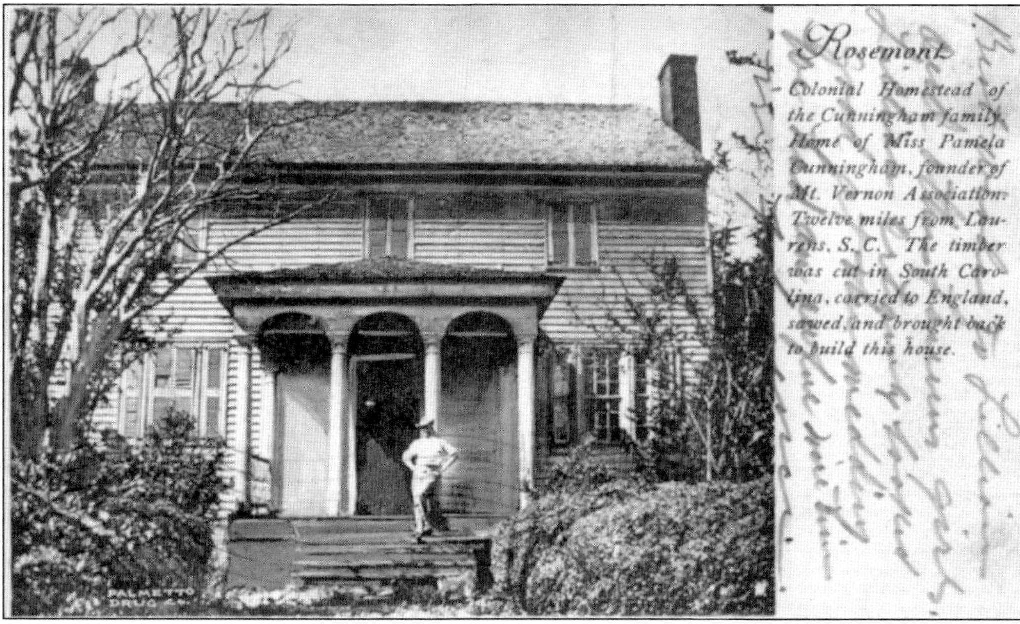

Built in 1790 by Patrick Cunningham, Rosemont was located several miles below Waterloo on the Saluda River. Logs were cut on the estate, sent to Charleston, and thence to England to be sawed into boards that were used to build the mansion. The blinds were also made in England, while the brick for the chimneys was made on the grounds by English workmen. Nails and hinges for the home were made in a blacksmith's shop on-site. Rosemont was surrounded by a large formal garden. The mansion gained additional fame as the home of Ann Pamela Cunningham, who organized the Mount Vernon Association for the preservation of George Washington's home as a national shrine. Rosemont was destroyed by a fire in 1930 that also claimed the life of its owner, Hugh Banks Cunningham. (Above courtesy Laurens County Library; below courtesy Libby C. Rhodes.)

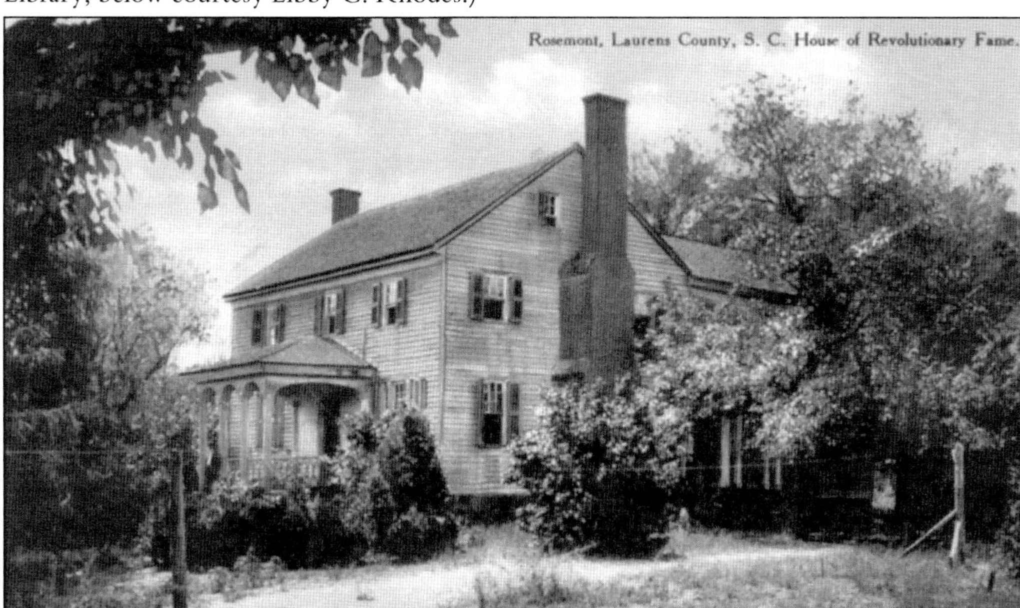

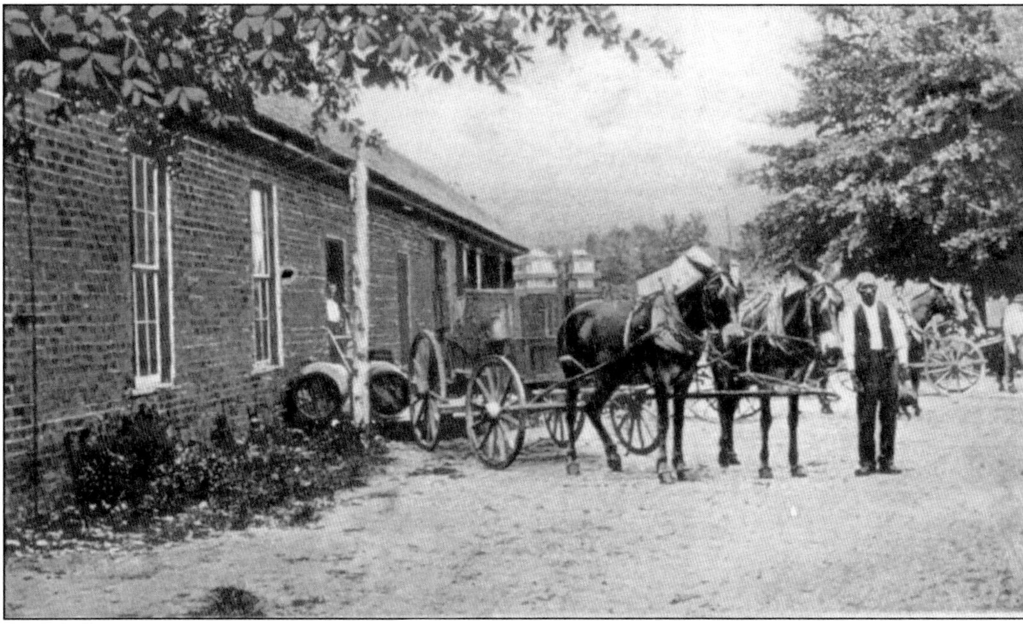

Harris Lithia Springs Hotel was located southeast of Waterloo on the Cross Hill Road. Guests came from New York and other large cities and resided in the hotel, sometimes for a month, to partake of the medicinal waters and enjoy weekend dances at the pavilion. The resort consisted of the hotel, which could accommodate 250 guests, a store, pool room, and ballroom. Surreys transported guests to and from the railroad stations in Waterloo and Cross Hill and also carried supplies and mail. In 1900, the *Laurensville Herald* read, "Hotel is now open for guests. If you come in the spring and drink the water freely and if you are not very much benefited or cured, we will board you free." The Harris Spring Hotel, a large frame building, was completely destroyed by fire in 1930. (Above courtesy Richard B. Taylor; below courtesy Kathryn W. Johnson.)

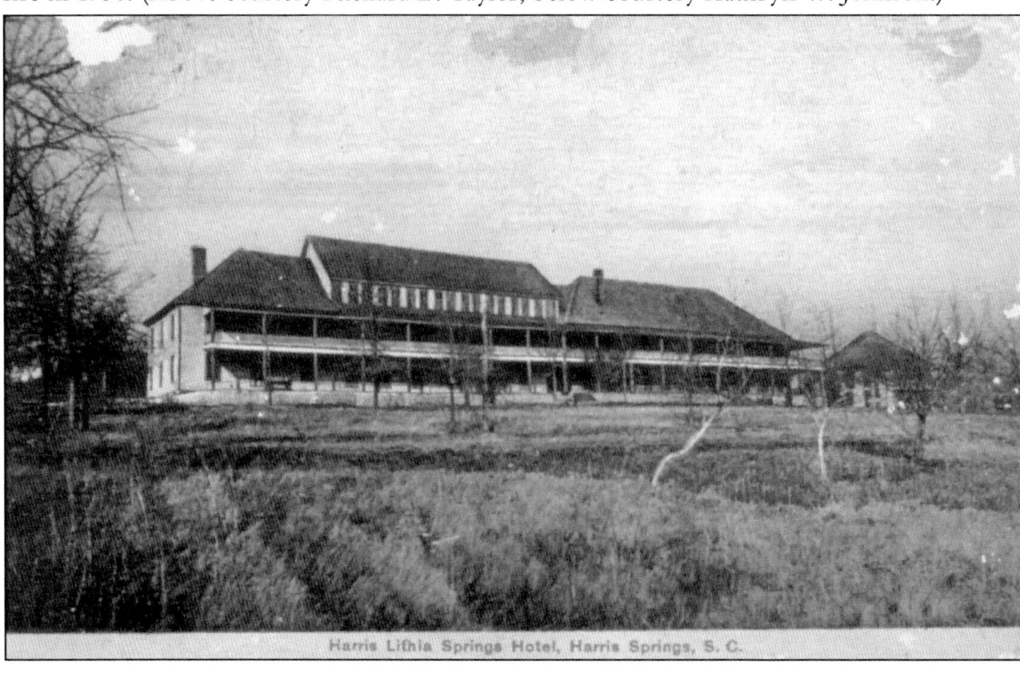

J. T. Harris was the owner of Harris Springs. He gave the springs his name and constructed the resort that officially opened in 1892. Harris Springs was born, and even today, the name continues to be remembered in Laurens County. The hotel's luxuries included a pagoda covering the spring, hot and cold baths, a livery stable, electric lights, and telephone connections. At one time, a post office was located inside the resort so that guests could send and receive mail at the hotel. A large porch wrapped around the hotel both upstairs and down. The dance floor was described as being "smooth as glass," and dances were held at the resort every evening during summer months. An orchestra from Charleston stayed the entire summer to play for the dances. (Above courtesy Billie E. Lawson Jr.; below courtesy South Caroliniana Library, University of South Carolina, Columbia.)

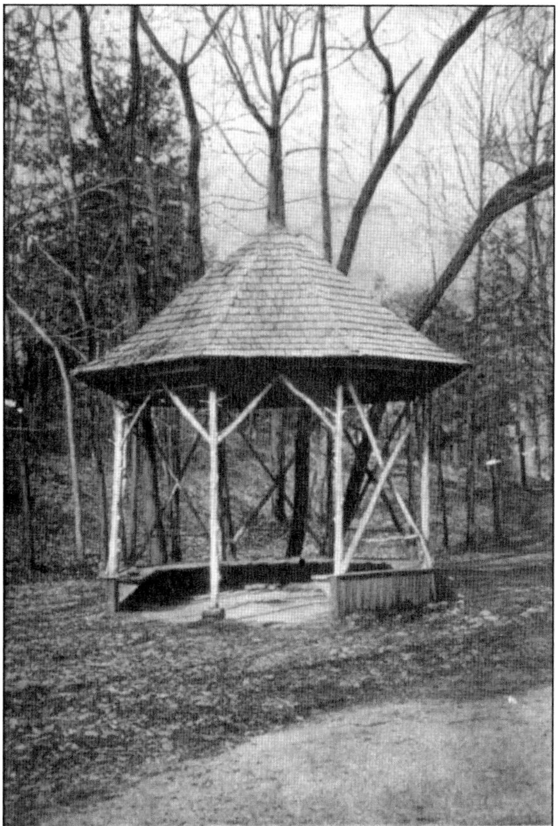

Sulphur Spring, Harris Lithia Springs, Harris Springs, S. C.

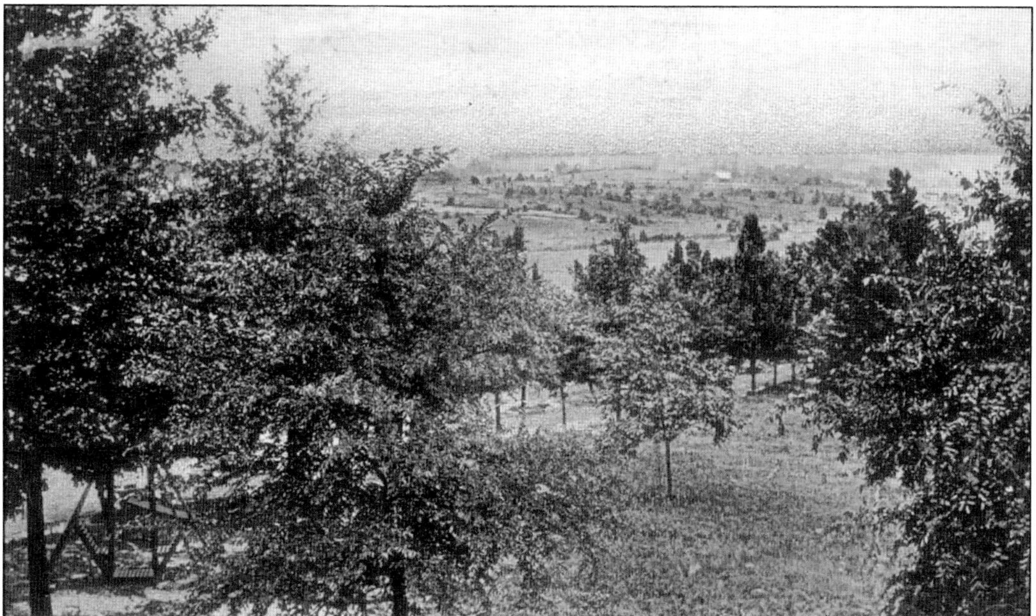

View East from Hotel Veranda, Harris Springs, S. C.

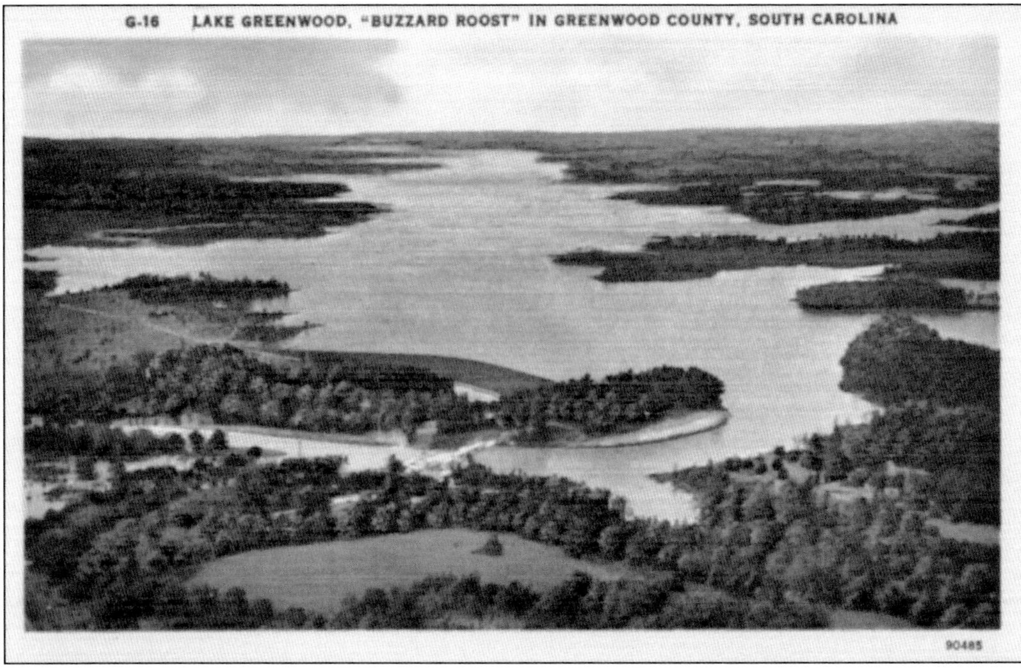

Lake Greenwood was formed after a dam was built on the Saluda River in 1938 by Greenwood County for the purpose of electric power; it became known as the "Buzzard Roost" project. The Greenwood County Electric Power System serves municipal and industrial customers in Greenwood, Laurens, Abbeville, and Newberry Counties. Lake Greenwood has a shoreline of approximately 200 miles and covers approximately 12,000 acres. The lake provides recreation in the form of fishing and boating for Laurens County residents. The eastern shore of Lake Greenwood is in Laurens County. (Courtesy Elaine Martin.)

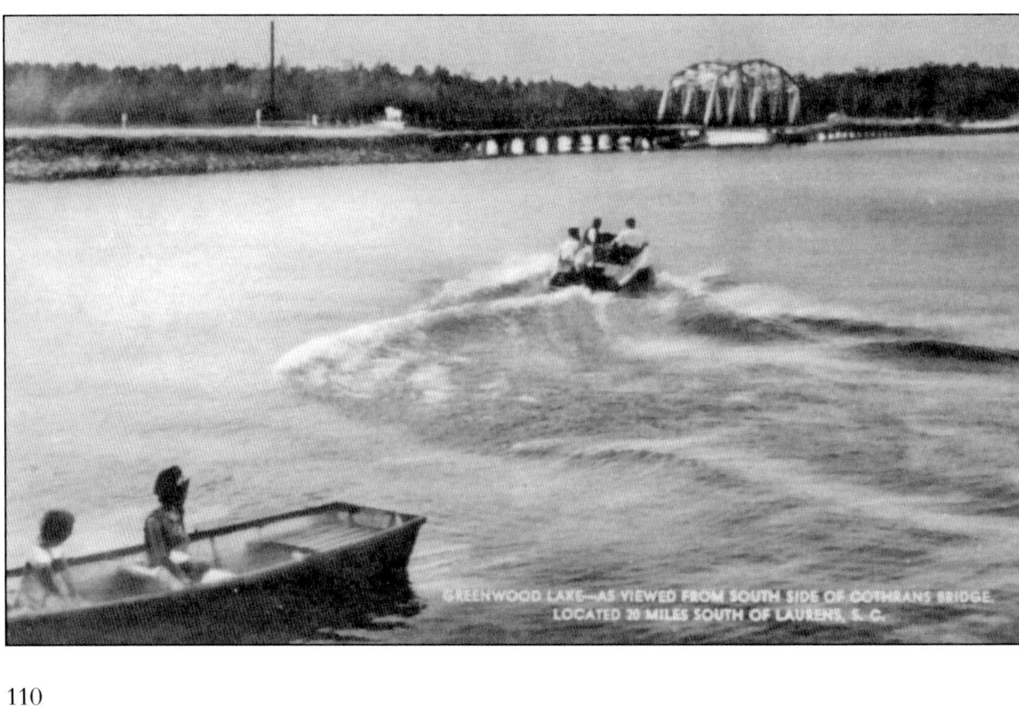

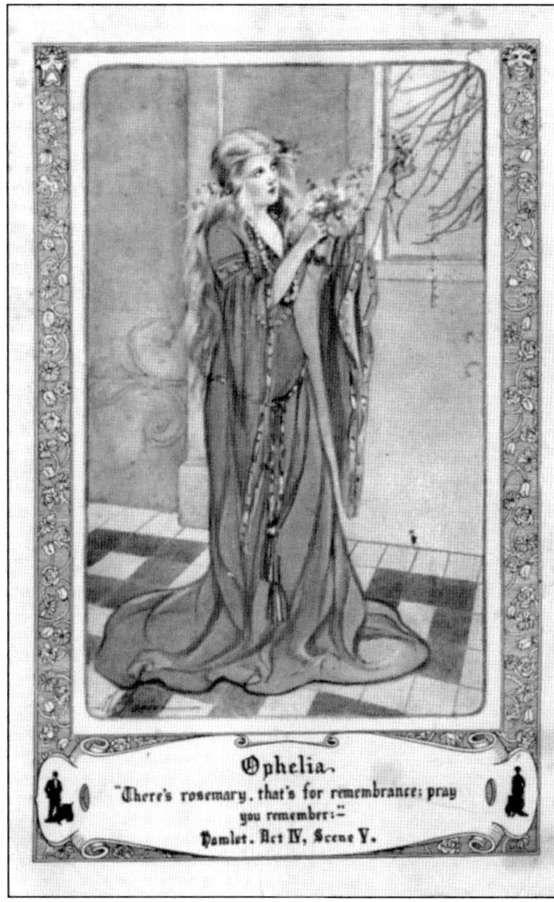

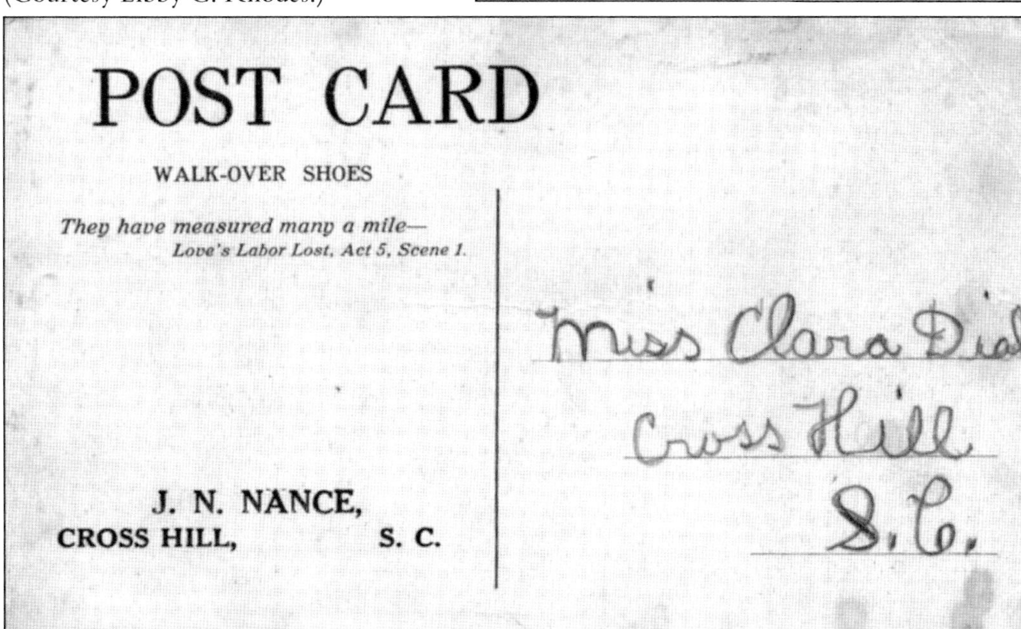

Advertising Walk-Over shoes, this postcard came from the J. N. Nance Store in Cross Hill. In the late 1800s, cotton was king and Cross Hill farmers were prospering. The small railroad town was flourishing, complete with a bank, two drugstores, five doctors, a newspaper, two gins, a knitting mill, boarding houses, and various general stores. The streets were named and laid off in a one-mile radius from the railroad. Elm trees were planted on both sides of the streets with sidewalks laid off. Land was given for the railroad and town by Mary McGowan Miller. The boll weevil and the Depression hit Cross Hill in the 1920s, and many people left their plows and mules behind to seek employment elsewhere. The town of Cross Hill is still incorporated. (Courtesy Libby C. Rhodes.)

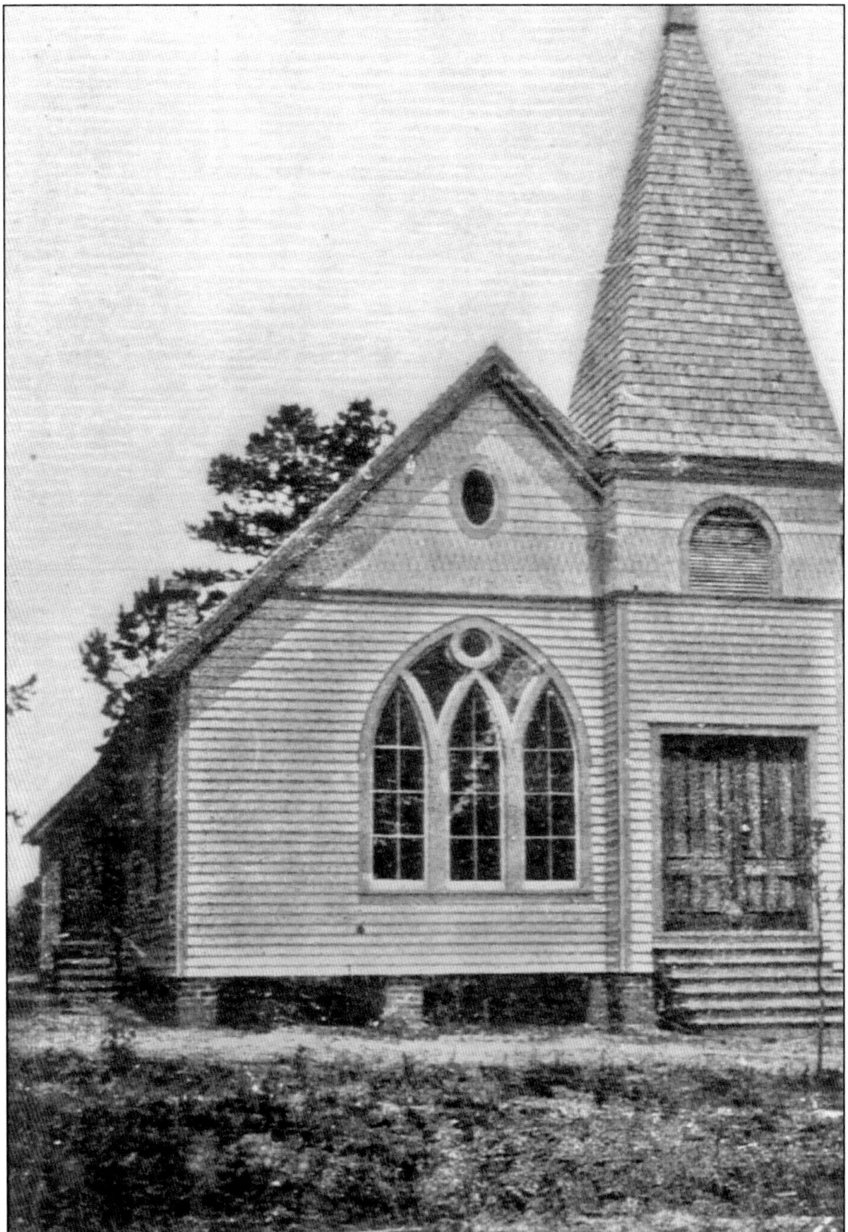

Mountville was so named because of a steep mountain-like hill rising from a little stream called Ginger Creek that joined Beaverdam Creek. In 1892, the Seaboard Railroad was completed and came through Mountville. With the coming of the railroad, the town thrived. Homes and business establishments were erected. Churches—Universalist, Presbyterian, and Methodist—were established. A school was built to serve the educational needs of the town's children. Mountville was complete with a post office and bank. The town maintained a healthy growth until after 1900, when automobiles arrived and detracted trade to larger cities. The Universalist church shown above was built in 1910 using materials that were donated from churches in Chappells and Saluda. (Courtesy South Caroliniana Library, University of South Carolina, Columbia.)

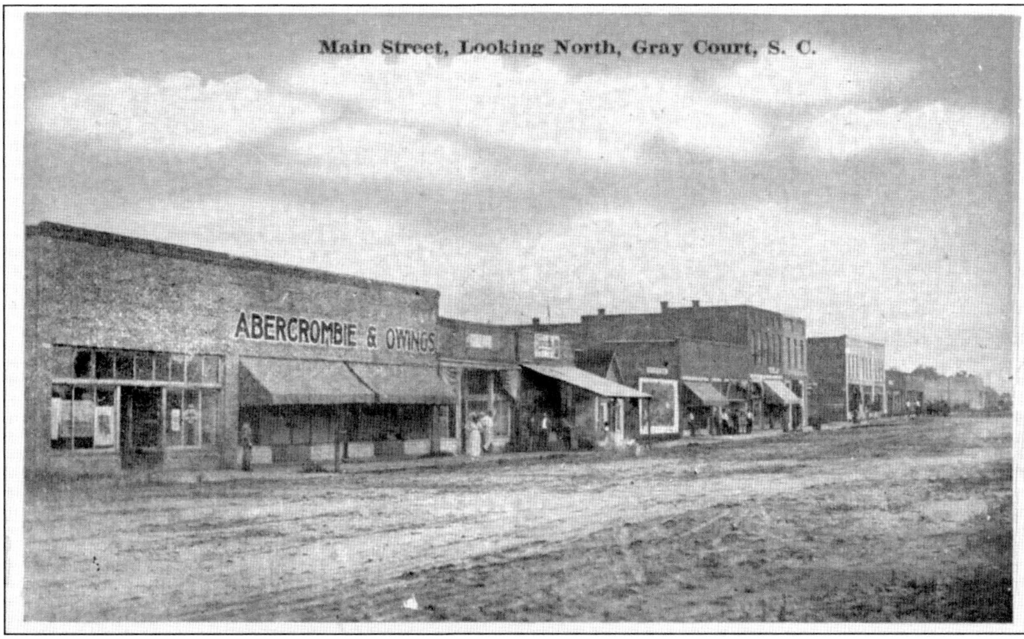

The arrival of the Charleston and Western Carolina Railroad in 1886 helped to make Gray Court, originally called Dorrohville, an agricultural trading center. Robert Gray gave land for the town and depot. He also was the first depot agent; therefore, the town was named in his honor. With the depot, located on Main Street, the town became a bustling little farming town that was especially lively on weekends. People gathered on Main Street to shop, board the train, and visit with neighbors. Grocery, clothing, general merchandise, dry goods, and hardware stores lined Main Street, as well as a hat shop. In the early days, two banks, two drugstores, a car dealership, a blacksmith shop, and three doctors were vital parts of the town. This early postcard shows the depot at the end of Gray Court's Main Street. (Above courtesy Elaine Martin; below courtesy Laurens County Library.)

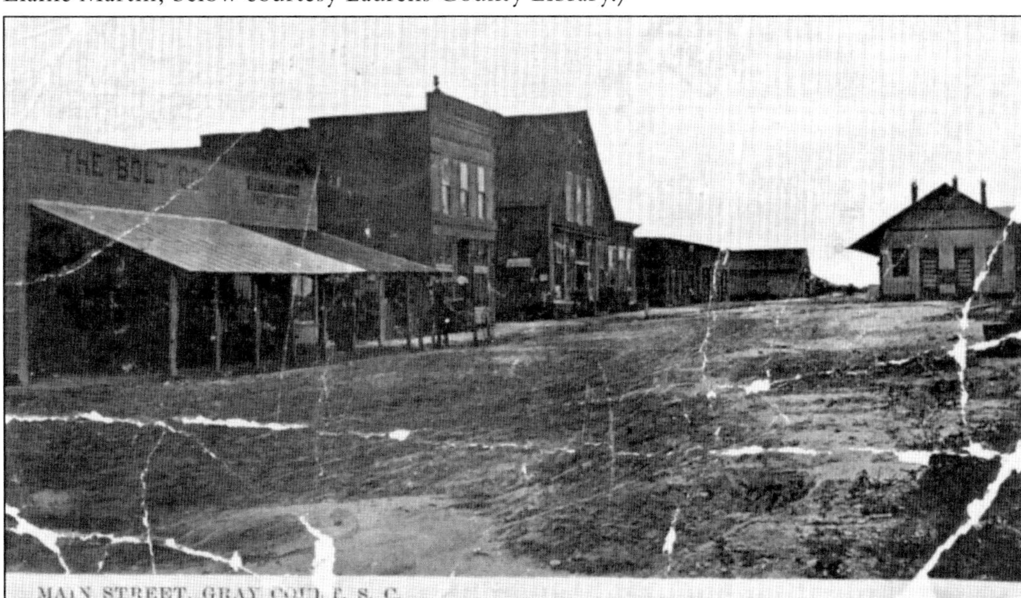

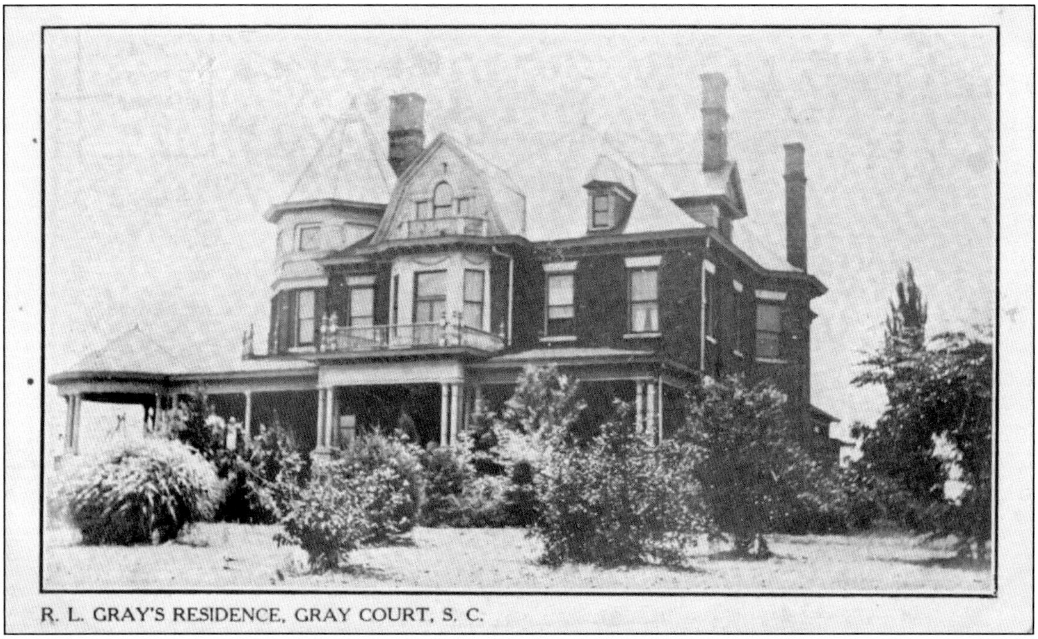

Robert L. Gray built this 14-room Victorian mansion in 1900 for his wife, the former Emma Dial. Located in Gray Court, the house contained 12 fireplaces, 6 chimneys, and stained-glass windows, and the foundation was constructed of granite slabs from a local quarry. The house was modeled after the residence of Mrs. Dial's uncle, Sen. Nathaniel B. Dial of Laurens. The house was destroyed by fire *c.* 1954. (Courtesy Richard B. Taylor Jr.)

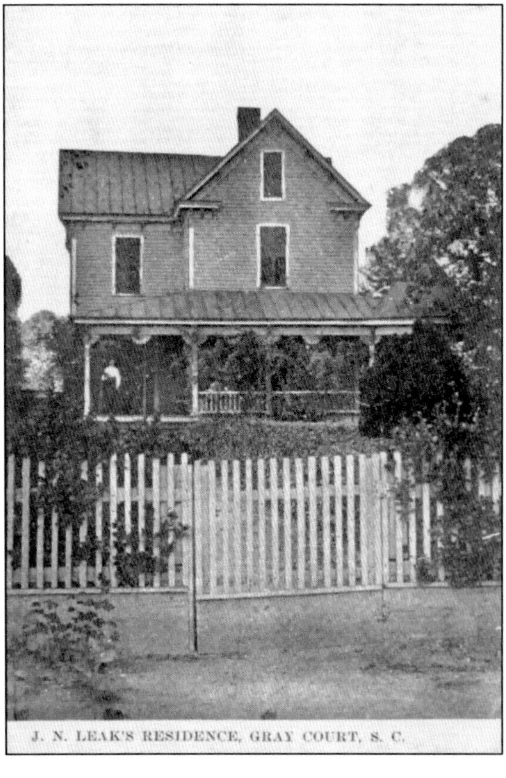

Located in Gray Court, this house was constructed in the early 1800s by Dr. Jerome Christopher, who also used his house as an office. He was Gray Court's first resident physician. Dr. Christopher often called on his patients in a horse and buggy. He also served as an alderman for the town of Gray Court. Through the years, the Leake, Shell, Martin, and Vandaveer families have also called the Victorian house "home." (Courtesy Elaine Martin.)

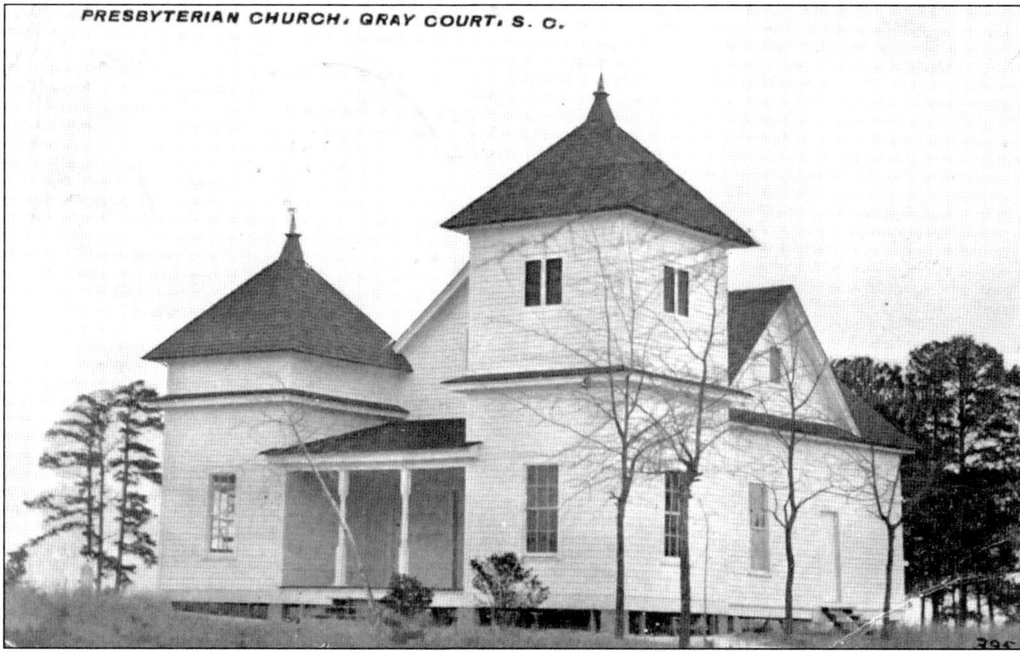

The Dorrohville Presbyterian Church was the first church to be built in Gray Court. The church was organized in 1865, and at the time, the small community was known as Dorroh because the post office was located in the Dorroh family home. The Dorroh, Peden, and Garrison families were early members of the Presbyterian church. The church no longer stands, but the cemetery remains on Georgia Road. (Courtesy Richard B. Taylor Jr.)

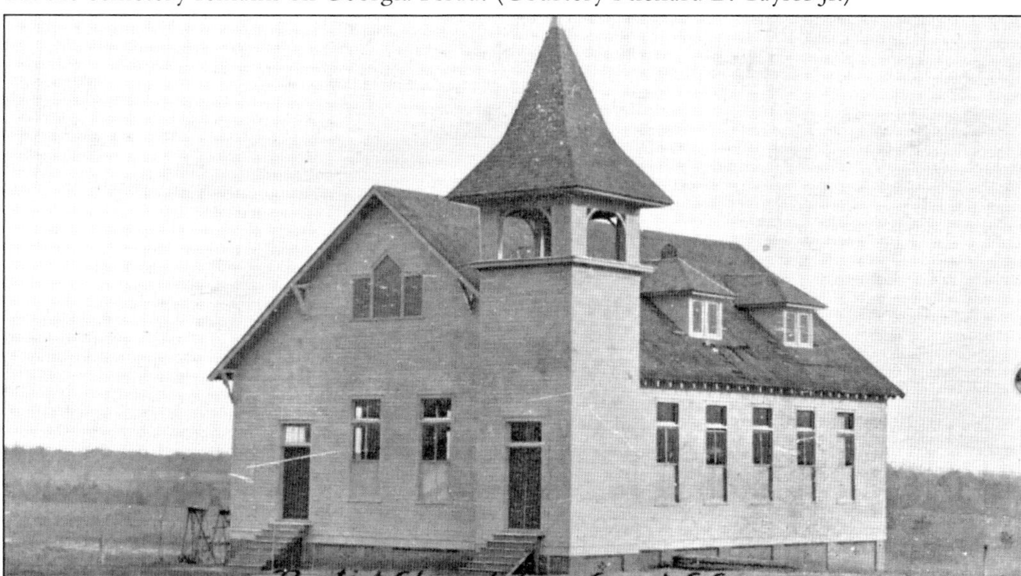

A group of Baptists met in the Gray Court–Owings School building and, after a sermon by Rev. H. L. Baggot, held an informal conference, during which they resolved to unite in the constitution of a Baptist church. In September 1912, the group of 39 officially organized the Gray Court Baptist Church; by November of that year, a building had been constructed and the first worship service held. (Courtesy Elaine Martin.)

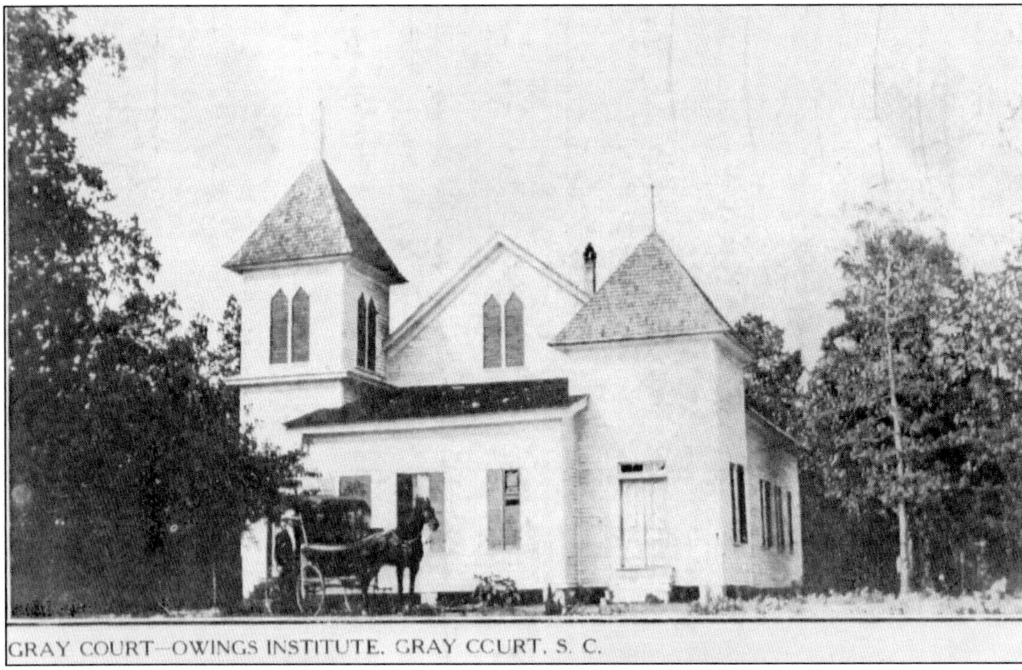

The caption on this postcard reads Gray Court–Owings Institute. However, the frame building is the Gray Court Methodist Church. Located just off Main Street in Gray Court, the church was organized in 1899 and remodeled in 1904. A group of Methodists believed that Gray Court needed a Methodist church; therefore, the church was organized from the nearby Dials Methodist Church. (Courtesy South Caroliniana Library, University of South Carolina, Columbia.)

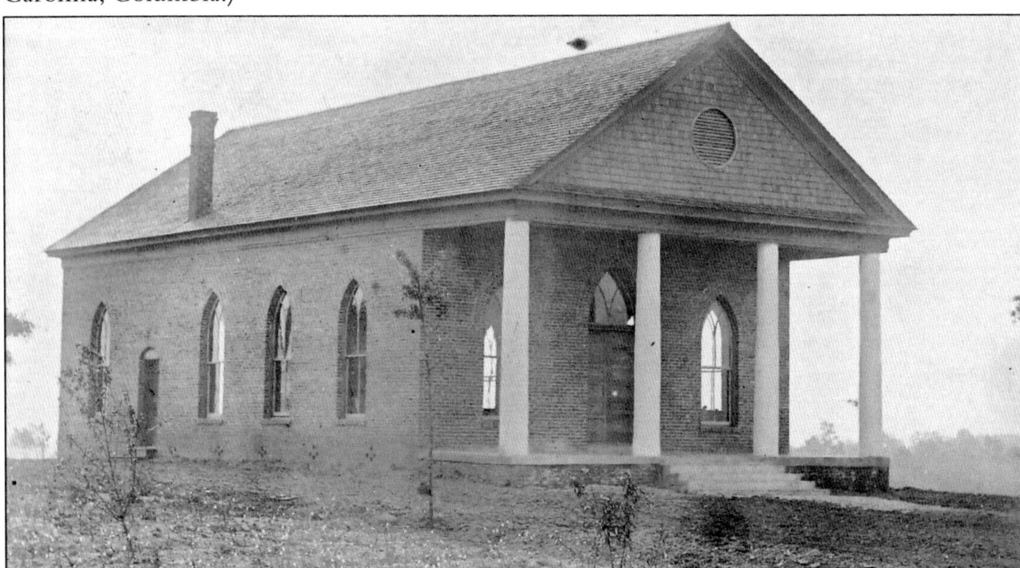

Owings Presbyterian Church was organized in 1911. A brick structure was constructed in 1912 to serve the religious needs of the congregation. Members from Harmony Presbyterian Church and Fairview Presbyterian Church formed the small church in the town of Owings. (Courtesy South Caroliniana Library, University of South Carolina, Columbia.)

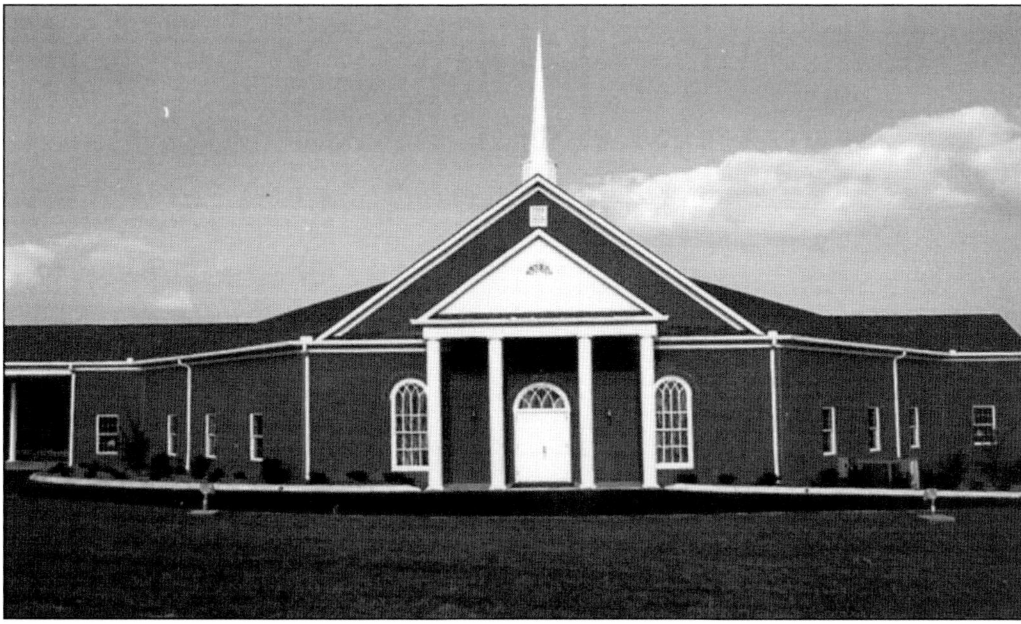

With only 18 members, Rabon Creek Baptist Church had its beginning in 1823 as a branch of Warrior Creek Baptist Church. With 39 members, the church was constituted on August 7, 1828. The first pastor was Jonathan DeWeese, who served until 1836. Four church buildings have served the congregation. The present church was dedicated on October 3, 1999. (Courtesy Elaine Martin.)

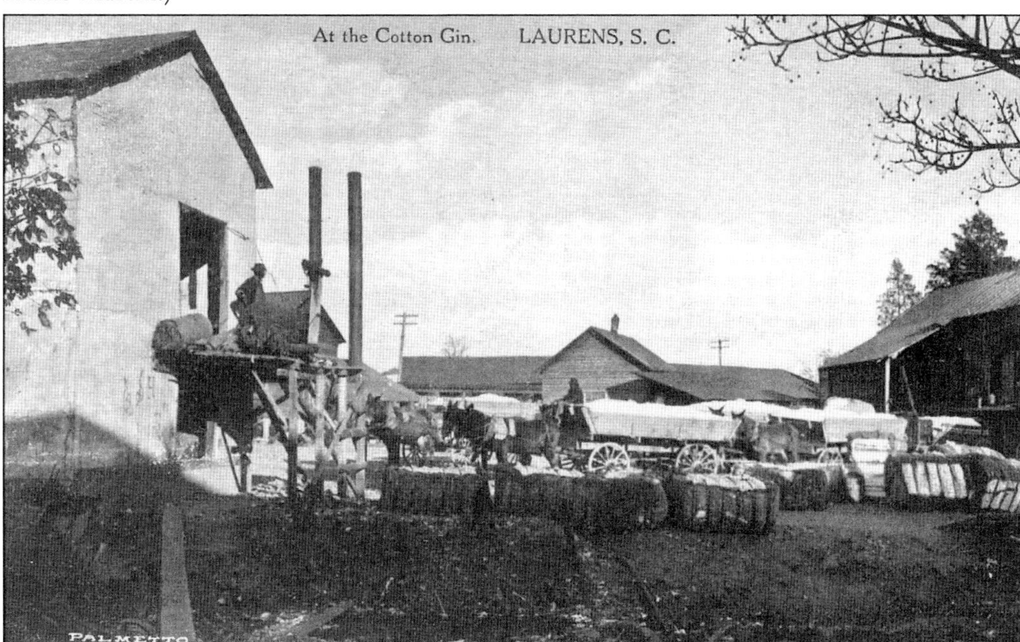

Cotton gins were once common in rural Laurens County. Because Laurens was an agricultural county, every small town had a gin. It was a popular gathering place for farmers. Sadly a day at the cotton gin is a thing of the past. (Courtesy South Caroliniana Library, University of South Carolina, Columbia.)

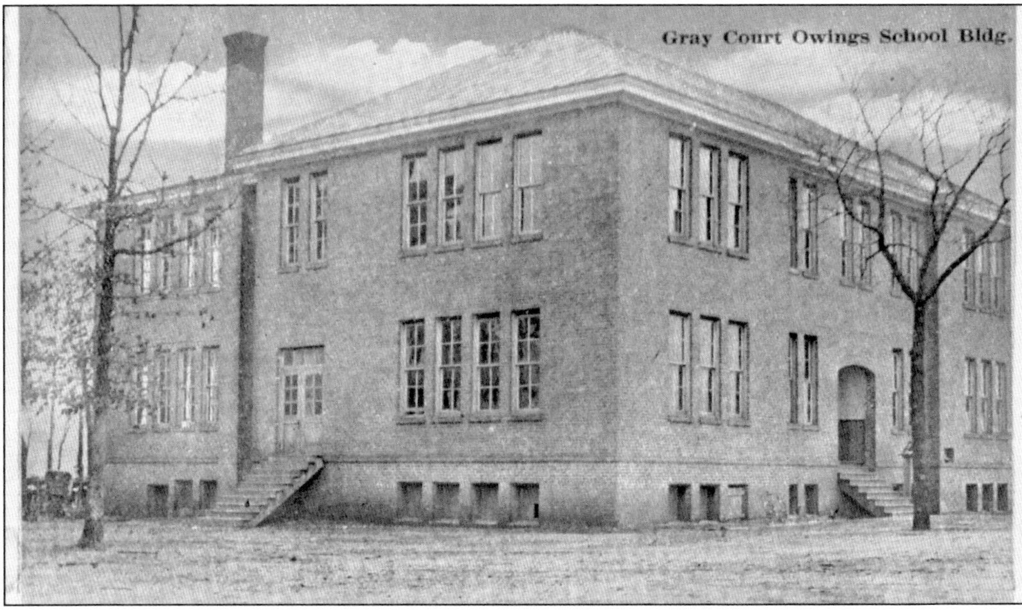

Located between the small towns of Gray Court and Owings, the Gray Court–Owings School building was erected in 1914 to serve the educational needs of students from upper Laurens County. Students attended grades 1 through 10 in the two-story brick structure. In 1928, an auditorium was added, and later a gymnasium was constructed. The Gray Court–Owings School continues to serve students from the area. (Courtesy Elaine Martin.)

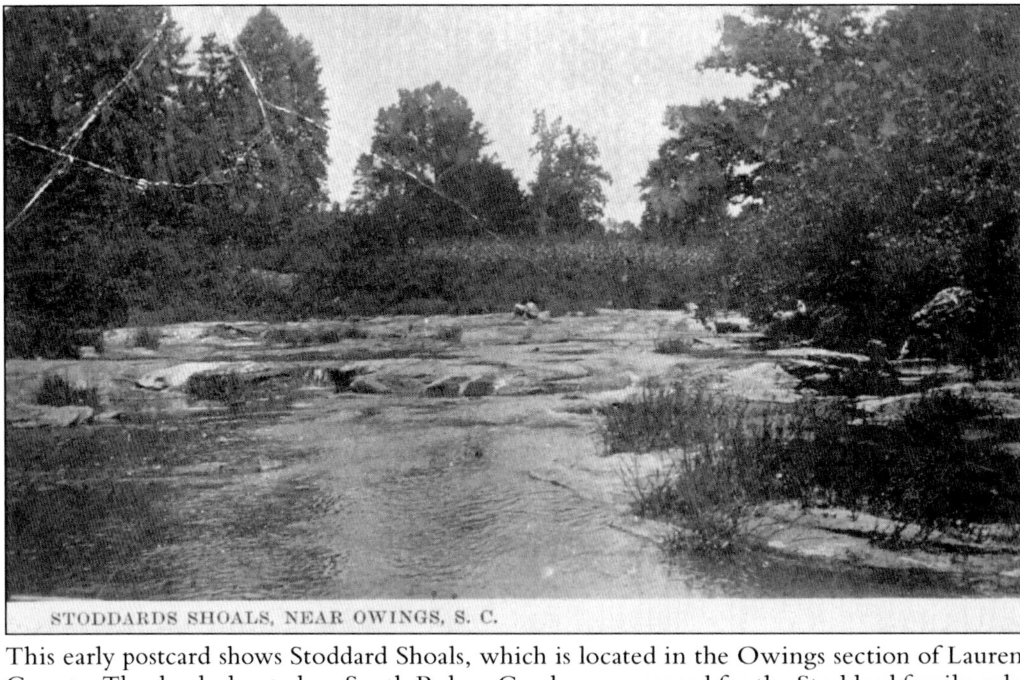

This early postcard shows Stoddard Shoals, which is located in the Owings section of Laurens County. The shoals, located on South Rabon Creek, were named for the Stoddard family, who were early settlers in the area. In the early 1900s, young people visited the shoals for picnics, swimming, and other social gatherings. It was also a favored spot for church social outings. (Courtesy Elaine Martin.)

Five

Real People
City Dwellers and Country Folk

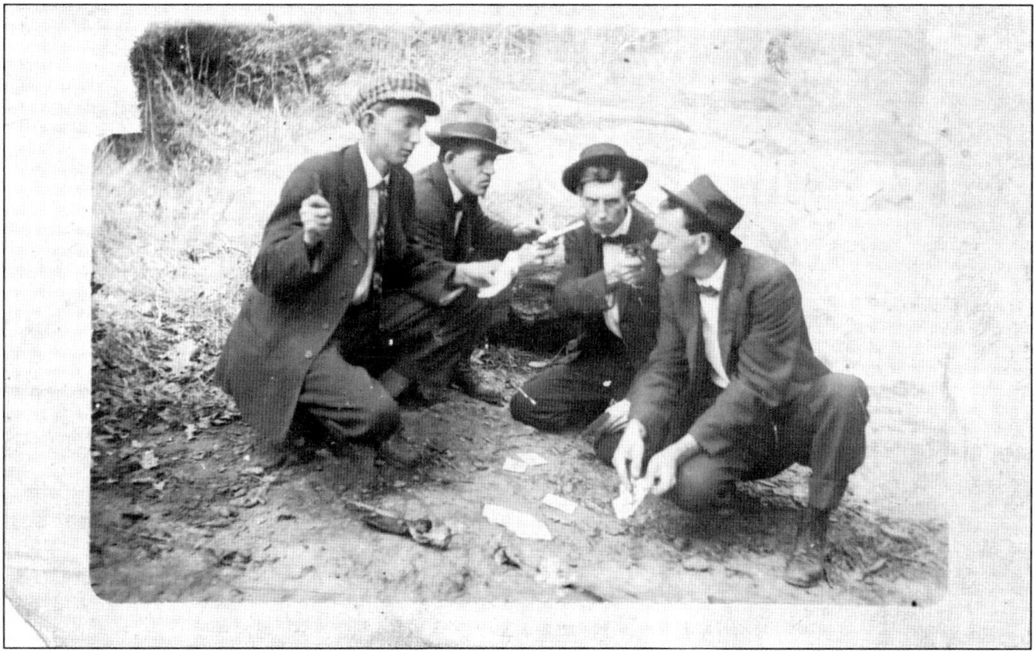

Itinerant photographers traveled the country roads of Laurens County and captured real people at work and at play. Today these images fill photo albums and boxes and are treasured family heirlooms. This group of young men, including (from left to right) Robert Herbert Coats, unidentified, James Julian Coats Sr., and unidentified, all of Cross Hill, staged a make-believe card game and argument and then actually brandished their pistols for the photographer. What fun they must have had carrying out the drama for the photograph. Little did they know that one day their photograph would grace the page of a postcard book and be looked upon by their great-great-grandsons. (Courtesy Libby C. Rhodes.)

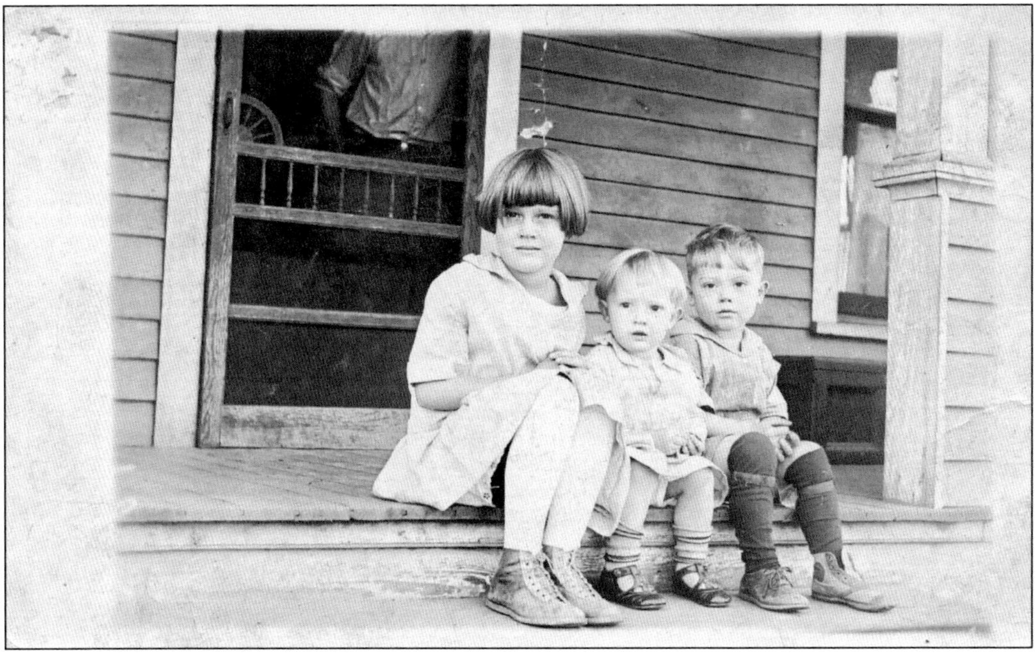

Sitting all in a row on the front porch steps are, from left to right, Ruth Johnson White, Mildred Johnson Clark, and Conway Johnson. They are children of Stanley Conway and Annie Rollins Johnson of Laurens. (Courtesy Kathryn W. Johnson.)

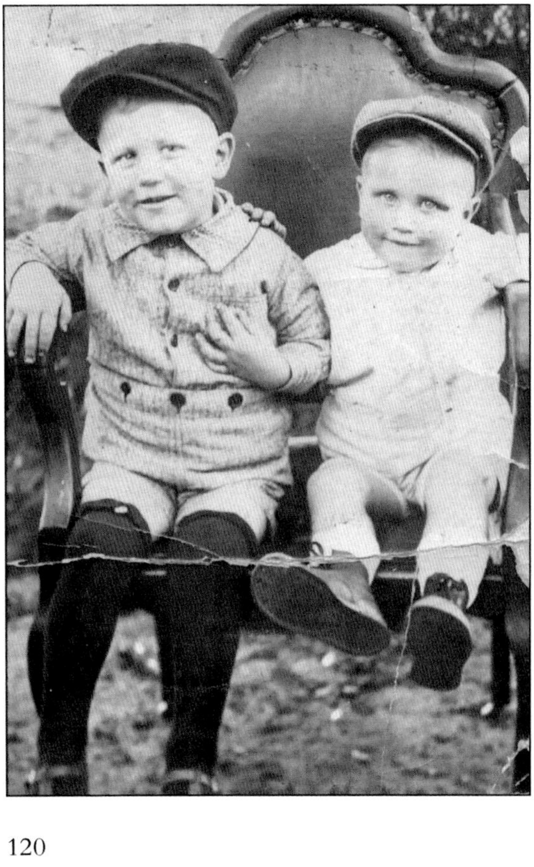

Frank Tucker, left, was born in 1924, and his brother, Furman Tucker, was born in 1926. They were sons of Fred and Florence Steen Tucker. This photograph was taken at the Tucker family farm on the Enoree River in northern Laurens County. The Tucker family later moved to Gray Court. (Courtesy Dianne T. Culbertson.)

Neighborhood children were captured by a photographer on East Main Street in Laurens. From left to right, they are (first row) Emily Taylor Bramlet, Forest Hugh Coleman, and unidentified; (second row) John K. Taylor, Mary Taylor, and Hilda Taylor; (third row) Margaret Coleman, Margaret Taylor Pratt, and Louis Taylor Hannahan. The parents of the Coleman children were Forest Hugh and Alice Coleman, and the parents of the Taylor children were William Lafayette and Emma M. Taylor. (Courtesy Elaine Martin.)

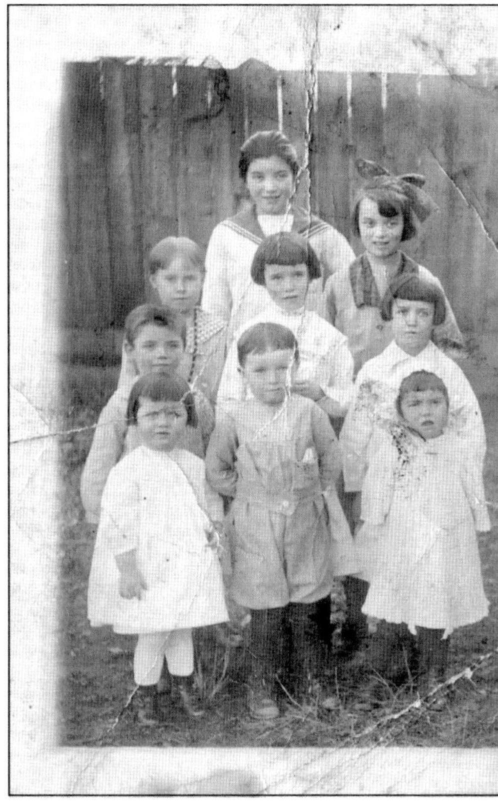

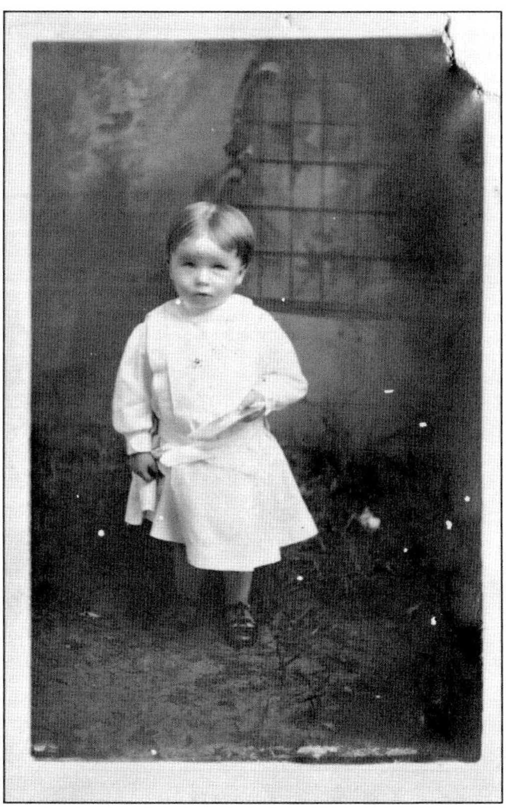

Forest Hugh Coleman Jr., son of Forest Hugh and Alice Stone Coleman, was a Laurens native and graduate of Clemson College. He was killed in France during World War II. He was married to the former Caroline Burroughs and is survived by a son, Forest Hugh Coleman III, and a daughter, Sue Coleman Brownlee. (Courtesy Elaine Martin.)

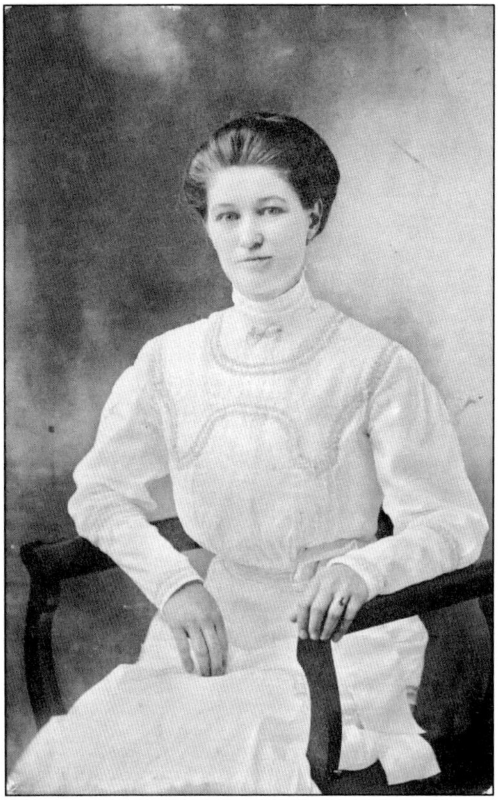

A stunning bride, the former Fay Culbertson of Laurens County, posed for the photographer in her wedding dress. She was married to James Bailey Benjamin on April 16, 1911. (Courtesy Willie Fay Lawson.)

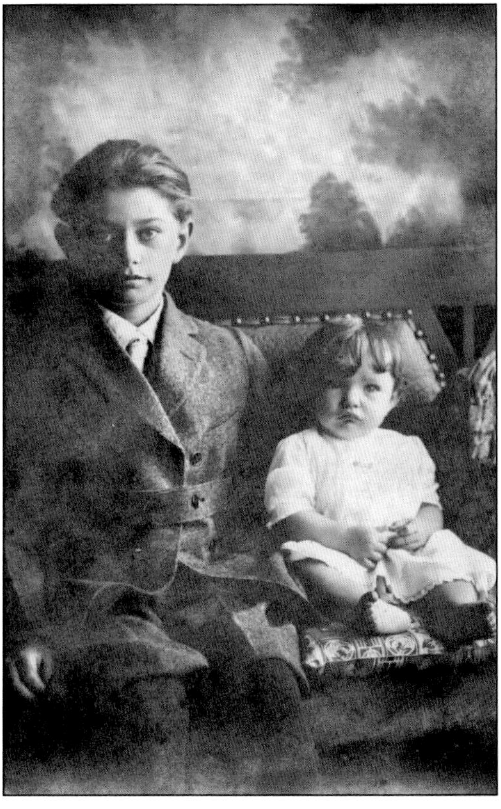

Dressed in their Sunday best and sitting for the photographer are John R. Benjamin and his younger sister, Nancy Benjamin. They are children of James Bailey and Fay Culbertson Benjamin of Laurens County. (Courtesy Willie Fay Lawson.)

The photographer simply removed the pitcher and added the baby to come up with a bath-time postcard photograph. The baby is Pauline Bolt, daughter of James Toliver and Bertha Elizabeth Wells Bolt. She later became the wife of Charles Franklin Dunaway Jr. (Courtesy Julius D. Bolt.)

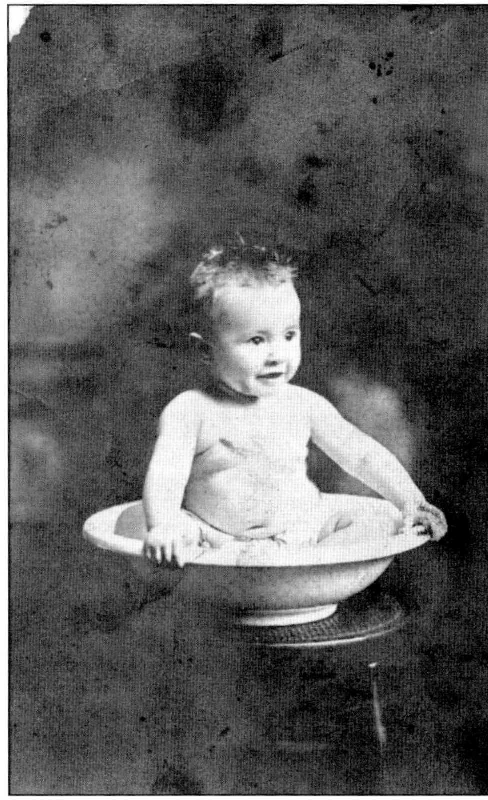

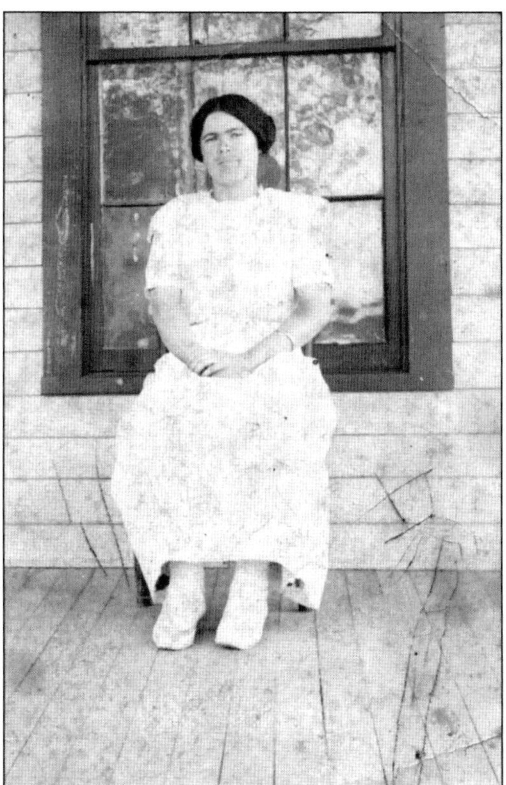

Nancy Caroline Bolt was photographed while sitting on the front porch. The daughter of James Dunklin and Amadora "Dora" Lindley Bolt, she later became the wife of John Hill McNinch and the mother of 10 children. (Courtesy Julius D. Bolt.)

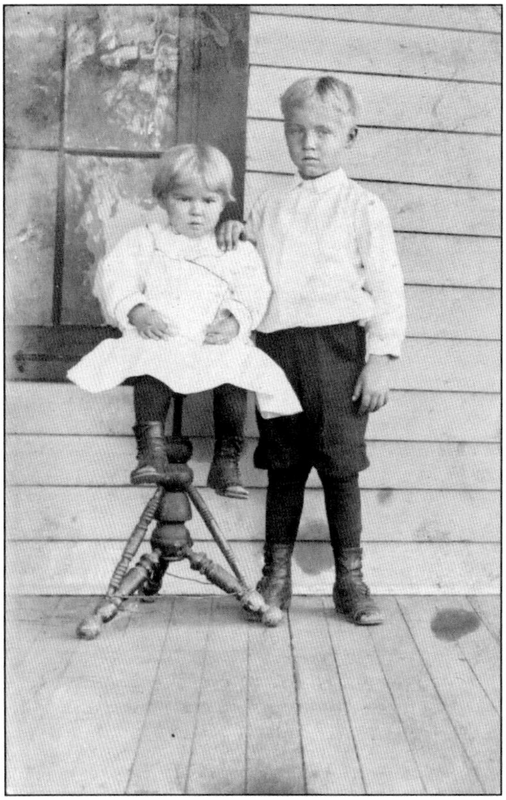

A traveling photographer captured this picture of Jesse Clarence and Dora Jennet Bolt, children of James Toliver and Bertha Elizabeth Wells Bolt. The younger sister sits on an organ stool that was moved from the parlor to the front porch, while her older brother stands beside her. Jesse later married Katherine Lula Wethers, and Dora married William Charles "Willie" Riddle. (Courtesy Julius D. Bolt.)

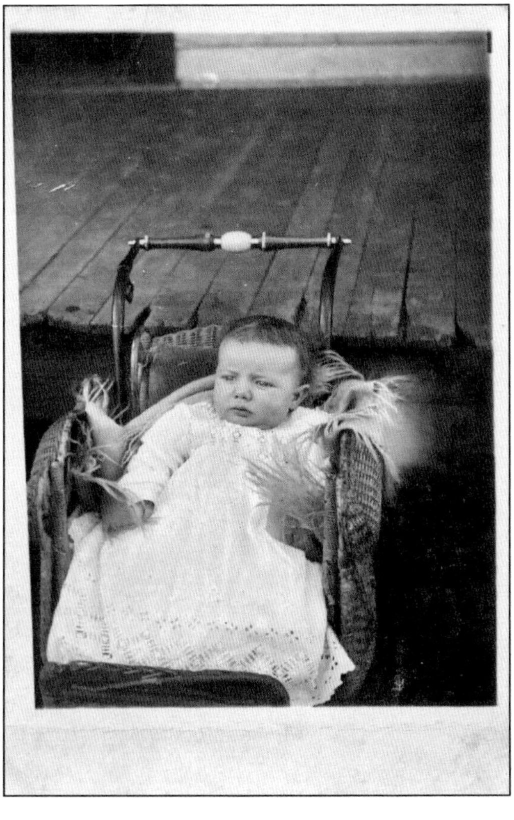

While wrapped in a woolen shawl and sitting in his wicker baby carriage, Jack William Bolt Sr., son of James Toliver and Bertha Elizabeth Wells Bolt, was a perfect model for this photograph postcard. He later married Carmetta Annett Upchurch. (Courtesy Julius D. Bolt.)

A World War II sailor, the late Matthew E. Weathers Sr., dressed in his uniform, was the perfect subject for a photograph postcard. He was a son of Dess and Cordia Weathers, the husband of Frances C. Weathers, and the father of Kathryn Weathers Johnson. (Courtesy Kathryn W. Johnson.)

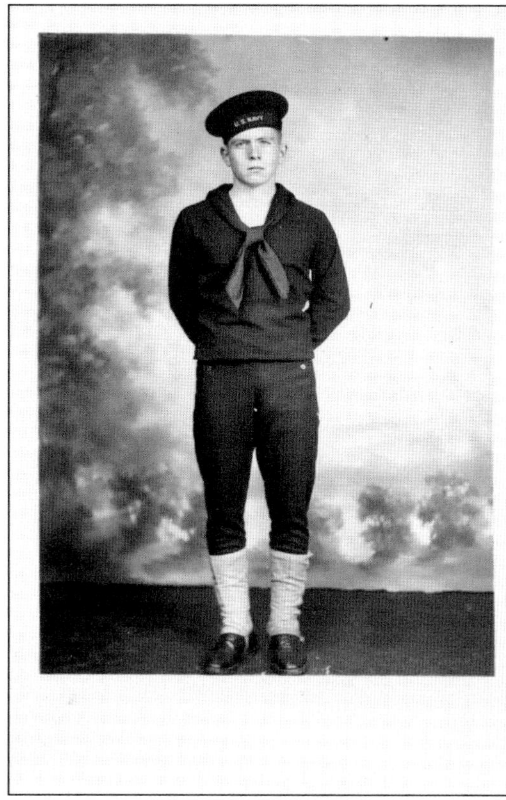

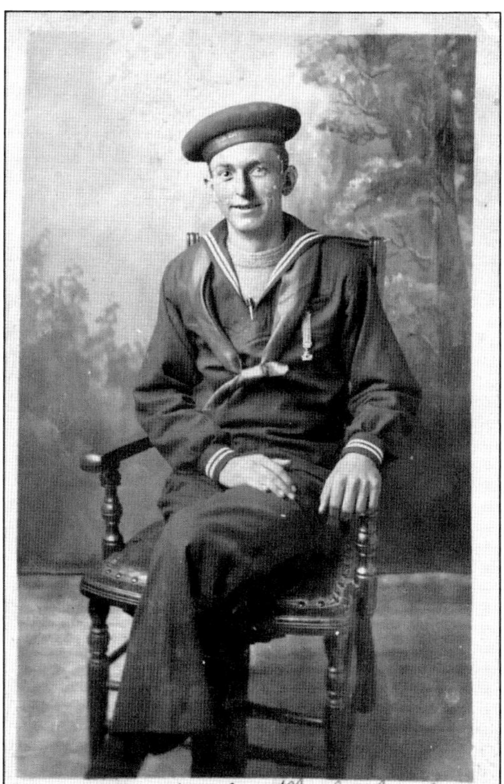

The late J. Wesley Fowler served as a Merchant Marine during World War I. The Laurens native later served as a deputy sheriff for Laurens County, was a member of the Woodmen of the World, and was a trustee of Mount Pleasant Baptist Church. He was the father of Mrs. Jerry Stoddard and Mrs. Barron Culbertson. (Courtesy Bobbie Stoddard.)

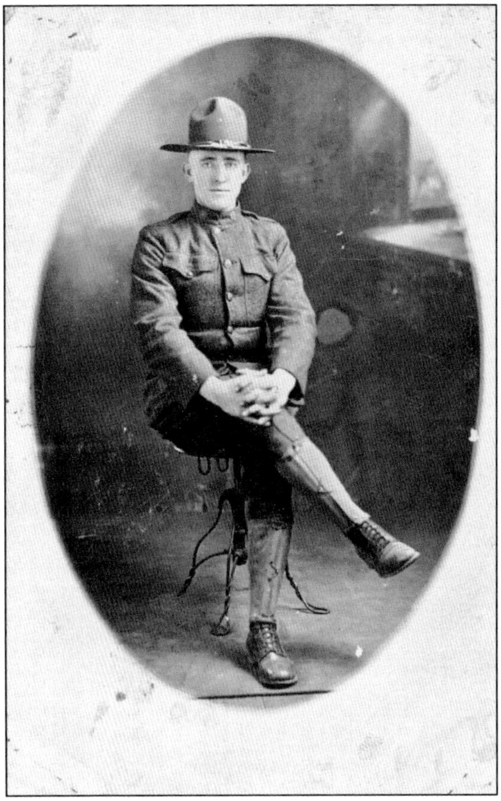

Born in 1892 in Laurens County, Clarence W. Wells was a son of Beaufort G. and Louria Alice Nickels Wells. He was first married to Maude Darnell and later to Lucy Busby Perdue. Wells served as a private first class in World War I and was honorably discharged in 1919. (Courtesy Julius D. Bolt.)

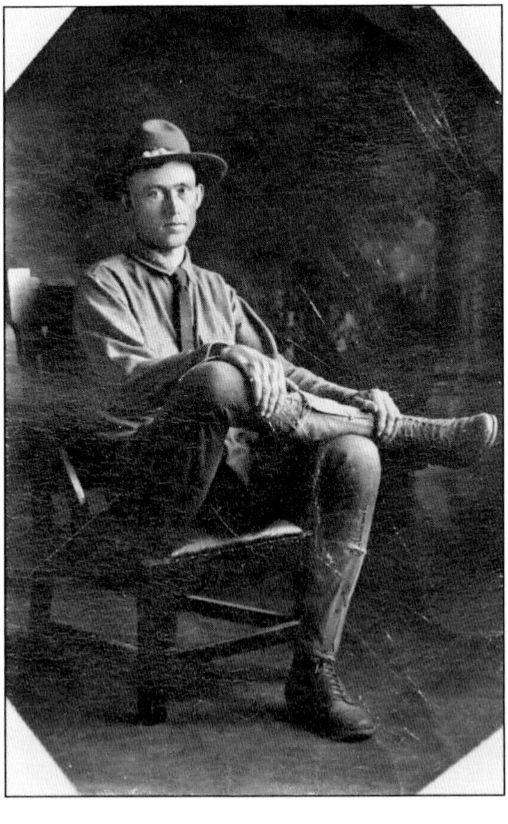

Jay Bolt was born in Laurens County in 1891. He entered the army in Company A, served his country during World War I, and was honorably discharged in 1919. Bolt was a son of James Dunklin and Amadora "Dora" Lindley Bolt. He was the husband of Clara Inez Knight Bolt. (Courtesy Julius D. Bolt.)

Robert Herbert Coats, son of Robert Vandorn and Lydia Hazel Coats, was born in 1894 in Cross Hill. A member of Company C Infantry, he served as a private first class in World War I. After a tour of duty in France, he was honorably discharged in May 1919. He was married to the former Ruby Monroe, and they were the parents of five sons. (Courtesy Libby C. Rhodes.)

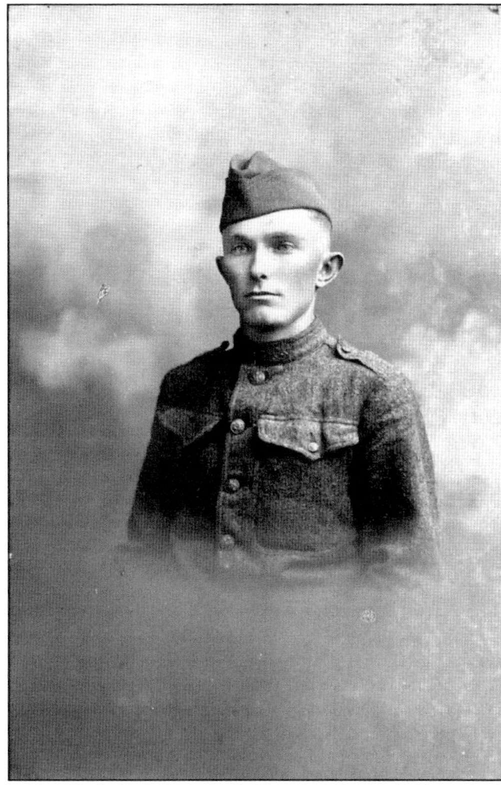

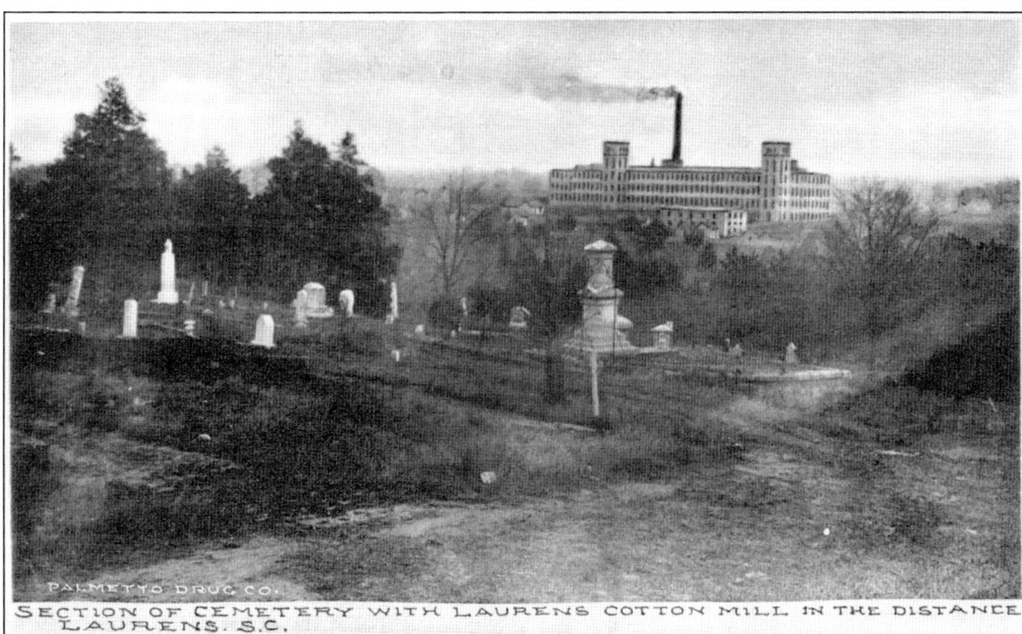

Monuments in the Laurens City Cemetery mark the graves of men, women, and children of Laurens County. Overlooking Little River, the cemetery is a reminder of those who have gone before us, the ones who called Laurens County home. (Courtesy Frances C. Weathers.)